The Political Geography of Contemporary Britain

Edited by

John Mohan
Queen Mary College, London

M
MACMILLAN

First published 1989

Published by
MACMILLAN EDUCATION LTD
Houndmills, Basingstoke, Hampshire RG21 2XS
and London
Companies and representatives
throughout the world

Typeset by Latimer Trend & Company Ltd, Plymouth

Printed in the People's Republic of China

British Library Cataloguing in Publication Data
The Political geography of contemporary Britain
1. Great Britain. Politics. Geographical
aspects
I. Mohan, John
320.1'2'0941
ISBN 0–333–47022–2 (hardcover)
ISBN 0–333–47023–0 (paperback)

Contents

v

List of Figures

List of Tables

Introduction

For some thirty years from 1945 the economic and social geography of Britain was shaped by a broad consensus comprising, among other things, commitments to full employment, Keynesian techniques of economic management, the welfare state, and a strong regional policy. That consensus has been challenged in the past decade; some challenges have been fundamental, such as the abandonment of any commitment to full employment, while in other policy areas challenges have been partial and less successful (for instance in health care). These changes have had profound effects on the human geography of contemporary Britain and, in order adequately to understand this human geography, an account is necessary of the processes which caused this consensus to break up.

The notion of a consensus is, of course, a difficult one: complete bipartisan agreement between political parties never existed, and differences of emphasis and substance have pervaded all policy areas (as Gamble demonstrates). Nor should the influence of the post-1979 Conservative governments be overestimated, since discontinuities in policy were apparent before then, while, for some of the authors in this volume differences between governments of whatever political persuasion have been of minor importance (e.g. Whitelegg, who argues that Conservative and Labour governments have developed policies which have served the needs of the car and the motor vehicle industry above all else, or Hudson, for whom profitability criteria for the nationalised industries are much older than Thatcherism). The authors all attempt to specify both the key discontinuities in policy, to trace the political forces that brought them about, and to separate political changes from secular trends (e.g. Lowe and Flynn, who note that post-1973 awareness of resource scarcity produced decisive shifts in environmental policy).

Initially, six chapters set the scene by providing contextual material for the analyses of specific policy issues. Gamble considers the extent to which Thatcherism is in fact a new form of politics and whether it has broken decisively with the post-war consensus. Taylor then argues that in order adequately to understand the changing human geography of Britain we need to comprehend Britain's changing position within the capitalist world economy. He traces Britain's declining role as a world power and links this to its changing material circumstances – notably the increased dominance of finance capital. He argues that Britain will be caught between two major geopolitical alliances: the Pacific Rim (the USA, China and Japan) and a European bloc straddling the Iron Curtain and including the Soviet Union. He concludes that, far from seeking to maintain its role as a world power, Britain would be better off more fully integrated into the European bloc.

Britain's changing role in the world economy is important in understanding its present human geography, but equally important are the internal geopolitics of nationalism, uneven development and the spatial distribution of electoral support. In this respect Anderson examines the thesis that the problems of maintaining territorial cohesion could lead to the 'break-up' of the British state. In his view the main impact of peripheral nationalisms will be on the relative strength of the major political parties, not on the cohesion of the state. However, he argues that an increasingly strident *British* nationalism could disrupt international relations, provoke further nationalist reactions in Scotland, Wales and Northern Ireland and, because of its links with racism, help produce more unrest in the inner cities. Linked to the question of territorial cohesion is the issue of the changing spatial polarisation of the electorate, analysed by Johnston and Pattie. They review the changing electoral map and the various interpretations of the reasons for the changes. They note the lack of a mandate for Conservative rule in the peripheral regions and argue that the Conservatives may develop strategies to 'recolonise' the periphery in order to sustain their legitimacy. One area the Conservatives have sought to 'recolonise' has been the inner city, but they have done so by what Duncan and Goodwin argue is a deliberate and spatially selective attack on the powers and policies of local government. This, they claim, is motivated less by economic considerations than by an attempt to circumscribe the ability of the local state to promote alternatives to central policy. In their view, the 'local government crisis' is an attempt to 'still the voices of alternative interpretations and oppositional representation which arise through uneven social and spatial development'.

The problems of managing uneven development and, in particular, deindustrialisation, are then discussed by Martin who constrasts Keynesian and Thatcherite efforts to manage industrial collapse. One basic problem with Keynesian policies was that no coherent policy – in terms of promoting industrial competitiveness, investment and innovation – was ever produced. In reacting against Keynesianism, the Conservatives have revived free-market capitalism in such a way that manufacturing has been pushed into a position where it is possibly beyond revival. Their strategy is not convincing in its assumption that market forces will promote renewal in the old industrial areas, not least because of the counter-regional subsidies received by much of South East England in the form of defence expenditures, infrastructural investments and tax reductions. Major developments such as the Channel Tunnel will favour the South East still more, to the detriment of Scotland, Wales, Northern Ireland and the north of England generally (as Whitelegg notes, it is unlikely that the improved cross-London links necessary to spread the benefits of the Tunnel will be built). Martin also notes that the re-emergence of inflationary pressures in the South East may well hinder the Government's anti-inflationary strategy.

The remaining chapters move from these broad considerations to analyses of specific issues. Three key themes run through these chapters: the changing boundary between the private and the public sectors; the changing character of the state and of state intervention; and the emergence of a 'politics of inequality'.

The first of these themes – the changing boundary between the public and the private sector – is central to Hudson's discussion of nationalised industry policy and to Martin's examination of de-industrialisation, where the key issue is the extent to which the market is to play a decisive role in shaping the economic fortunes of different regions and communities. It is also apparent in other chapters, notably Hamnett's discussion of housing policy. The promotion of owner occupation and the sale of council housing have produced an important shift in the tenure composition of the housing stock. These policies are also regarded by Hamnett as efforts to 'wean the electorate away from the siren song of socialism' and to weaken political support for collective solutions to housing problems. Indeed some London councils, as Hamnett notes, actually see the promotion of council house sales as a way of weakening the basis of support for Labour within their jurisdiction. Likewise, Whitelegg notes the impact of deregulation on transport policy and observes the effect of running transport systems in a commercial fashion, as in the attempts to make BR reduce its dependency on public funds. Similar points could be made about health care policy where, although the private sector is still numerically small, it has assumed greater ideological significance as there is a growing constituency – heavily spatially concentrated – which can avail itself of private health care. McDowell approaches this issue from a different standpoint for she refers to the changing boundary between the public sphere of work and formal politics, and the private sphere of the family and the home. She argues that current political developments are based on an ideology which seeks to limit women's participation in the public sphere and to confine them to the 'private' sphere by relying on their unpaid labour as sources of care.

Secondly, there is the changing character of the state and the changing nature of state intervention. The attempts to 'roll back' the state are well known and are apparent in chapters dealing with, for example, environmental regulation (Lowe and Flynn), nationalised industries (Hudson), deindustrialisation (Martin), transport (White-legg), and housing (Hamnett). Simultaneously, state policy-making has become more centralised with attempts being made to limit local autonomy on several issues. The 'local government crisis' (Duncan and Goodwin) is the most notable example, but this is also true of health care (Mohan) and policing (Fyfe), where numerous examples can be cited of restrictions on the capacity of local agencies to carry through their declared policies. Indeed the view has been advanced that the promotion of the 'free economy' demands a 'strong state' and that this can entail the abolition of local democracy. This is apparent through the setting-up of agencies designed to promote urban redevelopment with minimal local interference (Duncan and Goodwin) or in the proposals to devolve housing management to non-elected organisations (Hamnett). These developments are par-alleled by greater coercion, most notably evident in the policing tactics designed to control urban disorders and industrial unrest. Fyfe notes that the notion of a geography of policing is a novel one which sits uneasily with the commonly held view of the police as a neutral protector of the common good, but he does show that policing tactics have been carefully orchestrated towards specific places at particular times. Massey and Painter also make the point that the Government's attacks on trade unions have been targeted spatially towards the old industrial heartlands, a view echoed in Hudson's contribution.

Thirdly, a key feature of the last ten years has been the emergence of a systematic politics of inequality. Gamble describes this and reviews the interpretation of Thatcherism as a 'two-nation' politics, in which attempts are made to consolidate and protect support from key social groups and geographical areas (notably the financial and services sector, the professional and managerial groups, and the 'South') while marginalising the unemployed, those working in the public sector and manufacturing, and in the 'North' more generally. One reason for this has been the spatial polarisation of the electorate, which has allowed policies to be pursued which effectively ignore large sections of the country. Two groups most affected by this are ethnic communities and women. Smith traces the emergence of a new 'segregationism', informed by neo-classical economics and a revived British nationalism in the guise of a one-nation Conservatism. This explains the position of black people in housing and labour markets as a function of the operation of market forces, portrays national unity as incompatible with multiculturalism, and dismisses unrest and resistance by black communities as law and order issues, rather than as reactions to structural inequalities and institutionalised discrimination. It therefore denies efforts to remove social and spatial inequalities in black people's life chances. McDowell argues that the position of women has worsened in the 1980s owing to a combination of the coincidence of wider social and economic changes with the three terms of office of a radical right-wing Government committed to reduced welfare spending. Changes in the labour market, some the result of wider international developments, some resulting from governmental policy, have caused the increased 'feminisation' of poverty. The growing inequalities between those with access to private services and those constrained to depend on the public sector are also clear from the discussions of transport, health care and housing policy.

A further point addressed by some of these contributions relates to the expansion and geography of important social forces and

political movements. Thus Anderson analyses the actual and potential role of nationalist movements in terms of threatening the
coherence of the state. Duncan and Goodwin note how local
government has become a force for promoting opposition to central
government policies, to the point where central government has
deliberately targeted its policies on specific local authorities. Massey
and Painter consider the changing geography of trade unions and
argue that their decline results from the impact of three factors:
economic recession, longer-term changes in economic structure, and
the attacks launched by successive Conservative governments on the
unions. Lowe and Flynn consider the growth and political significance of environmental movements. These are often specific to
particular places, for example the recent emergence of a group of
Conservative MPs opposed to the adverse impact of unchecked
economic growth in South East England. They note that this could
have an important impact on the future direction of Conservative
policy, a view apparently confirmed in late 1988 by the rumours of
an impending 'greening' of the Government's policies.

Overall, the book forms a comprehensive introduction and
sourcebook for those concerned with understanding the changing
human geography of Britain. Its chapters cover a wide range of
topics in economic and social geography, and it highlights the
essentially political factors without which any explanation of this
human geography would be incomplete. As such, it is hoped that it
will be of value to all those interested in the political dimensions of
spatial issues in Britain.

JOHN MOHAN

Acknowledgements

The editor and publishers wish to thank the following who have kindly given permission for the use of previously published or copyright material: Basil Blackwell Ltd for the use of a diagram from *Losing the Fight Against Crime*, edited by R. Kinsey, J. Lea and J. Young (1986); the Nationwide Anglia Building Society for a figure from their publication *House Prices: the North–South Divide* (1987); the Policy Studies Institute for a table on the development of car ownership in Britain, which first appeared in Plowden, S. (1985) *Transport Reform: Changing the Rules*; the Longman Group UK for a table, 'State Hegemony and Kondratieff Cycles', from Taylor, P. J. (1985) *Political Geography: World-Economy, Nation State and Locality*, and for two tables from Johnston, R. J., Pattie, C. J. and Allsopp, J. (1988) *A Nation Dividing? The Electoral Map of Britain, 1979–87*; the editor of *Marxism Today* for the artwork for figures from 'Mapping Out the Unions' by D. Massey and N. Miles, *Marxism Today*, May 1984; and the Controller of Her Majesty's Stationery Office for a figure, 'Percentage Distribution of Women by Occupational Grouping, Great Britain, 1986', from Equal Opportunities Commission (1986) *Women and Men in Britain: a Statistical Profile*.

The editor is also grateful for the financial support of an ESRC Postdoctoral Research Fellowship (grant no. A23320076) from 1986 to 1989.

Any edited collection depends on the support of its contributors and the editor greatly appreciates the authors' enthusiasm for the project and for their willingness to respond to his requests for editorial amendments, cuts and so forth. Finally, the editor would like to thank Steven Kennedy of Macmillan for his editorial advice and encouragement.

1
Thatcherism and the New Politics

Andrew Gamble

The End of Consensus

During the 1970s British politics was unusually turbulent. As discontent multiplied and dissatisfaction with the conduct of government increased, so political debate became more polarised and few public institutions escaped censure and challenge. Many politicians and commentators across the political spectrum began to speak of turning-points and crises. The rise of Thatcherism and the fragmentation of the Left were signs of significant changes in British politics.

At the centre of this turbulence was the weakening of the authority of the state. This had both internal and external causes. The apparent inability of successive governments to respond to a number of deep-seated problems convinced many on both Left and Right that a radical overhaul of the objectives and institutions of government had become necessary if government was to regain effectiveness and legitimacy.

The most important internal reason for the sapping of confidence in government was the performance of the economy. Governments seemed unable to manage the economy successfully and to extricate themselves from an increasingly destructive cycle of short-term crises and policy failure. The modernisation programmes launched by the governments of Macmillan, Wilson and Heath during the 1960s and 1970s did not succeed in their main objective – reversing Britain's relative economic decline. This experience did more than anything else to destroy faith in the institutions and policy priorities governments had broadly accepted since the 1940s.

The failure of the British economy to grow as rapidly as its main rivals was explained in several ways: the split between the financial

1

and industrial sectors in the British economy; the preservation of the military and political trappings of a great power; the level and range of public spending; the scope of government responsibilities and interventions; the extent of power wielded by the trade unions; and the pervasive anti-enterprise culture at all levels of British society (Coates and Hillard, 1986; Gamble, 1985; Wiener, 1981).

Political debate, however, increasingly ranged over other aspects of modernisation as well, focusing for example on the government's response to cultural and social change. In the 1960s there were changes in the law on capital punishment, juvenile offenders, homosexuality, divorce, and abortion, as well as the re-organisation of state education along comprehensive lines. For their opponents these changes were associated with a climate of permissiveness, declining standards, the erosion of respect for authority and the undermining of the family and the school. The weakening of these institutions threatened the maintenance of order in society. For their supporters the changes were viewed as extending the social rights of citizenship, and as only the first instalment of more radical changes.

The post-war consensus was therefore already beginning to break down by the mid-1970s because the policies that it legitimated were considered both ineffective and increasingly harmful. A New Right in the Conservative Party, whose concerns were voiced by politicians like Enoch Powell, and a new socialist Left in the Labour Party began to map out sharp alternatives to the established policy priorities of both major parties.

How far this process might have gone and how successfully the party leaderships might have contained it was not tested, because the entire context of British politics was transformed in the 1970s by the end of the long boom, the emergence of recession, and the weakening of the position of the United States as the hegemonic power in the world system.

These changes obliged all national governments to abandon the framework for policy which had existed since the 1940s and to adjust to new conditions. The exhaustion of the established modes of investment and industrial organisation, changes in the international division of labour, and the deployment of important new technological systems, created the space for new political responses and agendas. When these changes were combined with local discontents over the objectives and performance of government, as in Britain, radical elements of both Left and Right were able to seize the initiative (these changes are analysed in Lash and Urry, 1987).

Thatcherism first emerged as one of these radical initiatives. It needs to be analysed in the context of these changes in the world order. It was never purely a local British phenomenon, although naturally it was shaped by local British concerns and events. Despite its widespread use, however, the term 'Thatcherism' remains controversial. Doubts have been cast on both the novelty, the coherence, and the radicalism of Thatcherism as a political project and on the existence of a post-war consensus which Thatcherism claimed to overturn (Jessop *et al.*, 1984; Riddell, 1983; G. Thompson, 1986).

Much of this criticism has been valuable. Attributing excessive importance to Thatcherism in transforming the world has to be avoided; talk of watersheds and new eras needs to be examined carefully. Thatcherism is best understood as a *project* to create a new hegemony, not as that new hegemony itself. It can be analysed as an ideological doctrine, as a political statecraft, and as an economic programme. It fully reflects the institutional complexities and contradictions of the world in which the Thatcherites are obliged to operate. But grasping the detail of the events, ideas and policies that make up Thatcherism makes the general concept more rather than less useful. The longer Thatcherism has persisted, the more its overall logic has become apparent. Often against expectations it has proved capable of overcoming reverses and renewing its radical momentum (for analyses of Thatcherism see Bulpitt, 1985; Gamble, 1988; Hall and Jacques, 1983; Jenkins, 1987; Kavanagh, 1987).

The notion of a consensus is a difficult one. If the term is taken to mean complete bipartisan agreement between members of the main political parties on all substantive aspects of policy, then plainly no true consensus ever existed. But it has also been argued that even when parties have pursued similar policies this may be due not to policy coincidence or convergence, nor to any consensus on values and objectives, but to particular circumstances and pressures.

These are not, however, decisive objections to the idea of a post-war consensus. The term is still useful if it is recognised that there was no complete consensus but rather an accommodation between different interests and values, which set a framework and priorities for post-war policy to which all parties in practice adhered. The origins of the consensus of the 1950s and 1960s must therefore be sought in the political settlement of the 1940s. This settlement was conceived as a temporary and limited programme of reforms but, assisted by trends in the development of the world economy and inter-state relationships it proved more durable, only beginning to come apart in the 1970s.

The 1940s political settlement embraced both external and domestic policy. Central to the former were the commitments to the Atlantic Alliance and NATO, the decision to withdraw from the empire, and the acceptance of the need to progress towards a new international economic order based on multilateral trade and currency convertibility. Central to the latter were the extension of the sphere of legitimate government intervention and an expansion of its scale. This involved not just the acceptance by government of responsibility for the level of unemployment and economic activity, but the establishment of collective welfare provision in health and social security, the enlargement of the public sector, and the consolidation of government initiatives to remedy regional inequalities and to ensure national and local planning of land use and industrial development (for the character of the consensus see Beer, 1965; Blake, 1985; Brett, 1985).

The 1940s settlement proved a lasting one, partly because Labour lost office in 1951 and was prevented from advancing to the next stage of collectivising the economy, and partly because the Conservatives back in office showed no inclination to implement their manifesto pledge to set the people free, and made little attempt either to dismantle collective welfare or to reverse measures of public ownership. They were broadly content to administer the enlarged and extended state and to continue the bipartisan foreign policy.

The Political Geography of the Consensus

The 1940s settlement proved durable precisely because its main assumptions and priorities proved strong enough to survive changes of the parties in government and changes in leadership. But critics of the concept of consensus have rightly noted that the consistency and continuity evident in many areas of policy owed less to positive agreement between the parties than to the constraints imposed by international military and trading relationships. The exceptional growth of the world economy during the 1950s and 1960s also created feelings of optimism and complacency about the institutional structure and policy priorities of the post-war world. Ideology was at an end and the good society was in operation.

In Britain the consensus was underpinned by a particular territorial code and by particular political institutions. Both Labour and the Conservatives were national parties seeking power at the centre of a unitary state and deploying national ideologies and national appeals to win support throughout the country. With few exceptions, parties contested all seats at every general election. Support for the parties was not evenly spread, but it was remarkably stable, as was the percentage of the popular vote which each party polled. Despite the persistence of a third party vote, the two main parties dominated electoral politics, winning between 90 and 95 per cent of all votes cast in general elections. From 1950 until 1974 the two main parties each polled over 40 per cent of the votes at each election, and the gap between them was always narrow, making the expectation of a regular alternation of the parties in government credible.

The national appeal of the Conservatives identified the party with the established order, the defence of the Union at home and the empire abroad, while Labour was identified with the institutions of the Labour movement and the industrial and political struggles for social justice. Both parties had a clear conception of citizenship, its rights and duties, which potentially included everyone in the population, with very few exceptions, although the Conservative vision of the nation was more hierarchical and less egalitarian.

The institutional basis for these 'one-nation' political projects was the existence of London as the metropolitan centre of both a highly integrated and homogeneous national territory (with the exception of Ireland), and of a substantial world empire. At the same time the United Kingdom economy as a whole, with London again playing a crucial co-ordinating role, was the centre of a cosmopolitan economy, a rapidly expanding world trading and financial network.

The post-war consensus depended for its stability on the maintenance of the external relationships that sustained the domestic economy. In the post-war period, however, the needs of the domestic and the cosmopolitan economies increasingly diverged. With the withdrawal from empire and the gradual erosion of Britian's importance as a world power (see Chapter 2) the necessity of remedying the weaknesses of the domestic economy became more apparent. The inability of successive governments to do so while maintaining the institutional legacies of British Unionism and British Labourism eventually undermined both and contributed to the crisis of identity they suffered in the 1970s (see Brett, 1985; Coates and Hillard, 1986).

The Rise of Thatcherism

The immediate reason for the rise of Thatcherism in the Conservative Party was the failure of the Heath Government to win re-election in 1974. Heath's refusal to stand down from the leadership even after a further defeat in October 1974, and the reluctance of senior Conservatives to challenge him, gave a free run to a challenger from the Right. The opportunity was taken up first by Keith Joseph and, when he dropped out, by Margaret Thatcher.

Thatcher was an unlikely challenger, both because she was a woman in a very male-dominated party and profession, and because she had only limited experience of high office. What made her bid credible was that it coincided with a strong feeling in the party that a change in the leadership had become necessary.

At the same time the demoralisation and disorientation that the events of 1973 and 1974 had created within the Conservative Party meant that many Conservatives were receptive not just to the idea of a change in leadership but to a radical overhaul of the party's attitudes and policies. Many of the old formulae of conservative politics were clearly exhausted. The Heath Government had sought to redefine the national appeal of the Conservatives following the withdrawal from empire, by giving priority to membership of the European Community, and indicating that Britain's European links should in future take priority over all others, even the special ties between Britain and the United States.

The Heath Government, in line with its post-imperial and European thinking, also delivered a severe blow to Unionism by imposing first direct rule and then power-sharing on Northern Ireland. The formal break that followed between the Ulster Unionists and the Conservative Party prevented the Conservatives being the largest single party in Parliament in February 1974, and was a factor in the slide in the party's share of the vote to 35 per cent in October 1974, the lowest proportion of the vote it has won at any general election so far this century.

The Heath Government also had a radical strategy for the modernisation of the British economy, but many of its policies, particularly its attempt to legislate a new framework for industrial relations (the Industrial Relations Act of 1971), and its desire to end subsidies for industrial 'lame ducks' such as Upper Clyde Ship-builders, encountered considerable resistance.

When unemployment began to rise sharply and industrial invest-ment remained sluggish, the Government turned away from reliance on market-oriented policies, and became more interventionist. The economy was reflated in the Budget of 1972 and the Government attempted to control inflation by seeking agreement between employers and the unions. When these talks failed it imposed a statutory incomes policy.

These changes were seized on by Enoch Powell and other Conser-vative critics as a U-turn and a betrayal of the 1970 manifesto. Most Conservatives, however, accepted them loyally at the time, including Thatcher and Joseph who remained members of Heath's Cabinet.

What damaged the record of the Heath Government was not the policy itself but the fact that the policy failed. This was largely for reasons outside Heath's control. The Barber boom was cut short by the quadrupling of oil prices in late 1973 and the beginnings of the world recession. The pay policy was on the whole successful. Most workers settled within the limits it prescribed. But the miners could not be accommodated; their work-to-rule brought power blackouts and the imposition of a three-day week on industry. The Heath Government then called an election, eighteen months before it needed to, on the explicit issue of Who Governs? The result was indecisive. No party won a majority, and the Conservatives actually polled more votes than any other party. But Labour won more seats, and was able to form a minority government and then to win an overall majority at a general election six months later.

The circumstances in which the Conservatives lost office in 1974 were crucial, both in providing the opportunity for Margaret Thatcher to seize the leadership and in creating the impetus for a wide-ranging reassessment of the party's record and policies. The New Right critique was made much more credible by the failure of the Heath Government, and a period of vigorous ideological dispute in the party commenced (on the Heath Government see Holmes, 1982).

The New Right

The New Right is a label attached to a diverse ideological and political movement. Although it has both liberal and conservative strands, they are united by a rejection of the assumptions underlying the policy regimes associated with social democracy in Britain and the New Deal and Great Society programmes in the United States (see Barry, 1987; Bosanquet, 1983; Green, 1987; Levitas, 1986).

One of the most important New Right ideas has been the concept of the overextension of the modern state. Governments have regularly pushed beyond the limits of their competence and the result has been extremely harmful to the preservation of social order. This has both liberal and conservative variants. The liberal argument has stressed the damage which unlimited government has done to the preservation of a market order, while conservatives are more concerned with how it has undermined authority throughout the institutions of civil society.

But although neo-liberals and neo-conservatives are often highly critical of one another they have little difficulty in recognising their common interest in destroying the political and intellectual credibility of the arguments supporting the maintenance of the extended state of social democracy.

They were assisted by the events of the 1960s and 1970s which discredited many collectivist and statist policies. The New Right attempted to use the policy failures of this period to justify the rejection of the whole intellectual framework which had underlain the extension of government responsibility in the economic and social field during the twentieth century.

New Right thinkers believe that the tide has finally turned against collectivism, and that after almost a hundred years of retreat, liberal ideas can once again become ascendant, capturing the moral high ground and the intellectual initiative.

The New Right includes both libertarians who think that all taxation is illegitimate and coercive, and neo-conservatives who believe the greatest problem is the breakdown of social discipline. But, as a political project, the centre of gravity in the New Right has always tended towards its authoritarian rather than its libertarian pole. The two central themes of the New Right project are that the economy should be free and the state strong. To make the economy free the state must be limited in its functions and its powers, but a limited state is not a weak state. The state must be strong enough to police the market order and ensure that the rules of market exchange are upheld and that no-one infringes them. It must also be able to confront and remove any obstacles that prevent markets working freely.

Under social democracy the economy has been fettered and the state weak. The chief reason why markets do not work is the extent of power exercised by private coercive groups, particularly trade unions. This is reflected firstly in the 'overmanning' of firms and the persistence of restrictive practices which lower efficiency. But much more is involved than just the bargaining strength of the two sides of industry. The power of the trade unions is one expression of a much deeper problem, the problem of modern democracy.

Democracy threatens both the market order and the authority of social institutions, because it constantly generates political pressures that are hostile to the preservation of stable systems of authority. Voters acquire 'excessive expectations' of what governments can achieve, and governments feel justified in expanding their activities and in taking responsibility for more and more areas of social life. As government grows so the scope of administrative decision-making expands and the scope of market allocation contracts. Lobbies and special interests multiply, since getting the right decision from the central bureaucracy has become vital.

The expansion of government itself is therefore what makes government weak. The state becomes a network of agencies which compete against one another and constantly strive to enlarge their own empires. Rational planning and co-ordination from the centre are increasingly difficult. Policy outcomes are often unplanned and arbitrary.

Hayek (1944) long ago warned that social democracy was an unstable half-way house betwen capitalism and socialism. Limited intervention would fail to produce the results expected and would generate demands for further intervention. The weak state of social democracy would lose all its legitimacy and be transformed into a totalitarian state, in which the state attempted to control everything.

From this perspective the 1940s settlement in Britain settled nothing. It was born of political stalemate rather than genuine accommodation and rested on unstable foundations which became steadily more precarious. It was responsible for the failures of economic management, the accelerating inflation and mounting unemployment, and the widespread dissatisfaction with the performance of nationalised industries and the quality of public services.

The harmful effects of the extended state of social democracy did not stop there. An expanded welfare programme encouraged a climate of dependency and undermined the authority and effectiveness of social institutions like the family. Everything could be left to the state. There was no need for self-reliance. This culture of dependency was further associated with a culture of permissiveness, the breaking away from the bonds of traditional social institutions and values.

Pinning the blame for permissiveness and the rising tide of crime, vandalism and public disorder on social democracy became central themes in New Right writing in the 1960s and 1970s. The priorities of post-war social democracy – such as maintaining full employment, providing universal welfare, and the idea of a mixed economy – were criticised because they were associated with large public-spending programmes, with a tax regime involving high marginal tax rates on income and wealth, and with the promotion of an ethos that was egalitarian, and therefore anti-capitalist.

What many on the New Right found most objectionable in social democracy was its conception of citizenship. The notion that all citizens should enjoy certain civil, political, and social rights made government intervention to secure those rights legitimate. It put the responsibility for creating the good society on political decision-making. The New Right believed that government could never acquire sufficient knowledge to plan society effectively, and that therefore the safest government was the government that was restricted as much as possible to the performance of a few basic functions.

Such a government needed to be strong in order to maintain the general rules that defined a market order and to protect the domains of those institutions, like private property and the family, on which the state's own authority rested. The objectives of the state are here defined as preserving a market order; the character of the state that does this is of much smaller concern. This is why although most of the New Right declare themselves democrats, they place liberty before democracy. Democracy is only a means, a particular type of government, whereas liberty is the essence of the market order, and can be maintained by authoritarian as well as democratic government. Democratic government may be the best form of government if it can be made to work. But, for the New Right, all forms of government are deeply flawed, and it is a choice between evils. Democracy has serious drawbacks because it leads to the generation of excessive expectations, the competitive bidding between political parties, the proliferation of special interests, and the growth of interventions in market processes which hinder efficient market allocation and the maximising of individual choice (see Buchanan, 1978; Hayek, 1960).

What the New Right seeks, therefore, is the placing of curbs on democracy to insulate the economy and civil society as much as possible from the harmful effects of 'politicisation'. Citizenship becomes defined in terms of the opportunities available to individuals in markets and no longer in terms of entitlements. There is no place for concepts of social justice in this view. Redistribution is illegitimate because it involves coercive interference in the outcomes of market exchange. Poverty, unemployment and disadvantage are no longer conditions demanding remedy through government programmes. All government is obliged to do is to ensure that all obstacles to the workings of markets are removed. Then the outcomes are not its responsibility but will depend on individual character and circumstance.

One of the main difficulties which the programme of the New Right has encountered as a political project is that it requires the dismantling of the institutions and policies of the extended state by the same political mechanism which they themselves have argued led to their creation in the first place. In the New Right view politicians and bureaucrats, if they are rational, cannot be enlightened. In pursuing their interests they will seek constantly to expand the activities over which they have control. It is this which leads to the constant presssure for the state to grow. If this process is to be reversed, either politicians and bureaucrats must start being enlightened and irrational, passing up opportunities to protect their interests, or a way must be found to make bureaucratic rationality supportive rather than corrosive of market order.

The Thatcher Government

These problems can be seen in the experience of the Thatcher

Government. It has managed to please relatively few of the New Right. The conservative New Right blames it for succumbing to liberal doctrines of free-market capitalism instead of concentrating on restoring limited government and social authority (Scruton, 1980), while the liberal New Right is critical of the timid nature of many of the measures which the Thatcher Government has carried through and its inability to shake itself free from the embrace of special interests; critics include Milton Friedman, George Gilder and Sir John Hoskyns. Many New Right critics regard the Thatcher Revolution as very incomplete.

A political project, however, should not be judged solely against the blueprints of its ideologues. What also matters are the practical changes that accompany its implementation. There have been several important shifts in the policy agenda and in the framework within which policy is discussed since the 1960s.

One of the most fundamental changes has been the redrawing of the boundaries between the public and private sectors. This has involved not simply rolling back the state. In order to roll back the state in some areas it has had to be rolled forward in others. State power has become more centralised and more concentrated under the Thatcher Government. The coercive apparatus of the state has been enlarged and deployed more openly (see Chapter 14).

Many of the targets of the new state policy have been the institutions of the Labour movement and the discredited corporatist order. The denationalisation of public enterprises (see Chapter 7) and the privatisation of public services (see Chapters 11 and 12) have eroded one of the main institutional bases of Labourism, and reduced the scope for national economic management. The scrapping of boards and quangos has been aimed in part at reducing the influence of the trade unions within national policy-making. The promotion of further internationalisation of the British economy through the abolition of exchange controls and the encouragement of inward investment also represent the abandonment of national economic planning.

Most far-reaching of all has been the attack upon the trade union movement itself (see Chapter 8). Trade union bills in 1980, 1982 and 1984 curtailed the freedom of unions to take action against employers and withdrew some of the immunities which have been in force since 1906. At the same time the severity of the recessions in 1974–6 and 1979–81 saw unemployment double to 1.5 million and then double again to more than 3 million. Against this background of widespread bankruptcies and a major shake-out of labour, trade unions experienced a rapid fall in membership and a decline in their bargaining position in most industries. Employers increasingly took the initiative in pushing through changes in manning levels and work practices, and the Government backed management in the public sector with the necessary resources and police to face down strikes. The most important and symbolic success for this policy came with the miners' strike in 1984–5.

Apart from the trade unions, major targets for government action were the powers and budgets of local authorities (see Chapter 5). The Thatcher Government continued the policy begun by Labour of seeking to re-establish central control over the local state. Grant penalties, and then rate-capping, were introduced, and a long struggle ensued. The Government abolished the metropolitan counties and the GLC (Greater London Council) altogether in 1986, and then announced in its manifesto for the 1987 election that it planned to change the funding of local authorities by substituting a community charge (a poll tax) for the rates (a system of property taxes). In many of its other plans – in education, housing, inner city redevelopment through Urban Development Corporations – the Government took or planned new powers to bypass local government. The era of collaboration between central and local government, with the centre content to delegate many powers to local authorities, appeared to be ending.

One Nation or Two?

Thatcherism has often been seen as an onslaught upon Labourism, but it was also an onslaught on that other great political force which has sustained British politics in the era of mass democracy: Unionism. The Conservative Party has traditionally sought to be a national party and has aimed to win support in all regions and from all classes. As the party of the Union and the empire it made a broad appeal to all sections of the nation. Under Baldwin, Churchill, Butler and Macmillan the party also came to identify itself with the emerging collectivist consensus on economic and social policy.

The rapid erosion of the foundations of the 1940s settlement and the changing character of the world economy and Britain's place within it made the old Unionist formulas outmoded. The empire was gone, even if the Falklands War was a powerful echo of it. Unionism was plainly disintegrating as a national political force, with the defection from the Conservative camp of both Ulster and Scotland, and the waning of Conservative support in Britain's major cities.

However, the area where the Conservative Party under Margaret Thatcher's leadership has most clearly repudiated the old consensus is in the social sphere. The social democratic conception of citizenship has been rejected. The nation which Thatcherism seeks to build is based not on the equal rights of citizenship guaranteed through state action but on the property rights of individuals.

The idea of popular capitalism is not a new idea for Conservatism; it was promoted strongly in the 1950s. But at that time it was a complement rather than a rival to collectivist welfare provision. By encouraging the growth of home ownership and share ownership the Thatcher Government seeks to align its electoral interests with its ideological plans for reshaping British society.

In practice, as several observers have noted, the Thatcher Government has been pursuing a two-nation strategy (Jessop *et al.*, 1984; Krieger, 1986; Overbeek, 1988). There is the nation of the future and the nation of the past; the nation of independence and self-reliance, and the nation of dependence and subsidy; the nation of the employed and prosperous, and the nation of unemployed and the poor. The message of Thatcherism is quite unlike the soothing social democratic message of Unionism and Labourism which suggested (whatever the reality) that the state was seeking to remedy or reduce inequalities and ensure that all citizens, as far as possible, had equal opportunities. The novelty and radicalism of Thatcherism lies in the rejection of those ideas. Inequality is welcomed and praised, and promoted through fiscal policy. The nation of subsidy and dependence is no longer to be propped up: it is to be reconstructed. The South is to swallow the North.

The Thatcher Government has identified itself with the buoyant and expanding internationalised sector of the economy, abandoning any hope that the sector of declining and uncompetitive traditional industries can be preserved. The problem for political management is that there are great difficulties in absorbing the population sustained by the old industrial manufacturing economy into the new. This is why the Manpower Services Commission (MSC), at first earmarked for closure, was reprieved and then greatly expanded.

In order to free the internationalised sector of the economy, the shackles of high taxation and high public-spending programmes on welfare need to be thrown off. The restructuring of public spending, industrial relations and many social institutions, in order to give maximum opportunity to the international sector, has required the strengthening of the state's powers to permit adequate policing and surveillance of the dependent populations which are outside the new prosperity. This project has so far been crowned with success. Aided by the boom initiated by the United States between 1982 and 1987, the internationalised sector of the British economy has performed strongly. Oil revenues and asset sales have helped swell the boom in revenues and permitted a budget strategy aimed at protecting and improving the living standards of those in secure employment. The British electoral system and the geographical concentration of Conservative support has ensured confirmation of the Conservatives in office in 1983 and 1987, even though their share of the vote is only 42 to 43 per cent.

Two-nation politics has so far proved a winning formula, but doubts remain about its durability. Margaret Thatcher has begun to speak of Britain as the first post-socialist society, and many supporters of her Government have described her victory in 1979 as an event which has permanently changed the British political landscape (e.g. Cosgrave, 1985; Holmes, 1985).

In assessing these claims it is necessary to distinguish between the changes that can be ascribed to the operation of political parties and those that are the result of broader changes to which all parties are obliged to adapt. Under Margaret Thatcher's leadership the Conservatives have been very skilful at identifying themselves with many of the new forces and developments of the 1980s. This has allowed them to present themselves as a modern party, in tune with new ideas, in contrast to the traditional and old-fashioned ideas and beliefs of their opponents.

The new politics of the 1970s and 1980s does not impose a simple strait-jacket on political forces. In other countries the themes of the new politics have been adopted and adapted by political forces with very different ideological alignments. Britain is rather unusual for the degree of dominance which the Conservatives appear to have established. Some of the changes over which they have presided, particularly the further internationalisation of the economy and the changes in industrial and occupational structure, appear irreversible. Changes in the balance of power between labour and capital, however, and the level and character of government intervention in the economy are less likely to prove permanent, unless the Conservatives find the secret of being eternally in office or succeed in permanently marginalising the Labour Party. Between 1981 and 1983 the possibility that Labour might be replaced by the Alliance, as the Liberals had once been replaced by Labour, was often canvassed. It looked a much less likely scenario in 1987.

The triumph of the Conservatives in 1987, despite the continuing unpopularity of many of their more radical policies, was a sign less of an impregnable political position than of the fragmentation of the opposition. Proposals to end this fragmentation through different kinds of electoral pact abounded by 1987, but there was never much likelihood of the political leaderships of Labour and the Alliance accepting them.

The strategy of the Labour Party under Neil Kinnock remained the restoration of Labour to its position as the alternative party of government in the old two-party system. An alternative strategy urged by some in the party was for Labour to embrace the cause of radical constitutional reform, and become the party of political modernisation, an area where the Conservatives had never tried to tread. By accepting that Britain had become a multi-party system it would both make many Alliance supporters more likely to vote Labour in constituencies where Labour had a chance of winning, and attack the heart of the Conservative political ascendancy.

Rebuilding opposition to Thatcherism in terms of widening democracy and extending citizenship rights, deploying arguments on fairness, openness, the extension of life chances, and new forms of government regulation of the economy, seemed the most likely route by which the political initiative would be wrested from Thatcherism. But the key remained the economy and its performance. After the stock market crash in 1987 the future of the Lawson boom began to assume critical importance for the future of the Thatcherite project. Without the cushion of increasing prosperity, part of the Conservatives' electoral support looked vulnerable. In 1988 many Conservatives, including the Prime Minister, became concerned that the new consensus rested too much on self-interest and too little on moral conviction. The ability of Thatcherism to continue to hold the political initiative and to set the terms of the political debate will depend on how far it can retain its support if the boom ends and the economy turns down. After surviving the storms of 1979–81, Thatcherism by 1987 had proved enormously successful as a political project. Ministers could justifiably claim that the decline had been halted. But whether the decline had been permanently reversed remained uncertain. The prospects for Thatcherism were clouded also. The depth of support for its themes of popular capitalism and the enterprise economy were still to be tested through hard times.

2
Britain's Changing Role in the World-Economy

Peter J. Taylor

Britain has lost an empire but has not yet found a role.

> Dean Acheson (former US Secretary of State) 1962.

We are a world power and a world influence or we are nothing

> Harold Wilson (newly elected Prime Minister) 1964.

The general premise upon which this chapter is based is that it is impossible to understand any country in the modern world separately from its position within the capitalist world-economy and geopolitical order. The specific premise that is developed is that it is impossible to analyse Britain apart from its domination of the world-economy and geopolitical order in the mid nineteenth century. The unique role that Britain played at that time and the subsequent decline from such exalted power continues to dominate any consideration of the nature of Britain today.

The world-economy is a global system of production and exchange operating through the prime motive of ceaseless capital accumulation (Wallerstein, 1983). One consequence of the logic of accumulation is uneven development in both space and time. Hence the world-economy is characterised by a distinctive spatial structure of core and periphery and a regular temporal pattern of medium-length cycles of growth and stagnation (Kondratieff waves). Both dimensions of uneven development provide a changing mixture of constraints and opportunities for the various actors in the world-economy. One set of actors, the territorial states, operate to enhance opportunities and curtail constraints in three main ways (Wallerstein, 1984). First, they define the legal framework for social relations within their boundaries. Second, they attempt to influence events beyond their boundaries. Third, they control flows across their boundaries – of commodities, labour and finance. The degree to which each state can successfully operate to enhance its position varies with the power of the state. This depends upon the material base of the state – how much world production it controls – and its position in the inter-state system where it can enhance its power by combining in treaties and alliances.

All states operate in the world-economy in the same basic way, but they vary immensely in the power they command. Each individual state has to come to terms with its power within this framework. It has to map out roles to play within the 'great game' that is international politics. Each role involves a view of the nature of the world-system and how the country fits into that system. This self-image becomes the guiding principle of how government should operate. In extreme cases such roles and their self-images are overthrown with the state in political revolutions. But roles can also be changed peacefully, as states adjust to their changing material base. In such cases two or more roles may compete for the attention of the politicians and public. This is because a particular role can be pursued after its original functions have objectively ceased. Such relict roles can continue to be influential. It is the thesis of this essay that in Britain such relict roles have severely distorted adjustment to the country's changing material base (for a discussion of the influence of these relict roles on Britain's internal structure, see Massey, 1986).

The most distinctive role of all is that of hegemony (Wallerstein, 1984: 37–46). In rare instances a very special circumstance occurs where one country is qualitatively superior to all the others. Objectively hegemonic states are identified when they have an economic lead over all rivals in terms of production, commerce and finance. This material base is projected into other spheres of world affairs. They are politically dominant, not in terms of a formal global imperium, but by maintaining a control of the system to ensure that no viable alternative coalition of rivals emerges. Similarly they are militarily dominant, not because they interfere to coerce across the whole system, but because they maintain the strategic points safeguarding the system. *Pax Britannia* of the mid nineteenth century remains the classic case of state hegemony: 'the workshop of the world', 'a nation of shopkeepers', the world's bankers in the City of

London, balancing power in Europe, and the Royal Navy ruling the waves, all added up to hegemonic power.

The features that make up hegemony do not disappear overnight. First to go is the productive edge that a country has over its rivals. Imitations and new technologies soon lead to rivals catching up and overtaking the erstwhile hegemonic state. Without its productive lead, commercial superiority is obviously threatened. The fall in economic power has consequences for political power as the balancing act becomes more difficult and then finally becomes impossible. Furthermore the relative decline of the material base means that the military sphere is inevitably affected, as maintaining a hegemonic-like military posture becomes excessively expensive. And finally, the last to succumb to rival challengers, the financial sector can no longer act as the world's banker. All of this happened to Britain in the period between its hegemony and the end of the First World War.

Wallerstein has related the rise and fall of hegemonic states to the cyclical nature of the world-economy (Research Working Group, 1979). The temporal pattern of growth and stagnation represented by Kondratieff waves produces cycles of approximately fifty years, each incorporating an A-phase of growth and a B-phase of stagnation. Such cycles are commonly traced back to the industrial revolution of the late eighteenth century. The period since has been described in terms of four Kondratieff waves – in this scheme the world-economy has been experiencing Kondratieff phase IVB since about 1970. Wallerstein has combined these material cycles with British and US hegemony as shown in Table 2.1. The Kondratieff waves are 'paired' into British and American 'centuries' of dominance. In the first A-phase of each sequence a period of ascending hegemony is identified when one state is emerging as the container of the most efficient production processes in the world-economy. When the world-economy moves into the next B-phase only this one state is in a position to take advantage of the more limited opportunities during the widespread stagnation. This phase is identified with hegemonic victory as it becomes clear to all which state is the most powerful in the world. With the next upturn in the world-economy we reach the phase of hegemonic maturity as the hegemonic state dominates the world-economy and the inter-state system. But this success cannot last and in the next B-phase we come to the stage of declining hegemony as other major states 'catch-up' economically

Table 2.1   State hegemony and Kondratieff cycles

	'Great Britain's century'		'The American century'
Kondratieff Cycle I	—1790–8— A_1 *Ascending Hegemony*	Rivalry with France (Napoleonic Wars) Productive efficiency: industrial revolution	**Kondratieff Cycle III** — —1890–6— A_1 *Ascending Hegemony* — Rivalry with Germany Productive efficiency: mass production techniques
	—1815–25— B_1 *Hegemonic Victory*	Commercial victory in Latin America and control of India: workshop of the world	—1890–6— B_1 *Hegemonic Victory* — Commercial victory in the final collapse of British free trade system and decisive military defeat of Germany
Kondratieff Cycle II	—1844–51— A_2 *Hegemonic maturity*	Era of Free Trade: London becomes financial centre of the world economy	**Kondratieff Cycle IV** — —1940–5— A_2 *Hegemonic maturity* — Liberal economic system of Bretton Woods based upon the dollar: New York new financial centre of the world
	—1870–5— B_2 *Declining Hegemony*	Classical age of imperialism as European powers and USA rival Britain. 'New' industrial revolution emerging outside Britain	—1967–73— B_2 *Declining Hegemony* — Reversal to protectionist practices to counteract Japan and European rivals
	—1980–6—		—?—

Source: P. J. Taylor (1985) p. 57.

and become serious challengers in an era of intense rivalry. Both British and US hegemony seem to conform to this pattern. Our concern is with the legacy of one hegemony (Britain's) in the era of another hegemony (the USA's).

The more exalted the role the greater its legacy. Hence the attempt to maintain a hegemonic role would be expected to influence a state throughout the trauma of its decline. This is certainly the case with Britain. As Britain's politicians and state officials tried to match Britain's role to its dwindling resources they were continually confronted with a self-image they could no longer sustain. Four post-hegemonic roles are identified below, all of which have been influenced by Britain's nineteenth-century hegemony. They are, in order of their appearance: 'Greater Britain', still ranked first but now as an imperial economic bloc leader; 'Hegemonic Mate', now accepting a lower rank as first lieutenant to the USA, the new hegemonic power; 'Regional Power', eschewing a world role and finding a haven in Europe; and 'Little England', finally exorcising the hegemonic spirit and accepting 'ordinary' status in the world. Although we will describe them chronologically, in reality they make up a kaleidoscope of fluctuating positions. Churchill recognised this when he viewed Britain's post-war situation as three interlocking circles – Atlantic, Empire, Europe – with Britain in a pivotal position. This was his way of maintaining a view of Britain's importance in the world after hegemony. Like all British politicians of the twentieth century, Churchill had to grapple with the dilemma of selling decline to a public raised on memories of hegemony. How this was achieved is a fascinating story.

Role One: Hegemonic Power and its Legacy

The rise of Britain as hegemonic power came in opposition to the old imperialism and mercantilism of the eighteenth century. The symbolic date for the overthrowing of the old order is the repeal of the Corn Laws in 1846. Through the middle decades of the nineteenth century Britain pursued a free trade policy and sought, with initial success, to persuade others to conform to the new liberal world order. Britain was attempting to create a world of free trading nations whose roles would be defined by their comparative advantage. It was assumed that this meant Britain would produce industrial goods for other countries who would send Britain food and raw materials. In short, Britain was seeking a world as one large functional region centred on itself. The self-interest incorporated in this world view was masked by an ideology of liberalism. In practice Britain combined a formal empire centred on India with an informal empire (economic dominance without political control) in Latin America, safeguarded by the Royal Navy.

There is no equivalent date to 1846 for symbolically signalling the end of British hegemony. Britain was hegemonic through the A-phase (growth) of the Victorian Kondratieff cycle, but during the B-phase (stagnation) of the final quarter of the nineteenth century Britain was overtaken in productive efficiency by the USA and Germany in key sectors such as engineering and chemicals (Taylor, 1985: 57). Both rival countries led a general movement away from free trade towards protectionism. Associated with this was the new imperialism, most notably in Africa. Britain gained most territory from this process but the fact that she had even to contemplate joining in a scramble for Africa indicated a fall from hegemony to mere rivalry. Politically the end of hegemony was signalled by the end of the 'free hand' in British foreign policy and the signing of defence agreements first with Japan and then with France and Russia between 1902 and 1907: Britain was no longer confident in her balancing act on either the European or world stage (Bartlett, 1984: 40).

The end of British hegemony was confirmed by the First World War. The immense costs of the war resulted in liquidating assets throughout the world and dependence on US finances. Even then Britain was shown to be incapable of winning the war without the addition of American troops. By 1919 Britain, the victor, was nevertheless clearly in no position to reconstruct its dominant power position. The League of Nations was a recognition that a new world order could not be built under one country's dominance. In 1922, in the Washington Treaty, Britain conceded parity to the US Navy, hence terminating more than a century of Royal Naval superiority (Bartlett, 1984: 132). In 1925 Britain returned to the Gold Standard with disastrous consequences, especially for the traditional export-ing industries of the North. The General Strike of 1926 was one result. In 1932 all this changed as the Gold Standard was abandoned along with free trade. The system of imperial preferences struck at the very heart of Britain's hegemonic role. After 1932 hegemonic-type policies were pale shadows of their former selves. From this time onwards the hegemonic legacy is to be found only in resonances that capture some of Britain's past grandeur, but always as a pathetic imitation.

Three instances of this resonance can be easily identified. In 1938, at Munich, Britain found herself representing not just her empire but a large section of world opinion in her attempts to prevent war in Europe. The traditional diplomatic approach to a challenge from Europe was finally found to be severely wanting. But to understand Britain's desperate search for peace at this time it must be realised that she had most to lose from war: another full-scale European war like 1914–18 would ring the death-knell to any lingering British ambitions for world leadership (Gamble, 1981: 59). In the event, the Second World War crippled Britain even more than the First World War, and by 1945 even parity with the USA was no longer an option.

The second example is the Suez fiasco of 1956. This Anglo–French attack on Egypt was in the grand tradition of maintaining the world's waterways for trade. The attack went ahead, however, without the knowledge of the Americans, the new hegemonic power. By using its economic might to engineer a run on sterling, the USA ruthlessly brought its allies to heel (Watt, 1984: 133). A whole new world had been created and Britain had stepped out of line. The result was political humiliation.

Twenty-six years later a very different outcome occurred in the Falklands/Malvinas conflict. Again acting without the USA, but this time in continuous consultation, Britain was able to bring off a military victory on the other side of the globe. Britain could claim to be a 'world power' once again. As Nairn (1983: 283) has so cogently put it: ' "Decline" vanished on April 3rd, psychologically speaking'. The Falklands cannot compare with India as a new centre of empire but the resonances of the past were clear for all to see as the naval task force returned to Portsmouth in triumph and celebration.

What does this hegemonic role mean in the post-hegemonic period? We must remember that during its decline Britain has been a *status quo* power (Northedge, 1974: 303): a situation of no change suits Britain as, in crudest terms, it translates into one of no further decline. In the true hegemonic role of a century ago, British self-interest was masked by a liberal vision of progress and freedom. In the post-hegemonic period the resonance of that past is found when

Britain fights the underdogs (be they Boers, Germans or Argentinians) with a sincere clarion call for justice!

Role Two: Greater Britain, the Imperial Leader

The opposite of a liberal world order is a world of economic blocs. This is what the new imperialism and protectionism of the late nineteenth century was creating. One role that Britain could take was to join in this battle of the blocs and abandon its free trade policy. And of course Britain was in a very good position in any economic warfare. Although giving way to the USA in the Americas, Britain still had the largest formal empire in the world, covering a quarter of all the land and people of the world. Hence the idea of a functional region centred on Britain could be created, but on a smaller scale than the liberal version. Certainly in 1900 Britain could abandon its hegemonic role, assume an imperial role, and still remain the most powerful state in the world. The temptation was there but ultimately it was largely resisted.

The idea of a global federation to form one state is usually traced to Seeley's *The Expansion of England* published in 1885 (Northedge, 1974: 207). But a coherent political movement to change Britain's role did not appear until 1903 with Chamberlain's launching of the tariff reform campaign (Gamble, 1981: 172). Initially unable to convert the Conservative Party, when they did fight the 1910 and 1923 elections on a tariff reform platform they lost. When the change did come as imperial preferences in 1932 it was a result of the global economic collapse rather than any campaign for change. In short, Britain's change of role was not part of a carefully planned change of strategy; rather it was forced on the Government by the severe constraints of a Kondratieff B-phase. In any case the time for integrated association or even federation had long passed. Although in 1914 Britain's declaration of war included all the empire, by 1919 at the Paris peace talks no co-ordinated empire position was achieved. In the year before imperial preferences were agreed, the white Dominions were formally given independence under the British crown. Nevertheless in the 1930s the British Empire, at last, constituted the largest economic bloc in the world.

The existence of the empire enabled Britain to claim superpower status along with the USA and USSR at the end of the Second

World War. But the position was fragile. As we shall see when discussing Britain's relations with the USA below, the opening up of the empire was one of the prime objectives of the new hegemonic power. In 1947 imperial preferences were made subject to the new GATT (General Agreement on Tariffs and Trade) rules so that Britain's brief role as an economic bloc leader had soon come to an end.

The legacy of Britain as imperial leader can be found, of course, in the Commonwealth. After Indian independence in 1947 a way was found for the new republic to remain in the Commonwealth with the Queen as symbolic head of the latter. Certainly in Labour Party visions of a 'third way' between American capitalism and Russian communism, the welfare state of their social democracy was considered transferable to the empire (Barker, 1983: 84). But such dreams soon passed. As more and more colonies became independent and joined the Commonwealth its nature changed profoundly. Whereas in 1939 the Commonwealth of the settler Dominions shared many geopolitical assumptions with Britain, including a faith in the British Navy, the new Commonwealth was a multi-racial association of states, most of whom did not share Britain's view of the world (Northedge, 1974: 229). Indian leadership of the non-aligned movement is the most obvious departure of a Commonwealth state from British foreign policy. This was most clear in the former's severe condemnation of Britain's Suez adventure. In 1965 two Commonwealth countries went to war – India and Pakistan – and peace was brought not through Commonwealth channels but by Britain's Cold War adversary the USSR. In 1983 the USA invaded Grenada, a Commonwealth country, and forgot to inform the Queen, who was still head of state. These episodes highlight the looseness of association that is the Commonwealth of Nations. The *coup de grâce* of empire is usually taken to be Britain's accession to the European Economic Community in 1973.

Are there therefore any resonances of Britain as imperial leader today? Although the Falklands campaign is sometimes portrayed in these terms – the empire strikes back! – it was, of course, a national effort with no Commonwealth connections at all. The major operation of the Commonwealth has been as a means of communicating to Britain 'Third World' concerns over decolonisation, Rhodesia and South Africa. Hence, rather than being a 'leader', Britain is typically the state under pressure to conform. But when all is said and done the Commonwealth survives, meets regularly and attempts to influence world events. It may be a far cry from the federation or economic bloc of the early dreamers, but it still symbolises Britain's imperial past. Many economic linkages remain important, giving Britain a role in the Third World it would not otherwise have. The empire may be buried but British imperialism is hardly dead and gone.

Role Three: Hegemonic Mate or the 'Special Relationship'

In this role Britain remains a major world power but is no longer number one. As the economic and military might of the USA became overwhelming in the mid twentieth century a new hegemonic power had arrived, and Britain, like all other countries, had to adjust accordingly. Viewing the new hegemonic state as young, wilful and inexperienced in the subtlety of world affairs, Britain offered its immense experience in return for the 'special relationship' with the USA. This preserved Britain's world status as a sort of mixture of advisor and trusty deputy. Cultural affinities are emphasised, as in Churchill's lauding of the 'English-speaking peoples': Britain was merely passing on the baton of progress to its cousins across the sea.

The beginnings of America devising a hegemonic role can be found during the First World War when President Wilson was expecting to use British and French financial dependence to ensure an 'American peace' (Watt, 1984: 32). In the event Germany capitulated too early for the US scheme and Wilson was defeated domestically. This left the severe US–Britain rivalry of the inter-war years – 'the great non-war of the twentieth century' (Taylor, 1987: 23) – culminating with the British reversal to imperial preferences. In the Second World War the latter became a prime target of American policy from the original Atlantic Charter of 1941 through to the loan negotiations of 1945 (Reynolds, 1981; Kolko and Kolko, 1973; Northedge, 1974: 185). With the end of the lend-lease scheme Britain was forced to go to the USA for a loan to start post-war reconstruction. The terms were harsh, but Britain accepted them since the alternative of little or no reconstruction was unpalatable. Among several conditions Britain had to agree to dismantle imperial preferences, ensuring American business access to the markets of the British Empire. This was, as some critics dubbed it, 'Britain's economic Munich'. It demonstrated US hegemonic power and Britain's fall from grace.

Britain remained a powerful state, however. With Russia devastated, France recently occupied and Germany, Japan and Italy defeated, Britain came out of the war in a strong position. When the term 'superpower' was first coined in 1944 it was used to include Britain as well as the USA and USSR. By 1947, however, the 'Big Three' had been clearly reduced to a bi-polar contest of just two superpowers in the emerging Cold War (E. Barker, 1983: 69). In that year Britain informed the USA that it could not afford to maintain its military commitments in Greece and Turkey. The taking-over of these commitments by the USA led directly to President Truman's speech in which he defined his 'doctrine' of USSR 'containment' (Rothwell, 1982). A crisis in sterling and Indian independence left Britain clearly inferior to the two superpowers. But as the USA deputy Britain continued to play a subordinate leadership role, first in organising the European response to the Marshall Plan in 1948, and then in the formation of NATO in 1949. Britain may no longer have been a member of the Big Three but she was still number three in the world.

One of the reasons why Britain fitted so easily into its 'hegemonic mate' role was because the economic policies the USA pursued as hegemonic power were essentially the same as those of Britain as hegemonic power a century earlier. Britain had stayed loyal to a liberal world economy until 1932, so that the new US policies could still be seen as a return to 'our' policies: Britain had finally converted the USA to the correct way of organising the world!

But behind the continuity there was a profound paradox that was to be Britain's undoing. The terms of the special relationship left Britain with a world-wide pattern of commitment to be paid for from a material base far removed from hegemonic status (Gamble, 1981: 107–13). In fact in real terms Britain was spending more overseas in the early post-war years than it ever had in the nineteenth century. This foreign policy coincided with a domestic policy that created the welfare state. The combined burden on the economy was never fully costed. There was no national economic plan to accommodate the needs of this new Britain. Something had to give and the result was Britain's notorious 'stop-go economy' (Blank, 1977; Jessop, 1980). As the inflationary pressures of these expenditures grew, demand was cut and with the resulting high interest rates this harmed the prospects of the manufacturing sector. As deflation took hold the constraints were relaxed to ensure unemployment remained at socially acceptable levels. A very uneven pattern of growth provided the seeds for crisis.

The special relationship disappeared in the 1960s. Harold Macmillan was the last prime minister to act out Britain's number three role in organising the 1960 superpower summit. British troops had fought in Korea in the early 1950s but were not alongside the USA in Vietnam in the 1960s. America was let down in its hour of need: the special relationship was dead. In 1967 financial pressures finally forced Britain to abandon its commitments 'east of Suez'. Britain was no longer a world power but a regional power in Europe and the Mediterranean.

With the demise of US hegemony in the current Kondratieff B-phase, a strange reassembly of the special relationship has occurred. Britain and the USA are blood cousins again, brought together by a New Right rhetoric (Reaganomics and Thatcherism) combining a return to liberal economic orthodoxy and belligerent foreign policy. In the economic sphere co-operation has been difficult, but in terms of foreign policy the 'iron lady' has fitted perfectly into the new Cold War against the 'evil empire' that is the USSR. The symbolic cementing of the new special relationship came in 1986 when Britain facilitated the US bombing of Libya, against the protests of its European neighbours.

Role Four: Regional Power in a European Haven

Britain's fourth role was a product of economic league tables. In the late 1950s and 1960s all western European countries, except in the poorer Mediterranean zone, overtook Britain in terms of per capita gross national product. Within little more than a decade Britain had fallen from being world number three to being denigrated as the 'sick man of Europe'. In these circumstances what more obvious choice of role was there than that of joining the conspicuous success going on just across the Channel? Here on Britain's doorstep was another potential superpower. At last a choice had to be made from among Churchill's three circles and only the Europe option seemed to offer a realistic prospect of economic security.

The decision to carve out a dominant European role for Britain was not an easy one. There was a tradition of detachment from European affairs: Britain was in but not of Europe (Northedge, 1974: 142–5). It had only become involved in Europe to counter threats to its world roles. This dominated Britain's relations with its western European neighbours in the early post-war years. At this time Britain was still the leading European power and played this role in the development of the Marshall Plan with the setting up of the Organisation of European Economic Co-operation in 1948. In the same year Britain led the formation of the Brussels Group dealing with defence issues. In all this organisational activity Britain opposed the 'federalists' who wanted to move towards a 'United States of Europe'. In 1949, the Council of Europe was set up in a form that did not offend Britain's anti-federalist position.

The turning point in Britain's relations with Western Europe came with the Schuman Plan (Northedge, 1974: 155). This proposed integrating the coal, iron and steel industries of West Germany and France under a supra-national authority so as to make future war between them materially impossible. In 1950 the European Coal and Steel Commission was formed, with the Benelux countries and Italy joining France and Germany. These six countries went on to create the European Economic Community (EEC) in 1957, which aimed at long-term political integration as well as short- and medium-term economic harmonisation. Both were anathema to Britain. The single outside tariff, for instance, would have forced Britain as a member to discriminate against Commonwealth countries. In response Britain formed in 1958 the much looser European Free Trade Association with other non-EEC countries and which had no common external tariff. For a short while Western Europe was divided into two economic blocs. But in reality EFTA was no substitute for the much larger EEC.

By 1960 Britain was beginning to reassess its role, as the relative lack of post-war economic success came to dominate the political agenda. Negotiations and applications to join the EEC in 1961 and 1967 were vetoed by French President de Gaulle. This further compounded British humiliation. The veto was largely on the grounds that Britain was insufficiently 'European'. As an 'oceanic power' she would act as a sort of American 'Trojan horse' within the EEC. Hence British entry to Europe had to await the fall of de Gaulle, and accession only finally arrived in 1973. A decade of uncertainty seemed over.

In the event the delayed timing was unfortunate. The growth the EEC had enjoyed slowed down with the rest of the world-economy as the Kondratieff cycle changed phases. A new British Government renegotiated terms and a referendum confirmed membership in 1975. Although the 'No' supporters emphasised loss of British sovereignty by membership, the 'Yes' majority exploited fears of 'a lonely Britain' (Childs, 1986: 253), lost in a turbulent world. The latter won a two-to-one majority confirming a popular lack of faith in Britain's ability to go it alone in the world any more. Ironically within one year the economic security the EEC offered was found wanting as another economic crisis led to the International Monetary Fund insisting on public expenditure cuts as conditions for a loan. Britain was being treated like a Third World country. Its sovereignty in 1976 was probably more at risk from the IMF than the EEC. Either way it soon became clear that British hopes of an economic revival based on European competition came to nothing. The new role was not stemming the long tide of British decline.

In the 1980s the European Community is not a major issue in British politics. In the 1984 European election, for instance, only 33 per cent of the British electorate bothered to vote, compared with an average of over 60 per cent elsewhere. Traditional British fears of federalism have proved unfounded as moves towards political integration have not progressed. In fact the 'community' continues to operate as a collection of states with varying national interests. Britain's European role continues to be an enigma.

Role Five: Little England in a Brave New Plural World

As a way of concluding this chapter, I am going to discuss a role that has never actually existed. Its potential, however, highlights the problems inherent in the roles that have existed. Quite simply the story told above is one of post-hegemonic trauma. What role could Britain have that truly exorcised its hegemonic legacy? A little utopian thinking can reveal both the constraints of the past and the potentials of the future.

Let us begin with the constraints because they are indeed severe. Northedge (1974: 358–9) argues as follows:

It is important to see this British decline first in what may be called its world geopolitical context, that is, in terms of the ever changing balance of world forces as a whole... Because of the strength and ubiquity of these geopolitical forces hardly any action by a British government could have done anything to arrest or reverse the British decline... the decline of British power... (was) too geopolitically based.

Northedge is here referring to the period 1945–73, although we can see that his argument could be applied to the whole of the last century. There is a sense in which decline from hegemony is inevitable as we have argued: other countries will copy, initiate and innovate at the expense of the erstwhile leader. No one country can maintain a monopoly of efficiency in the world-economy in the medium run. What happened to Britain is now happening to the USA. But this does not mean that the vicious rivalry that followed British hegemony must repeat itself in the much more dangerous nuclear world of the late twentieth century.

One scenario which does predict a new world of economic blocs is Wallerstein's (1988) 'geopolitical shift'. He envisages a pattern of alliances pitting the Pacific Rim bloc (USA–Japan–China) against a European bloc (Western Europe–Eastern Europe–USSR). Such a bi-polar world contradicts the ideological assumptions of the Cold War. As such it represents an important bonus for a Europe that can be 'united' again by the drawing back of the Iron Curtain. For Britain, however, the picture is far from rosy. It is stranded between its global and Atlantic faces and its European linkages. In this scenario Britain's future is worse than a simple extrapolation of recent decline: Britain will be left 'lonely' and consequently helpless, a pawn for the two new power blocs to use as they will. Actually I believe this scenario to be as depressing for Europe as it is for Britain.

This 'full' European bloc can be viewed as the consequence of a process of European integration that has been operating since the world-economy began. From small dynastic units to nation-states to the European Community, the trans-Iron-Curtain bloc is a next stage in a political superstructure conforming to the increasing scale requirements of capital. But there are other trends which do not conform to the creation of bigger and bigger political units. The 'minor' nationalisms of Europe that never managed to create their own nation-states have made a comeback in the last few decades. Instead of disappearing, as all models of political development predicted, they have survived and prospered to challenge the modern European state (Williams, 1980). A Europe of smaller units is also incorporated in the programme of the new European-wide peace movement: imposed peace by large political units can be a peace not worth having (Voûte, 1987). And finally, for all the comparisons made with the countries of the European Community, the first European countries to overtake Britain in the 'economic league table', and which continue to head it, are Sweden and Switzerland. In Eastern Europe the most successful country economically has been Finland. In these terms at least, small is beautiful: hence the call for the Swedenisation of Western Europe and the Finlandisation of Eastern Europe (E. P. Thompson, 1987: 32). This is an alternative Europe without economic blocs and geopolitical imperatives.

Only in such an alternative Europe can Britain be freed of its hegemonic legacy. Today that legacy is expressed in 'Thatcherism', with its not-so-subtle combination of elements of the first four roles identified above. The temporary political success of this particular phenomenon should not lead us to forget that the material conditions that have cut short Britain's world role throughout this century continue unabated. Only finance capital remains as an element of world power (still firmly number two). But finance capital does not require a territory occupied by 56 million people. It would be better off if London were converted to a city state such as Singapore!

Nairn (1977) has long predicted the break-up of the territorial state of Britain. In his analysis Scotland and Wales will follow Ireland in separating from the antique imperial English state of Great Britain. The rise of such nationalism in the 1970s has subsided, but Thatcherism and its domestic divisiveness has put it back on the agenda with the collapse of the Scottish Conservative Party in the 1987 general election. But where will this leave England? According to Nairn (1983: 288) 'The *real* England is irredeemably Tory'. And yet the widening north–south divide in Britain, both political and economic, is not drawn along the England–Scotland boundary. The material conditions exist for a break-up of England between a 'finance South' and a 'industrial North'. This is not currently on the political agenda but there must be a limit to the relative decline of northern England and the maintenance of loyalty to the state that oversees that decline (see also Chapter 3). A divided England would be the surest way of ending Britain's hegemonic legacy. In any case the break-up of Britain would fit neatly into a Europe of small countries. The hallmark, even logo, of Thatcherism – that there is no alternative – must be confronted. A political geography of Europe as a single economic bloc is one alternative to the continuation of the Cold War politics of Thatcherism. It is in fact what Hitler tried to create before the Cold War. A pluralist Europe of many countries in which the components of the British state take their place is a far more palatable political geography to look forward to. This is Britain's fifth role, which can be created from the ashes of Thatcherism.

3
Nationalisms in a Disunited Kingdom

James Anderson

The United Kingdom of Great Britain and Northern Ireland is spectacularly ramshackle and lop-sided. As its cumbersome title suggests, it falls well short of the modern – and nationalist – ideal of the homogeneous nation-state. The ideal is that the territory of the nation and that of the state should be one and the same: to each nation its own state, each state the expression of a single nation, a happy coincidence of cultural community and political sovereignty. For nationalists the territorial boundaries of nations and states should coincide, and clearly they do not in the case of the UK. It encompasses Scottish, Welsh, Irish and other identities such as that of Northern Ireland Protestants, imperfectly bound together by a wider but incomplete sense of Britishness. England, with over 80 per cent of the total UK population, is very much the political 'centre' (though there is increasingly a case for confining that term to the South-East of England). Scotland, Wales and Northern Ireland are politically its 'peripheries', and the need to claim 'unitedness' in the title hints perhaps at the imperfect unity of a *multi*-national state in which the three 'peripheries' differ markedly not just from the 'centre' but from each other.

This chapter examines the thesis that the failure to meet the nation-state ideal will lead to the break-up of the UK. It briefly describes the ramshackle character of the state and it outlines the resurgence of its nationalisms since the 1960s, in order to speculate on their likely political implications.

The modern conception of the nation-state – of a geographical fit between cultural community and political organisation – emerged from absolutist states such as England, France and Spain in late feudal times and only became codified as nationalist doctrine at the time of the French Revolution. Although nationalism has been used for all sorts of political purposes, progressive and reactionary, the ideal has a democratic element which helps explain nationalism's widespread appeal (see J. Anderson, 1986: 124–42). The nineteenth century liberal democrat John Stuart Mill brings out this element in his *Considerations of Representative Government* (1872):

> It is, in general, a necessary condition of free institutions that the boundaries of government should coincide in the main with those of nationality... Where the sentiment of nationality exists in any force, there is a *prima facie* case for uniting all the members of the nationality under the same government, and a government to themselves apart.

However, the problem – and Mill does not seem to have been aware of its seriousness – is that the boundaries of 'government' and 'nationality' frequently fail to coincide: governments refuse to alter existing state boundaries, and in any case different nationalities are often so geographically intermingled that national territories cannot be easily defined or agreed between the competing claims.

The ideal of the nation-state in fact comes from two, often conflicting, aspirations: the aspiration of states to speak for a single, unified nation, and the aspiration of nations for states of their own. Nationalisms are territorially-based forms of ideology and politics; they link historically and culturally defined 'nations' to political statehood, either as a reality or as an aspiration. Nationalists typically find their unifying symbols and criteria of 'belonging' in the particular history and geography of their territory – its culture, language, landscape, and so forth – and, despite antagonistic class relations within the nation, geographical proximity in a particular territory can also provide at least an illusion of a common economic interest (J. Anderson, 1988: 30–2). Thus states inculcate nationalist feelings to achieve legitimacy and maintain the unity of the whole population and its loyalty to what dominant groups define as the 'national interest'. Sovereignty is asserted over what is claimed as the whole 'national' territory, against the claims of autonomist or separatist groups within the state, as well as against political forces from outside it. State-sponsored nationalism (e.g. British nationalism) thus generally works against any significant territorial reorganisation of political units, in order to preserve what it claims is a nation-state. However, minority nations within the state (e.g. the Scots or the Irish) can follow a similar logic, though with very different results. Where they demand their own 'right to national self determination', either in the form of autonomous 'home rule' or in a completely separate state, the legitimacy and perhaps very survival of the existing state can be undermined:

> ...the state in its own defence tends to act as though it were a single and unified nation from the cultural point of view, and if in fact it is not this, it must endeavour to make the facts correspond to the ideal, regardless of the rights or liberties of those among its citizens who do not belong to the majority nation. On the other hand, every nation... which is not a national state must seek to become one... The history of self-determination is a history of the making of nations and the breaking of states (Cobban, 1944: 6, 50).

But does this mean that the UK is in danger of breaking up? It has after all been around in something like its present form for quite a long time.

The best-known analysis – indeed advocacy – of nationalism's potential for breaking up the UK is Nairn's *The Break-Up of Britain* (1977). Along with Perry Anderson and others, Nairn saw the disintegration of the British state as both inevitable and desirable because its archaic pre-industrial character was now a major obstacle to social and economic progress. Britain had not had a full and effective bourgeois revolution such as France experienced. The landed gentry and aristocracy had retained political power long after the Industrial Revolution; the internationally-oriented financial interests of the City of London still predominate politically over UK-based manufacturing interests; and the British state is peculiarly archaic in its lack of a written constitution, its reliance on monarchial legitimation, its treatment of the population as 'subjects' of the monarch rather than as 'citizens' with rights, and its secrecy and lack of genuine democracy, all of which render it unable to halt long-term economic and political decline.

The basis of this perspective, revived recently by Perry Anderson (1987), has been severely criticised (e.g. Barratt Brown, 1988; Callinicos, 1988), but of particular interest here is Nairn's thesis that it is the *multinational* character of this archaic state which offers the best hope of its break-up. Given the inability of the labour movement and Labour Party to confront and reform the essentially

Conservative British state, Nairn felt that the 'peripheral' nationalisms of Scotland, Wales, and above all Ireland, would be its
'gravedigger'.

Nationalism for Nairn was a response to *uneven development* – of
'underdeveloped' countries or regions which wanted freedom in
order to 'catch up' with more advanced and dominating ones (which
fits Ireland's historic relationship to Britain), or a response of
relatively advantaged or 'overdeveloped' areas which felt 'held
back' by the existing state (which could be made to fit the 1970s idea
that an independent Scotland could float free from a declining
British state on the revenues from North Sea oil – 'Scotland's oil'). It
was an elegant theory owing a lot to Ernest Gellner (1964), and it
has considerable appeal (not least to geographers). But uneven
development is a rather blunt instrument for explaining the development of nationalisms (see Orridge, 1981). It is not too difficult to
think of 'under-' or 'over-' developed regions which never even
began to create separate nationalisms, and the theory doesn't even
recognise the strongest of those which do exist in the UK: the British
nationalism of the British state.

Nairn developed his ideas in the mid-1970s, when nationalism in
Scotland and Wales was on the advance and Northern Ireland had
already experienced over five years of nationalist guerrilla war. The
authority of the central state seemed to be weakening, and there
were fears – hopes for some – which in retrospect seem greatly
exaggerated, that Britain was becoming 'ungovernable'. However,
these fears – and hopes – were turned around following the election
of Margaret Thatcher's Conservative Government in 1979. Earlier
that year referenda on the devolution of some central powers failed
to produce 'home rule' assemblies in Scotland and Wales (decisively
in the latter case, questionably in the former, as we shall see).
Separatist pressures subsided and Nairn subsequently admitted that
he had overstressed the 'gravedigger' role of peripheral nationalisms
(Nairn, 1981). But now he saw a more general crisis of the state: its
inability to halt Britain's industrial decline was becoming increasingly obvious, and the SDP (Social Democratic Party) split from the
Labour Party had seriously weakened the parliamentary opposition
to the Conservatives. These were the underlying structural realities
but 'an accumulation of contingent forces' was needed to 'produce
actual disorder', and in the UK these contingent forces were the

'peripheral' nationalisms and the ethnic conflicts of England's 'inner cities' (Nairn, 1981).

There had been serious conflict, mainly between minority communities and the police, in cities such as Bristol, Birmingham and London. It reflected the racism endemic in British nationalism – for nationalists like Enoch Powell a multiracial society was 'a non-identity', a denial of British nationhood (Levitas, 1986: 108–110; see also Chapter 9). In Northern Ireland, Government inflexibility in attempting to 'criminalise' the Provisional IRA allowed ten IRA prisoners demanding restoration of their political status to starve themselves to death. This greatly boosted militant nationalism and ushered in the IRA/Sinn Fein twin strategy of 'the armalite rifle and the ballot-box'. Even in Scotland and Wales nationalist pressures persisted despite the referendum results, exacerbated by 'Thatcherism's' ending of 'one-nation' Toryism (see Chapter 1). State-aided growth in the South-East of England (see Lovering and Boddy, 1988) contrasted with industrial decline and neglect elsewhere. Much of the Midlands and North of England also suffered from the so-called 'North–South Divide', but the political disaffection was especially marked in the 'peripheries', particularly in Northern Ireland, and in Scotland where the Tory vote virtually collapsed (see Chapter 4). Margaret Thatcher, self-proclaimed British nationalist and leader of the Conservative *and Unionist* Party, has been pursuing policies which boosted rival nationalisms and weakened 'the union'. This paradox seemed to support Nairn's hopes for peripheral nationalism, especially in view of the weakness of Labour on the one hand, and the ramshackle and apparently vulnerable character of the British state on the other.

Incomplete Unification

The different territories do not have fully standardised statistics and even their designations lack uniformity. Northern Ireland is a 'province' (sometimes incorrectly called 'Ulster', a province with nine counties, three of which are in the Irish Republic). It has its own civil service, education system, judiciary, and to some extent its own laws. It sends MPs to the UK parliament in London but from 1921 to 1972 it also had its own parliament; however, in 1974 this was replaced by direct rule and what is in effect a British colonial governor. Wales, by contrast, is a principality, integrated into the kingdom of England since 1536. Scotland is also a kingdom and although its parliament was dissolved in 1707 it has retained many of the trappings of a separate state (e.g. its own legal and education systems, its own banknotes, its own Presbyterian Church of Scotland and also its own Trades Union Congress which developed separately from the British TUC in London). Whereas England is administered by the specific departments of state – Education, Employment, Environment, etc – the peripheries are administered via their own sections of *central* government – the Scottish, Welsh, and Northern Ireland Offices. The Scottish Office was established in 1886; in contrast the Welsh Office, like the Wales TUC, was set up in response to nationalist pressure after 1960.

The *ad hoc* character of the UK reflects its different histories. The English kingdom developed from its South East core region between the tenth and fifteenth centuries, by which time it was a strongly unified state by contemporary European standards. However it was only in the late sixteenth century that the absolutist Tudor monarchy began to exert political control over the whole of Ireland, and even then Ireland, unlike Wales, retained separate political institutions. In contrast to the military conquest of Ireland, and before that Wales, the Scottish and English crowns were voluntarily joined in 1603 when James VI of Scotland became James I of England as well – and introduced the first 'national' flag; and it was by Acts of their two parliaments that the two kingdoms were united as Great Britain with a single parliament in 1707. The final episode in the creation of a unified state – the United Kingdom of Great Britain and Ireland – came in 1801 when the formally independent Irish Parliament was abolished following the military defeat of the first Irish nationalist uprising in 1798.

But if this entity was never fully unified in institutional terms, its unification was even more incomplete at the level of popular consciousness and cultural identity. Indeed attempts at cultural homogenisation were in some respects counterproductive. Religious uniformity and state churches were seen as important for state security, but it was the privileged position of episcopal Protestants in Ireland which led dissenting Presbyterians and Catholics to establish Irish nationalism; and the religious sectarianism of the Orange Order has been used against it ever since the 1790s. In Wales language has been the historic issue, with Welsh on the retreat from economic and political pressures since Welsh-speakers were banned from public office in 1536. But it was the sixteenth-century translation of the Bible into Welsh – actually in the interests of achieving a uniformly Protestant state – and the development of Methodism and opposition to the state episcopal church, which were mainly responsible for keeping the language alive. In 1900 about half the population of Wales could still speak Welsh; and halting its further decline in the twentieth century would be the single most important incentive for Welsh nationalists.

There were also major differences in how the three peripheries developed economically, again particularly marked in the Irish case. Scotland and Wales (or at least Central Scotland and South Wales), along with North-East Ulster around Belfast, shared fully in the economic benefits and political glories of the Industrial Revolution and the British Empire, whereas most of Ireland, including most of Ulster, did not. This uneven development, combined with the legacy of political and religious discrimination, resulted in the partitioning of Ireland in 1921, with twenty-six of its thirty-two counties breaking away in the first fissuring of the United Kingdom of Great Britain and Ireland which had been established in 1801. Now it became the United Kingdom of Great Britain and Northern Ireland, the latter comprising six counties rather than Ulster's nine in order to give it a more substantial built-in Protestant majority of roughly a million Protestants to half a million Catholics.

The British Parliament agreeing to Irish Home Rule provoked a serious constitutional crisis, with leading Conservatives encouraging armed opposition to what they saw as an affront and a threat to the British Empire. Their British nationalism (as distinct from English nationalism which was largely metamorphosed into the greater British identity) had developed from the mid-nineteenth century in relation to the expanding British Empire and in response to a growing inter-imperialist rivalry involving Germany, the USA and other countries. The new British identity was grafted on – successfully for the most part – to the existing cultural and political identities in Wales and Scotland, to give *dual* identities, Welsh or Scottish *and* British, whereas in Ireland successful grafting was largely confined to Protestants and the industrialised North East. In Wales the language issue, and in Scotland the trappings and memory of separate statehood, sustained weak nationalist movements, but even they generally identified with British imperialism, in contrast to many Welsh and Scottish nationalists today.

The Resurgence of Nationalisms

Despite the incomplete unification of the UK, the upsurge of its nationalisms in the 1960s came as a surprise. Centre of an Empire being transformed into a Commonwealth, the UK, far from appearing vulnerable, had indeed seemed a particularly successful case of political integration. Northern Ireland did have a separate political culture and its own parliament, but its problems seemed safely locked up there and the main issues of Irish 'Home Rule' long settled. It was widely believed that modern democratic government and a developed economy had made political separatism a thing of the past. Furthermore, with the extreme nationalism of the Nazis still fresh in people's memories, nationalism in general was widely seen as a dangerous anachronism. The world was becoming too interdependent for people's loyalties to be confined to historical 'nation states', never mind smaller regions within them. The future lay with supra-state bodies like the European Community, and some even saw the United Nations as the embryo of world government. In this 'brave new world' the sub-state nationalisms which did exist were easily dismissed as irrelevancies. Nationalists in Wales and Scotland got hardly any electoral support, and they tended to be seen as quaint irritants (as when in the early 1950s some Scots expropriated the Stone of Scone which an English king had taken from Scotland in the thirteenth century): anachronisms certainly, but in the 1950s not particularly dangerous ones. Yet within less than two decades there was a great resurgence of sub-state nationalism (and in countries such as Spain, France and Canada as well as the UK), and the disintegration of the multinational British state seemed a possibility.

The resurgence is reflected in the electoral statistics. The Scottish National Party's percentage share of the vote in Scotland, 1.3 per cent in 1945, rose to over 30 per cent in 1974 (only 6 percentage points behind Labour); while in Wales Plaid Cymru's share rose from 1.1 per cent in 1945 to over 19 per cent in 1970. In both cases their support fell back again, but it remained at much higher levels than before the resurgence (Table 3.1).

Table 3.1 Nationalist resurgence in Scotland and Wales:
Percentage share of the vote in selected UK general elections

Country/Political Parties	1945	1959	1970	1974 October	1979
SCOTLAND:	%	%	%	%	%
Nationalist	1.3	0.8	11.1	30.4	17.3
Conservative	41.0	47.2	38.0	24.7	31.4
Liberal	5.6	4.1	5.5	8.3	9.0
Labour	47.5	46.7	44.5	36.3	41.4
WALES:					
Nationalist	1.1	4.8	19.7	10.8	8.1
Conservative	23.9	32.6	27.7	23.9	32.2
Liberal	15.0	5.5	6.8	15.5	10.6
Labour	58.4	56.4	51.6	49.5	48.5

Both Plaid Cymru in Wales and the Scottish National Party achieved electoral 'breakthrough' from the catalytic effects of single by-election victories, in 1966 and 1967 respectively. The SNP (Scottish Nationalist Party) created something of a sensation by capturing what had been considered a safe Labour seat; and it achieved a peak of eleven MPs in October 1974.

There were particular reasons for a nationalist upsurge in each country: for instance a 'now or never' feeling about halting the language decline in the case of Wales – by 1960 Welsh-speakers were down to a quarter of the population, from a half in 1900. But the upsurge occurred in many different countries and stemmed from a more general mixture of economic, political and cultural factors, operating at an international as well as a national and regional level. The economic factors included the decline of regional economies and once-prosperous industrial areas, and increased penetration by multinational companies, which happened in Scotland, Wales and Northern Ireland in the 1960s and 1970s. Not only were economic matters increasingly seen as under the control of *external* interests – the parent companies of branch plants – but the displacement or

weakening of *local* industrial and commercial elites disrupted traditional political processes and channels of integration with the central
state. Cultural factors included the threat of terminal decline to
some languages, as in the Welsh case; but there were also other
revivals of indigenous culture more widely defined, particularly in
reaction to the increased import of mass culture – sometimes seen as
'Americanisation' – following the general arrival of television.

As for more directly political changes, there was a general increase
in state activity and politicisation around regional problems and
regional economic development (e.g. Regional Planning Councils
were set up in the 1960s), but having defined Scotland, Wales and
Northern Ireland (along with parts of England) as 'problem regions'
the central state proved unable to solve their economic problems. At
the same time states such as Britain and France were experiencing a
decline in their independent standing because of the loss of empires
and the growth of supra-state institutions, economic and military.
Thus with the decline of empire and of the UK as a world power (see
Chapter 2), the paramount British identity has been weakened in
Wales and Scotland (and even among a section of Protestants in
Northern Ireland who now favour an independent Ulster as the best
way of retaining their marginal privileges over Catholics).

In 1970 Rose found that in Scotland less than a third of those
sampled thought of themselves first as 'British', while for two-thirds
the primary identity was 'Scottish', and in Wales the respective
proportions were similar. In Northern Ireland only 29 per cent put
'British' first, 43 per cent putting 'Irish' and 21 per cent 'Ulster'
(quoted by Paddison, 1983: 70). The development of the European
Community meant that small states within it would now have
greater economic viability, and nationalists in countries such as
Wales and Scotland felt they could do better by dealing *directly* with
the Community rather than via the UK and London. In many cases
they derived encouragement from anti-colonial nationalist struggles
overseas, which also helps to explain a general strengthening of anti-
imperialist and left-wing elements in the revived nationalisms since
1960.

Subjective identities do not necessarily translate into political
action, however, and there was nothing automatic about these
various factors of uneven development leading to a nationalist
upsurge, much less to success in reaching nationalist objectives. But
they provided much more favourable grounds for nationalist parties
and politicians; they help explain the widespread nature of the

upsurge; and their continuing presence suggests that nationalist politics will continue to be important in the UK, though at what level is impossible to predict.

To appease nationalist pressure, the Labour Government, dependent on votes in Scotland and Wales (see Table 3.1), set up the Royal (Kilbrandon) Commission on the Constitution ('. . . in relation to the several countries, nations and regions of the United Kingdom') in 1969. In 1975, to avoid losing more support to the nationalists, it established Scottish and Welsh Development Agencies, and it announced plans for the devolution of some government functions to elected assemblies in Edinburgh and Cardiff. However the referenda on devolution in 1979 were far from being a success for Scottish, and particularly Welsh, nationalists (Table 3.2).

Table 3.2   Referenda on devolution, 1979

	Turnout as % of electorate	Yes as % of total votes	No as % of total votes
Scotland	64	52	48
Wales	58	20	80

The delay in holding the referenda and the form of assembly proposed (widely seen as little more than 'souped up' local government) had the (desired?) effect of deflating some of the nationalist support. An 'unfriendly' amendment required that, in order to effect change, a majority of 'Yes' votes had to constitute at least 40 per cent of those entitled to vote, so although a Scottish assembly was favoured by 52 per cent of those who voted they constituted only 33 per cent of the electorate and the 'assembly' was defeated. In Wales defeat was clear-cut. Here the nationalists' main support came from the Welsh-speaking rural west rather than the industrial heartland of mainly English-speaking South Wales; and given that Welsh was now a minority language it proved divisive rather than unifying in parts of Wales. Plaid Cymru failed to break Labour's electoral hold in the predominantly working-class and heavily populated industrial areas of the South, and here the proposed Welsh assembly was often identified with cultural parochialism. In Scotland too the nationalists faced more serious problems than 'unfriendly' amendments. Less than half the SNP's supporters were in favour of the party's ultimate goal of an independent Scotland. Two months after the referenda the Conservative Party, which was opposed on principle (British nationalist principle) to devolved assemblies, comfortably won the British general election; and the SNP lost nine of its eleven parliamentary seats.

Nationalism had declined from the heady days of the early 1970s. However, it was far from dead. In 1979 the SNP came second in many Scottish seats; and with continuing economic deprivation under a Conservative Government in the 1980s the Scottish labour movement became much more in favour of home rule than it had ever been in the 1970s. Wales got a Welsh-language channel on television after Plaid Cymru's leader Gwynfor Evans MP threatened a hunger-strike to the death. In the 1983 general election Plaid Cymru's share of the vote again declined a little, but the SNP's 11.8 per cent was comparable to its 1970 level (see Table 3.1); and this increased slightly to 14 per cent in the 1987 general election when the SNP gained three seats but lost two to give it a total of three, and Plaid Cymru gained one to give it three as well.

Neither, on this evidence, is likely to be the 'gravedigger' of the UK state in the foreseeable future, the role Nairn (1977) ascribed to them. Sub-state nationalisms are less of a threat to the central state than is often supposed, mainly because of opposition to them from *within* their own regions/countries. These regions have been *partially* integrated into the larger state; and if uneven development is a factor in the creation of separate and separatist nationalisms it also operates *within* their regions to undermine them, whether it is class and linguistic unevenness as in Wales, or a matter of religion and economic discrimination as in Ireland.

Welsh and Scottish nationalisms do however have a profound effect on developments within their respective countries, and on state-wide party politics, because of differential support for them. For instance, in Scotland in the 1987 general election the Conservative Party gained under a quarter of the vote, lost half its Scottish seats, and its MPs were reduced to ten. Labour, by contrast, gained over 40 per cent of the vote and over five times as many seats. While the Conservatives have been losing support in Scotland over the last three decades, it is Labour which has most to lose from a nationalist upsurge: to win a state-wide majority Labour depends on Scotland whereas the Conservatives do not. The same applies in Wales, though to a lesser extent because it has many fewer parliamentary seats. In 1979, for example, Conservative support in both Scotland and Wales was less than one-third, compared to nearly a half in much more populous England, but nearly half the Welsh votes went to Labour (see Table 3.1). An opinion poll in April 1988 found that 35 per cent of Scots now favoured complete independence, 42 per cent a devolved assembly, and only 20 per cent wanted the *status quo* (*Observer*, 26 June 1988).

In short the Conservative *and Unionist* Party, based largely in England, and particularly southern England, has in government stimulated separatist tendencies by default, but at the UK level these tendencies are much more of a threat to the Labour Party. It is split for instance over the issue of illegal refusal to pay the Scottish 'poll tax', some Labour MPs arguing that they should provoke a constitutional crisis because of the 'unrepresentativeness' of Conservative policy in Scotland (Hansard, 1988). The Labour leadership, however, opposes non-payment and instead stresses reliance on it being returned to power in a general election when it could legally revoke the tax. In the short term, the Scottish nationalists with less restrained opposition to the poll tax appear the likely winners – which could of course affect Labour's chances of forming a UK government – while the Conservatives have little left to lose in Scotland (indeed it has been suggested that it was for this reason that the poll tax was tried out first in Scotland).

The situation in Ireland is very different, in line with its different historical legacy. It is obviously more serious – two decades of guerrilla war, over 3,000 deaths, a war the British Army has said it cannot win. But at the same time this conflict is much more detached and separate from the mainstream of British politics. Neither the Conservatives nor Labour organise in or depend for votes on Northern Ireland. Whereas devolution for Wales or Scotland has been a means of maintaining the unity of the UK as far as central politicians are concerned, in the Northern Ireland case it has been more a means of keeping Irish matters out of British politics (and avoiding a constitutional crisis such as occurred before Ireland was partitioned – Northern Ireland Unionists had not wanted a separate parliament in 1921). Contrary to Nairn's general argument, the lack of integration may be a strength for the UK rather than a weakness where Northern Ireland is concerned.

Since the late 1960s the nationalist versus unionist conflict has dominated everything in Northern Ireland. Even here the nationalist share of the vote had dropped to 11 per cent in 1959 (though partly because of nationalist abstentions). The nationalist revival was basically due to the growing contradictions between, on the one hand, the growth of the British welfare state, the decline of traditional industries and the increasing penetration by multinationals in both parts of Ireland, and on the other hand a state where unionism had dominated totally since 1921 by reducing everything to a question of loyalty to the very existence of Northern Ireland. By 1979 the nationalist share of the vote had risen to 28 per cent while the Northern Ireland Labour Party (separate from the British Labour Party and contrasting with its strength in Scotland and Wales) was 'squeezed' to 1 per cent of the vote (from 17 per cent in 1945). But a major division emerged between the constitutional nationalists of the Social Democratic and Labour Party, and Sinn Fein, which is linked to the Provisional IRA; while the Unionist Party has severed its links with the British Conservative Party and split into two separate Unionist organisations. The Unionists are divided between wanting a restoration of a Northern Ireland parliament (which depends on the nationalist and Catholic minority having some share of power), or total integration with the rest of the UK (which none of the main British parties wants), while a minority associated with the Protestant paramilitaries favour the 'Independent Ulster' solution. The Anglo–Irish Agreement signed by the London and Dublin Governments in 1985, over the heads of the Ulster Unionists, gives the Irish Republic a consultative role in Northern Ireland affairs and is designed to create a devolved power-sharing between Unionists and constitutional nationalists in order to undercut the IRA. It is however opposed both by the Unionists and by the IRA.

The main forces in Northern Ireland are divided (and to some extent can be 'played off' against each other by the British state); and their separateness from so-called 'mainland Britain' has been increased by a conscious 'Ulsterisation' of the military conflict (e.g. a doubling in size of the Royal Ulster Constabulary, and the creation of the locally recruited Ulster Defence Regiment, to replace the regular British Army). The separateness is periodically mirrored by opinion polls which show that over half the people in Britian favour the reunification of Ireland and British withdrawal. And this logic has not been lost on the IRA. It too realises that in British politics Irish deaths are not as politically telling as English ones – hence its bombing campaigns in Britain and against the British Army in Europe. In 1984 it nearly succeeded in blowing up the British Prime Minister and much of her Cabinet at the Conservative Party Conference in Brighton. So while its impact in Britain is slight in purely political terms it has the potential for a serious impact through bombing and killing. On a political plane the conflict, with its allegations of a British Army 'shoot-to-kill' policy against suspects, its non-jury courts, and other erosions of civil liberties, has damaged the UK's reputation internationally. But because the Irish conflict is relatively detached, it does not at present threaten the stability of the UK state as such. Indeed given the extent to which Northern Ireland has now to be subsidised economically by Britain, the British state might be well rid of it – if only there could be guarantees that the Northern Ireland 'troubles' would not then spread to the whole of Ireland and to Britain itself.

We can conclude therefore that peripheral nationalisms will continue to be important in UK politics, but more for its separate parts than for the UK state as a whole. At state-wide level their main impact will probably continue to be on the relative strength of the main political parties rather than on the integrity of the state, the detached Irish case excepted. Rather than being an *alternative* to labour movement opposition to the state, as Nairn hypothesised, the major nationalist advances in the early 1970s coincided with and drew strength from an upsurge of labour militancy (which, with the miner's strike of 1974, brought down a Conservative Government).

On the other hand an increasingly strident British nationalism, now based predominantly in England, could both disrupt relations with the rest of Europe and provoke further nationalist reactions in Scotland, Wales and Ireland, as well as more unrest in England's inner cities. Current Government policy which appears to 'write off' some of the peripheries as economically dispensable, while indirectly subsidising the South East of England (e.g. roughly half of all Ministry of Defence procurement spending is in the South East compared to less than 1 per cent in Wales and Northern Ireland, and only 6 per cent in Scotland: Lovering and Boddy, 1988), could be storing up yet more problems for the future when 'Thatcherism' unravels. It is already producing serious inflation in the booming South East, and the situation will probably become more volatile when the 'cushion' of North Sea oil deflates in the 1990s. However, while the United Kingdom may not be as united as it once was, nor Great Britain as great, the state though ramshackle and archaic is unlikely to be forced apart in the foreseeable future.

4

The Changing Electoral Geography of Great Britain

R. J. Johnston and C. J. Pattie

A major feature of the electoral geography of Great Britain since the achievement of the universal adult franchise in 1928 has been the continuity in the geography of support for the various political parties, especially Conservative and Labour. There have been significant variations in the percentage of votes won by the parties over the six decades, but these have not affected the relative relief of the electoral map, though its amplitude has shifted up and down as support for a particular party either waxed or waned (Johnston, 1983).

This continuity has typically been accounted for by proposing a class cleavage between the blue-collar, manual workers (or working class), most of whom voted Labour, and the white-collar, non-manual workers (or middle class), almost all of whom voted Conservative; the Liberal party was mainly the recipient of temporary protest votes, and lacked continuity of support from particular segments of society. This class cleavage was generally assumed to be uniform throughout Great Britain; electors in the same class were assumed to vote the same way, wherever they lived (Bogdanor, 1983).

In the context of this simple cleavage or 'class equals party' model (Rose, 1982) change was also accounted for as a uniform national phenomenon. Central to this account was the concept of uniform swing (Butler and Stokes, 1969, 1974); in a two-party system, between any pair of elections the change in the percentage voting for one of the parties at the national level is reproduced in every constituency. Such uniformity suggests great similarity in the pattern of voting across the UK (excluding Northern Ireland), but uniformity of swing, expressed in percentage points, does not imply similar shifts in support (Johnston, 1981a). If the Conservative Party won 60 per cent of the votes in constituency X at the first election, then a swing against it of two points would mean a loss of 3.3 per cent of its supporters ($\frac{2}{60}$), whereas if it had only 30 per cent of the votes initially a two per cent swing would be a loss of 6.7 per cent ($\frac{2}{30}$). Thus uniformity of swing (the net outcome) has been associated with variability in proportional loss (the degree of 'leakage'); the stronger a party was in a constituency at the first election of a pair, the smaller its proportional loss of support.

During the early post-war decades, therefore, the electoral geography of Great Britain had two major characteristics: 1) a pattern of support for each party which paralleled the 'class geography' of the country and 2) swings between elections which saw parties lose support least, in relative terms, where they were already strong. This did not mean similar patterns of behaviour in every place, however; the class effect was usually magnified in the election results so that, for example, where the Conservative Party should have performed well on the basis of the class structure of the constituency it did even better, and vice versa (Butler and Stokes, 1974; Johnston, 1981b, 1985). This was usually accounted for by the concept of a 'neighbourhood effect', whereby members of the majority in an area are supposed to 'convert by conversation' a minority of those who might otherwise have voted for an opponent, but that concept is now claimed to be unrealistic (Dunleavy, 1979; Taylor, 1985; Johnston, 1986b).

Changing Bases of Electoral Behaviour

If the pattern of voting, and of changes in the pattern of voting, presented relatively few analytical problems for electoral analysts in the early post-war decades, the same cannot be said of the later years. Curtice and Steed (1982) identify 1955 as the watershed year, since when the 'class equals party' model has become less relevant. Different analysts stress two major sets of reasons for recent changes.

1. *Dealignment and growing electoral volatility.* This thesis (Sarlvik and Crewe, 1983; Crewe and Denver, 1985) argues that the traditional class cleavage has been broken, and that many more voters now

evaluate parties anew at each election in terms of their current policies/performance/leaders, rather than voting habitually for the same party, which was believed to occur in the past. The long-term process of *political socialisation*, by which people learn particular attitudes and partisan preferences that strongly condition their later behaviour, is being displaced as an influence on voting by the shorter-term processes of *political evaluation*, in which people care-fully evaluate competing party claims every time they vote. Such political evaluation is set in the context of a general set of political attitudes, which develop during a process of socialisation in child-hood and early adult years; but with both greater social mobility and rapid economic and social change requiring new political responses from parties, those attitude sets vary over time, as do the contexts in which they are applied. Thus people are no longer so closely identified with particular parties, and they are increasingly prepared to vote in ways inconsistent with their socialised general beliefs (or ideologies) because of their evaluation of the present party leaders and policies (Whiteley, 1986).

The dealignment thesis argues that the ability to predict electoral preferences from people's social and economic characteristics has declined (Crewe, 1986; Franklin, 1985); others claim that the class cleavage remains strong in Britain, but because there has been a decline in the size of Labour's traditional constituency, and a reduction in the proportion of the electorate who fit the standard class stereotypes (Johnston, 1986c), it must adopt policy directions that are attractive to a wider spectrum of the population (Heath, Jowell and Curtice, 1985, 1987a; Goldthorpe, 1988; but see Dun-leavy, 1987). A problem in evaluating these competing theses is the lack of studies designed for that purpose. Each major study of the British electorate (based on the data sets collected for the British Election Study) is in two parts. The first looks at the processes of political socialisation and cross-classifies vote against socio-eco-nomic characteristics, whereas the second looks at the links between votes, attitudes and party evaluations (see Butler and Stokes, 1969, 1974; Sarlvik and Crewe, 1983; Heath, Jowell and Curtice, 1985); unfortunately, the links between the two are rarely explored. White-ley (1983, 1984, 1986) has shown that voters' social attributes were poor predictors of their voting in 1979 and 1983; the most important were the degree to which people identified with a particular party and their evaluations of each party's record on salient (mainly economic) issues. Sanders, Ward, and Marsh (1987) contend that in 1983 it was voters' optimism about the short-term future of the economy that was the strongest influence on their decision whether or not to vote Conservative – optimistic people were more likely to vote for the incumbents; Heath, Jowell and Curtice (1987b) suggest that it was relative evaluations of the party leaders that influenced shifts in partisan preference after 1983.

The degree of voter volatility inherent in the dealignment thesis is not in the parties' interests; without stability of support from certain sections of the electorate, they must remobilise support frequently. Thus a brief period of dealignment is likely to lead the parties to seek a realignment, creating new stable electoral bases on which to found their new electoral appeals: Dunleavy (1979, 1980a, 1980b) suggests that such a new cleavage has developed in Britain around *consumption sectors*, with the Labour Party mobilising support among those dependent on the public (state) sector for education, health care, housing, and transport, whereas the Conservative Party promotes private sector provision and wins support from those who avail themselves of it (see also Dunleavy and Husbands, 1985, and Franklin and Page, 1984).

The dealignment thesis has been extended by Rose (1982; Rose and McAllister, 1986), who argues that the links between attitudes and partisan choice are now as weak as those between socio-economic characteristics and expressed preference. Neither socio-economic characteristics nor attitudes distinguish between the supporters of the various parties:

> On most issues an individual who held the dominant view of the electorate could be a Conservative, Alliance or Labour voter. . . The most common form of disagreement is within parties rather than between them. . . How a person votes is a poor guide to what a person thinks about most issues today (Rose and McAllister, 1986: 145–7).

This argument contradicts Heath, Jowell and Curtice's (1985, 1987b) case that each of the three main parties has an 'attitudinal heartland'. Discriminant analyses strongly favour the latter view; knowledge of peoples' attitudes allows successful predictions of how they voted (Johnson and Pattie, 1988).

2. *The new political agenda thesis.* These ideas focus on the changing political environment within which British voters make their electoral decisions. Until the 1960s there was considerable

consensus over major policy issues, such as the welfare state, between Conservative and Labour. That consensus has since broken down (see Chapter 1), leading to 'adversary politics' (Finer, 1975), in which the two parties offer substantially different policy packages and create uncertainty, if not insecurity, because each election could result in a major reversal of government policies.

One response to adversary politics in the early 1980s was the growth of a third, centrist grouping – the Alliance. Since the 1930s the occupier of that central ground, the Liberal Party, was mainly a recipient of protest votes (Himmelweit *et al.*, 1985). The size of the protest increased substantially at the two elections of 1974, however, implying dissatisfaction with adversary politics and a widespread feeling that the Conservative and Labour parties were out of touch with contemporary reality. The Liberal revival was then boosted in 1981 by the creation of the SDP (Social Democratic Party) and its decision to form an electoral Alliance platform with the Liberals, whereby the parties agreed not to compete against each other in any constituencies. The goal was to 'break the mould' of British politics, to destroy the class cleavage and create a centralist consensus. The Alliance's electoral success in 1983, winning 25.4 per cent of the votes cast, was based on substantial cross-class support (though its greatest support came from those in the professional and technical white-collar occupations). Furthermore, it involved the creation of a clear attitude–vote link; substantial numbers of Alliance voters were associated with a particular set of attitudes (libertarian, free market with a strong welfare state) suggesting that an Alliance vote was more than just a protest vote (Heath, Jowell and Curtice, 1985).

The creation and relative electoral success of the Alliance (reflected in votes won but not seats won, because it lacked a clear geographical heartland; its 25.4 per cent of the votes in 1983 brought only 23 of the 633 seats in Great Britain) was not the only change in the political agenda. In 1974 there was also a revival in the fortunes of the nationalist parties in Scotland and Wales (the Scottish National Party and Plaid Cymru), explained mainly by reference to local factors in the more rural areas (Agnew, 1984; Cooke, 1984; Agnew and Mercer, 1988). These nationalist revivals show an enhanced ability of those parties to mobilise support against the stranglehold on British politics held by the English Conservative and Labour parties, each of which is strongly centralised in orientation and organisation.

Growing Spatial Polarisation

These two accounts of the changing political and electoral agenda in Britain imply (with the exception of the growth of the nationalist parties) a continuation of the thesis that Britain has a uniform political culture. This is clearest in Crewe's work on dealignment which virtually ignores spatial variations in electoral volatility (Sarlvik and Crewe, 1983), though after the 1987 election he concluded that Labour is now a 'class party of the north' (*The Guardian*, 15 June 1987). Attitudes are developed and voters mobilised in a national context, it seems, mainly through the mass media and the structuring of the campaign by the parties.

The implication of a uniform national political culture for the geography of voting patterns is that either: 1) the greater electoral volatility is matched by a greater variability in the electoral map, or 2) the shifts are the same everywhere (with the exception of the nationalist parties), thereby maintaining the parameters of the traditional map. The geography of voting is of very minor relevance only to most analysts: McAllister (1987), for example, argues that once class and attitudes are are taken into account, spatial variations are trivial (see also Johnston, 1986a, 1986b).

Among British political scientists, three writers have focused on spatial variations in voting behaviour that indicate either new, spatial, cleavages or greater polarisation about the current cleavages. Miller (1977: 65) concluded from his study of the 1966 election that: 'The partisanship of individuals is influenced more by where they live than what they do'. After the 1983 election, he argued that polarisation at the constituency level had increased, so that people were apparently even more influenced by their local environment than by their membership of a particular occupational class (Miller, 1984).

Whereas Miller's work has been based almost entirely on regression analyses at the constituency scale, Curtice and Steed (1982, 1984, 1988) have focused on a coarser classification of constituencies, yet explored in more detail the reasons behind the identified changing geography. In 1982 they wrote that: 'the long-term change in the relative strength of the Conservative and Labour parties within constituencies has been marked by two major cleavages – between the North and the South, and between urban areas and rural areas (p. 256), extending this (following the 1983 election) to:

'There has been a long-term movement towards Labour in the North, in Scotland and in the most urban areas and towards the Conservatives in the rest of England and in rural areas. This pattern was continued in 1983 sharpening even further the socio-geographical cleavage between Conservative and Labour' (p. 338).

After the 1987 general election Curtice and Steed (1988) suggested that the long-term spatial trends had been altered somewhat. In particular, they noted that the growing urban–rural divide of previous elections had been halted, with Labour no longer dominating the inner cities. Instead, they suggest: 'Signs of an emerging centre-periphery cleavage, with the Conservatives doing better the closer a constituency to London, as well as a continuation of the core-periphery, North/South, cleavage, could be discerned' (p. 333).

This changing geography is identified by Berrington (1984) as a major unsolved puzzle for electoral analysts. Taylor (1979) showed that the growth of the Conservative share of the vote over the period 1955–79 was closely correlated with population change, suggesting differential migration with pro-Conservative voters moving to the economically buoyant areas and pro-Labour voters remaining in the depressed areas. Curtice and Steed (1982) argue that this alone is insufficient to account for the variations they have identified, and suggest that it could also result from changing social composition of constituencies (without differential migration), the differential spatial impact of third parties (the Liberals have traditionally won more votes from Labour in safe Conservative seats in the south and from Conservative in safe Labour seats in the north, for example), and greater voter response to spatial differentiation in patterns of economic and social well-being, consequent on the growth of the north–south divide in Britain's economic geography.

Increased Spatial Polarisation, 1979–87

Analyses of the 1983–7 trends suggest that the regional polarisation continued during the latest inter-election period – if anything, the pace accelerated (Denver, 1987; Johnston and Pattie, 1987). Here we extend those analyses, using two classifications of the 633 constituencies. (For the detailed statistical material, see Johnston, Pattie and Allsopp, 1988.) Our *geographical regionalisation* comprises twenty-two regions defined to separate out the urban and rural portions of the major regional divisions of the country and is thus

Table 4.1 Inter-election changes in the percentage of the electorate voting for each party, 1979–87, by geographical region

	Conservative			Labour			Alliance		
	79–83	83–87	79–87	79–83	83–87	79–87	79–83	83–87	79–87
Strathclyde	−3.3	−2.4	−5.7	−3.9	10.5	6.6	11.2	−4.0	7.2
East Scotland	−0.9	−0.9	−1.8	−4.6	7.9	3.3	11.0	−3.3	8.6
Rural Scotland	−0.3	−0.3	−0.6	−4.0	5.2	1.3	8.1	1.0	9.1
Rural North	−0.2	0.4	0.1	−7.1	3.7	−3.4	6.2	−0.9	5.2
Industrial North East	−2.3	−1.2	−3.6	−8.6	7.3	−1.3	9.6	−2.4	7.2
Merseyside	−5.0	−3.5	−8.5	−4.5	7.7	3.1	6.8	0.7	7.5
Greater Manchester	−4.0	0.8	−3.1	−6.3	4.6	−1.7	6.9	−1.8	5.1
Rest of North West	−2.5	0.4	−2.1	−5.7	4.9	−0.8	7.4	−2.1	5.3
West Yorks	−1.4	1.8	0.4	−8.2	5.6	−2.6	7.8	−2.8	5.0
South Yorks	−2.7	−1.4	−4.1	−7.9	7.8	−0.1	7.9	−2.5	5.4
Rural Wales	−0.1	0.7	0.6	−6.8	6.1	−0.7	6.1	−0.2	5.9
Industrial South Wales	−2.6	0.7	−1.9	−8.4	10.2	1.8	10.1	−4.2	5.9
West Midlands Conurbation	−3.4	1.4	−2.0	−6.2	2.9	−3.3	8.7	−1.9	6.7
Rest of West Midlands	0.3	1.2	1.5	−7.4	2.3	−5.1	8.3	−0.8	7.5
East Midlands	−0.3	2.8	2.5	−8.0	2.7	−5.3	7.6	−1.6	6.0
East Anglia	0.4	2.1	2.5	−8.8	1.5	−7.3	9.3	−1.2	8.0
Devon and Cornwall	−0.9	−1.1	−2.0	−6.8	4.3	−2.5	8.4	−2.0	6.4
Wessex	−0.1	1.8	1.7	−7.8	1.2	−6.6	7.9	0.9	8.8
Inner London	−3.8	2.6	−1.2	−7.4	3.2	−4.1	7.8	−0.1	7.7
Outer London	−3.2	3.7	0.5	−9.0	1.6	−7.3	8.3	−2.3	6.0
Outer Metropolitan	−0.5	2.9	2.4	−8.4	1.1	−7.3	8.5	−1.2	7.2
Outer South East	−0.4	1.8	1.4	−7.7	1.3	−6.4	8.1	0.4	8.5
National	−1.7	1.1	−0.6	−7.2	4.1	−3.1	8.3	−1.4	6.9

Source: Computed by the authors (see also Johnston, Pattie and Allsopp, 1988)

finer-grained than the Standard Regions conventionally used. Our *functional regionalisation*, based on a cluster analysis of 1981 census data (Crewe and Fox, 1984), identifies thirty-one separate groups of constituencies with common socio-economic and demographic characteristics. (The regions are listed in Tables 4.1 and 4.2. The names clearly identify them; further details are in Johnston, Pattie and Allsopp, 1988.)

Table 4.1 shows the change in the percentage of the electorate who voted Conservative, Labour and Alliance in each geographical region for the periods 1979–83, 1983–7 and 1979–87; table 4.2 provides similar data for the thirty-one functional regions. By geographical region, the general north–south divide is clearly evident in the changing pattern of support for both Conservative and Labour parties. Over the full eight-year period 1979–87, for example, the Conservative share of the electorate fell on average by 0.6 percentage points. In most of the regions north and west of a Severn–Wash line the fall was substantially greater (Rural North, Rural Wales and West Yorkshire were exceptions); south and east of that line the Conservative vote increased in all regions on average, except in Devon and Cornwall and in Inner London. Similarly, the Labour vote fell overall by 3.1 percentage points on average, but it increased in four of the northern regions and fell by less than the national average in five others there; it fell by more than the national average in nine of the ten southern regions. The Alliance vote increased more in southern than northern England, on average, though it increased by well above the average in Scotland.

The thirty-one functional regions also show substantial variations about the national averages (Table 4.2). In general terms, the more deprived regions are at the top of the table, and the economically more buoyant and prosperous are lower down. In most of the former (the major exception being the Black Country grouping) the Conservative loss was greater than average, whereas in many of the latter the Conservative vote grew between 1979 and 1987; increasingly its support came from those constituencies that were benefiting most from the industrial restructuring over which the Conservative governments of 1979 and 1983 presided. Complementing this, Labour lost fewer votes in the less prosperous regions, and its share of the poll increased substantially in three regions most of whose member constituencies are in Scotland. This suggests a growing spatial polarisation of the electorate that sees Conservative and

Table 4.2 Inter-election changes in the percentage of the electorate voting for each party, 1979–87, by functional region

	Conservative			Labour			Alliance		
	79–83	83–87	79–87	79–83	83–87	79–87	79–83	83–87	79–87
Inner city/immigrant	−3.2	3.0	−0.2	−6.9	2.6	−4.3	7.5	−1.4	6.2
Industrial/immigrant	−2.6	1.3	−1.3	−6.7	4.4	−2.3	7.3	−2.2	5.1
Poorest immigrant	−3.5	1.5	−2.0	−4.6	4.7	0.1	6.9	−4.8	2.1
Intermediate industrial	−1.8	0.9	−0.9	−8.1	4.5	−3.6	8.5	−1.8	6.7
Old industrial/mining	−2.4	1.3	−1.1	−8.1	7.1	−1.0	7.5	−3.2	4.4
Textile	−1.8	1.3	−0.5	−6.6	4.7	−1.9	6.6	−2.6	4.0
Poorest domestic	−2.6	0.4	−2.2	−8.4	10.6	2.2	8.2	−0.7	7.5
Conurban local authority	−3.3	−0.4	−3.7	−7.8	6.2	−1.6	8.2	−2.5	5.8
Black Co.	−2.2	2.6	0.5	−6.4	2.2	−4.1	9.1	−2.2	6.9
Maritime industrial	−3.4	−1.0	−4.4	−8.6	7.4	−1.2	10.0	−2.7	7.4
Poor inner city	−2.3	0.9	−1.4	−6.6	4.4	−2.2	7.8	−0.5	7.3
Clydeside	−4.1	−1.9	−5.0	−5.1	11.5	6.4	9.2	−3.7	5.6
Scottish industrial	−1.2	−2.1	−3.4	−3.4	9.7	6.3	12.8	−4.0	8.8
Scottish rural	−0.3	0.1	−0.2	−4.0	3.4	0.6	8.4	0.7	9.1

High status inner metropolitan	−5.4	2.3	−3.1	−5.6	3.4	−2.2	6.5	−1.7	4.7
Inner metropolitan	−4.4	2.0	−2.4	−6.6	4.1	−2.6	7.4	−0.7	6.7
Outer London	−3.3	3.4	0.2	−8.2	2.0	−6.2	8.3	−1.8	6.5
Very high status	−2.0	1.9	−0.1	−7.3	1.7	−5.6	7.3	−0.7	6.6
Conurban white collar	−4.0	1.0	−3.0	−7.3	3.4	−3.9	8.3	−0.6	7.7
City service	−3.3	0.1	−3.3	−7.7	4.5	−3.2	8.5	0.4	8.9
Resort/retirement	−1.0	1.2	0.2	−6.3	2.1	−4.3	6.1	0.6	6.7
Recent growth	0.9	1.2	2.1	−6.7	3.7	−3.1	11.1	−1.4	9.6
Stable ind.	−1.0	1.7	0.7	−8.0	3.6	−4.4	9.8	−2.5	7.4
Small towns	−0.4	1.2	0.8	−8.0	2.6	−5.4	7.7	−0.2	7.5
Southern urban	0.4	2.3	2.6	−8.4	0.9	−7.5	9.4	−0.2	9.2
Modest affluence	−1.5	0.9	−0.6	−8.5	3.2	−5.3	9.2	−1.1	8.1
Metropolitan industrial	−1.1	3.4	2.4	−9.8	2.9	−6.9	0.7	−3.2	6.5
Modest affluent Scotland	−1.8	−0.4	−2.2	−4.3	8.4	4.2	10.7	−3.7	7.0
Rapid growth	1.7	2.7	4.4	−7.7	1.9	−5.9	8.0	−1.6	6.4
Prosperous/non-industrial	−0.3	0.6	0.3	−7.1	2.5	−4.6	6.6	0.6	7.2
Agricultural	0.6	0.9	1.5	−6.5	2.2	−4.2	6.4	−0.3	6.1
National	−1.7	1.1	−0.6	−7.2	4.1	−3.1	8.3	−1.4	6.9

Source: Computed by the authors (see also Johnston, Pattie and Allsopp, 1988)

Labour increasingly drawing their support from particular geographical regions of Britain and also from particular types of constituency.

Accounting for the New Geography

The main reason for this growing spatial polarisation of the electorate since 1979 appears to be the changing economic geography of the country during that period. Several indices illustrate those changes: among the most directly apparent to the electorate are levels of unemployment and the prices of residential properties. During the period of Conservative rule, the official unemployment rate increased from 4.3 per cent in 1979 to a peak of 12.3 per cent in January 1986, and was at 10.4 per cent in June 1987. The increases were not uniform across the country, however, but were much higher in the northern and western regions (including Devon and Cornwall). The geography of property value changes was more or less a mirror image of that of unemployment. The 1980s have seen a great boom in the prices for residential units in the southern regions but property prices have increased much less elsewhere (see Chapter 12).

These two indicators may directly influence people's voting. Those made unemployed, those never able to get work, and those in a household where somebody either is or becomes out of work, will be quite likely to blame the Government and, if they previously voted Conservative, to switch to another party in protest. In contrast, those benefiting from the increased property prices could decide to vote Conservative to protect their enhanced equity holdings. More importantly, however, these indicators point to major geographical differences in social and economic circumstances across the country, differences that provide the contexts within which people evaluate the future and the promises of the contenders for political power.

Sanders, Ward and Marsh (1987) suggest that people's perceptions of their likely immediate futures have been major influences on their voting choice during the 1980s. A year before the 1983 general election, the Conservative Government was very unpopular with the electorate. The rapid recovery in its fortunes (as revealed by opinion polls) in mid-1982 was associated by many commentators with the

'Falklands factor': the successful campaign against Argentina and the firm image of the Prime Minister. But they suggest that the 'Falklands factor' was a minor influence for a few months only (see, however, Norpoth, 1987). The major cause of the revival in Conservative fortunes was a belief that economic recovery was beginning; an increasing proportion of the electorate responded optimistically to questions about their perceptions of their own and the country's economic future.

Such optimism was probably more common in the relatively prosperous regions of the country – those with low unemployment rates and rapidly increasing property prices. If so, the swing to the Conservative Party in the south and east (or to the Alliance as a second choice), but towards Labour in the north and west, is readily appreciated. Similarly, the poor performance of Labour in Greater London in 1987 (relative to its vote-winning in Merseyside and Strathclyde in particular) can be appreciated as a function of the relative strength of the London economy (despite major pockets of unemployment in some boroughs) rather than the claimed impact of the Conservative and Alliance campaigns against the so-called 'loony left' councils in some London boroughs and the targeting of London Labour Party candidates as left wing.

Table 4.3 presents data drawn from the 1979, 1983 and 1987 Gallup polls conducted on election day for the BBC, each of which included a question relating to respondents' perceived household financial situations over the previous twelve months. Those data show, for five aggregated regions: 1) the B:W ratio, between the number who thought things had got better and the number who thought things had got worse; and 2) the percentage voting Conservative, Labour and Alliance (Liberal in 1979) among those who thought things had got better, stayed about the same, and got worse. There were clear regional variations in people's levels of economic satisfaction, especially in 1983 and 1987 when southerners (including Londoners) were generally more satisfied than their northern counterparts. These variations were matched by voting in 1983 and 1987. (In 1979, the incumbent Government was Labour, and people who thought things had got better recently were more likely to vote Labour, especially in the northern regions.) In each region in 1983 and 1987, the less satisfied people were with their situations, the less likely they were to vote Conservative and the more likely they were to vote either Labour or Alliance. Given the spatial variations in

Table 4.3   Vote by perceptions of personal economic situation over the last twelve months and aggregated region

	Got better			The same			Got worse			B:W ratio
	C	L	A	C	L	A	C	L	A	
1979										
London	33	39	12	28	42	10	40	13	15	0.55
South	37	32	17	41	28	12	58	15	13	0.73
Midlands	31	48	9	41	26	8	60	13	7	0.85
North urban	20	50	8	29	39	6	40	21	13	0.99
Scotland/Wales	14	51	7	24	38	10	30	28	8	0.75
1983										
London	74	4	17	53	26	14	19	51	22	0.77
South	71	5	18	56	11	25	21	28	43	1.15
Midlands	54	16	15	41	26	17	21	39	26	0.61
North urban	60	15	20	47	23	18	16	49	26	0.61
Scotland/Wales	53	15	18	34	28	25	13	46	21	0.49
1987										
London	45	33	13	34	40	17	12	60	15	0.98
South	67	8	18	48	14	26	18	35	34	1.55
Midlands	59	17	17	44	27	19	17	42	22	1.29
North urban	43	22	25	33	34	20	10	58	17	0.75
Scotland/Wales	43	17	20	22	43	16	10	57	11	0.88

Source: Computed by the authors from BBC/Gallup survey tapes (see also Johnston, Pattie and Allsopp, 1988)

economic satisfaction, therefore, the voting pattern is clearly related to perceived economic well-being. But there were further inter-regional variations; dissatisfied southerners were twice as likely to vote Alliance as dissatisfied Scots and Welsh, for example, and people who thought things had stayed 'about the same' were more likely to vote for the incumbent government in the South and Midlands than were people with similar beliefs in London, the urban North, and Scotland and Wales.

These results suggest a growing local and regional consciousness regarding economic and social welfare in Britain during the 1980s.

This is probably an extension of trends that began in the 1950s, which clearly contradict the notion of a uniform British political culture promoted by many psephologists and by the political parties whose campaigning activity increasingly focuses on the national mass media and the projection of their leaders' images via television. The implication is that although most effort at mobilising voters – at influencing their processes of political evaluation – is national in its content, an increasing number of people are responding to this through their interpretations of the local rather than the national context.

The Implications of a New Electoral Geography

A number of important implications follow from the general trends outlined here. The first refers to the composition of Parliament, for over the post-war decades the south-eastern regions of Great Britain have returned an increasing proportion of Conservative MPs, and the northern and western regions a relatively larger number of Labour members. Parliament is itself spatially polarised: during the 1980s, the Labour party has represented very few constituencies in the South-East (excluding London), South-West, East Anglia and East Midlands regions, whereas Conservative representation in Scotland and Wales has halved.

This polarisation was accentuated by the performance of the Alliance in 1983 and 1987. (In 1979, when the Liberal Party stood alone, its vote was substantially concentrated in certain regions. In 1983, when it was joined by the SDP for the first time, it performed relatively well in most regions (Tables 4.1 and 4.2) apart from the English Midlands, and the degree of polarisation declined markedly. Four years later, its support was more concentrated spatially: see Johnston and Pattie, 1987).) In many of the more affluent constituencies the Alliance won second place in 1983 and 1987 and is being seen as the main challenger to the Conservative hegemony there at present: in the less affluent areas, on the other hand, the Alliance has had less long-term impact, and the Conservative Party remains the main challenger in Labour-held seats. (The impact of the creation of the Social and Liberal Democratic Party (SLD) in 1988 plus the continued existence of a small SDP is difficult to assess. It is assumed here that the SLD will inherit the majority of 1987 Alliance support.)

One consequence of this growing polarisation is a decline in the number of marginal seats which more than one party might hope to capture at an election (Curtice and Steed, 1986; Johnston, Pattie and Allsopp, 1988). Hence the Conservative hold on power has become firmer, because there are fewer seats where Labour could replace it. To some commentators, the best chance for Labour to form another government (unless it broadens its electoral base very substantially) is as the largest party following a major switch from Conservative to Alliance in the south and east. To others (including an increasing number of Labour supporters) the case for electoral reform is enhanced, as the only sure way of terminating Conservative hegemony of power. (The Conservative governments of 1979, 1983 and 1987 were elected with 43.9, 42.4, and 42.3 per cent of the votes cast respectively; their majorities in Parliament were 43, 144 and 101). Some believe that the best hope for Labour is to enter an electoral pact with the Alliance (e.g. Steed, 1987) while others argue for a major change in its policies so as to win over voters in the affluent south (Mitchell, 1987).

Political parties frequently interpret successes at a sequence of two or three elections as indicators that they are now the 'natural party of government', only to find that they are ousted soon after. Thus, although the Conservative Party has seemed to be deeply entrenched as the governing party of the United Kingdom throughout the 1980s, that government (like any other) cannot rest on its electoral laurels; it must continue to sustain its support and to ensure that its electoral base is substantially founded throughout the electorate. A polarised electorate is potentially unstable, since those segments denied access to power, which have little sympathy for the government's policies, and attract little response from the government, might find that their only route to influence and power is other than through the ballot box, with implications for the stability of the entire society and the legitimacy of the whole of the state apparatus (see Chapter 3).

In polarised societies, the development of movements against those who have a monopoly of power is frequently enhanced if either those involved are spatially identifiable (i.e. they are concentrated in certain areas at certain times, at least) or they can be mobilised through territorial strategies. In such situations the problems faced by those controlling the state apparatus are potentially greater than where the likely protestors are spatially scattered and thereby difficult to mobilise. In contemporary Britain, the growing territorial polarisation of the electorate therefore poses major potential difficulties to the elected government.

The result of the 1987 general election illustrates, on a minor scale, the sorts of problems than can arise. The Conservative Party won fewer seats in Scotland and Wales than ever before (10 out of 72 and 8 out of 38, respectively), and consequently found it difficult to staff the Scottish and Welsh Offices with local MPs. Labour members, as well as the nationalist parties, claim that this gives the Conservative Party no mandate at all to rule in those peripheral countries.

The separate identity of Scotland and Wales provides a substantial foundation for local interests to counter the Conservative hegemony in London. Such a strategy is not as readily available elsewhere, notably in the North of England, where Labour members are in a substantial majority. There, at present, the only route for contesting central government policies and decisions has been via elected local governments (as shown by Liverpool Metropolitan District Council and the South Yorkshire County Council), but central government has severely restricted the freedoms of local governments in recent years (see Chapter 5). Other mobilising apparatus may have to be identified, however, to launch potentially threatening strategies against the current Tory hegemony.

To counter opposition strategies to mobilise the electorate against it, the Conservative Party may seek to 'recolonise' the peripheral areas, where it retains substantial electoral support but lacks a major elected presence. Since 1979, Conservative governments have substantially reduced both the volume of regional aid and the areas for which that aid is available, arguing that restructuring of the local economies requires an openness to market forces rather than protection from them. The long-term consequences of that strategy might be a substantial restructuring of the economic and social infrastructure of the depressed areas, resulting in an economic renaissance. As yet, the economic and social polarisation of the country has not declined substantially, however; it may even have increased substantially. Consequently, the Government must consider how long it can wait before tackling the 'regional problem' with the sort of vigour it invested in the rhetoric of tackling the 'inner city problem' after its 1987 victory. The latter was in part a response to economic problems, but also to increased tension within many inner-city areas which was producing not only a disaffected electorate but also unrest that threatened the legitimacy of the state in certain areas. (Some observers felt that Margaret Thatcher used the term 'inner city' as a synonym for all 'deprived regions'). Such tensions and threats to legitimacy have been less apparent in the regions than in the inner cities since the 1987 election, but the clear vote against the Conservative Government in Scotland and Wales could stimulate growing challenges to rule by an English party lacking support in those peripheral countries – from the nationalist parties, from Labour, and from the SLD which has more seats in Scotland than in any other region. To counter such challenges, the Conservative Government may promote economic change in Scotland and Wales more vigorously, and in doing so it would be under great pressure to advance similar policies for the depressed areas of England. (After the 1987 general election, for example, the Secretary of State for Scotland, Malcolm Rifkind, argued for extension of the 'enterprise culture' in Scotland, to replace what he identified as its 'dependency culture'.)

One final implication of the changing electoral geography refers to the reform of the electoral system. The two 1974 results, which saw the Liberal Party win 18.8 per cent of the votes on average, but only 2 per cent of the seats, rekindled the cause of electoral reform. Proponents of proportional representation believe that such reform is the only way to restore consensus politics to Great Britain. The growing spatial polarisation of the electorate will aid their case, since the potential threat to state legitimacy that it contains could readily be countered by a parliament elected from multi-member constituencies on either the German or the Irish systems. Each party has significant voter support in most parts of the country, but wins substantial numbers of seats in only a few. Electoral reform would correct that imbalance, so that whichever party (or parties) were in power, the government would undoubtedly be more representative of all parts of the country than it is at present.

5
The Crisis of Local Government: Uneven Development and the Thatcher Administrations

Mark Goodwin and Simon Duncan

Introduction and Outline

Relations between local and central government have occupied a relatively peaceful backwater within British politics over most of the last fifty years. Despite occasional ripples of discontent, as when Labour-controlled Clay Cross refused to implement Conservative legislation on council house rents, or Conservative-run Tameside opposed Labour's comprehensive education policy, local government seemed deeply embedded in the post-war political consensus. With the coming of a fully fledged welfare state, a wide range of public services were provided and administered locally. Both major parties seemed happy with this system, and were content to give (when they occupied Westminster) and to receive (when they controlled town halls) local discretion over service provision. Even the major reform of local government undertaken under the Local Government Act of 1972 followed uncontested Whitehall commissions and aroused little debate. All this has now changed.

Over the past decade, local government has become a major political issue for left and right alike. The first two Thatcher administrations passed five major Acts dramatically altering the emphasis of local–central government relations, and carried a mass of allied legislation extending central control in individual policy areas such as housing, transport and civil defence.

The third Thatcher Government has already introduced major legislation which will break completely with the previous consensus on local government finance, public housing and education. This clear 'crisis' in the relationships between central and local government has taken an explicitly geographical form. Particular authorities in specific places have been affected more than others, and even very general legislation has had a widely uneven impact.

This may be expected of legislation designed to tackle the policies of certain local authorities. What is less obvious is the fact that uneven spatial development lies at the very root of the so-called 'local government problem'. Thus the current tensions and topicality of local–central relations do not result solely from a specific 'Thatcherite' ideology (although Conservative policies have given a significant push to the process). Instead they are the latest stage in a long history of conflict, which, although often dormant, is inherent in the very structure of local government and which, crucially, is activated and sustained through the uneven spatial development of social relations.

At the heart of the current crisis lies the desire by the centre to control and regulate the actions of local government – and in particular to limit the activities of certain Labour-controlled urban authorities. To understand this conflict, we need to be able to account firstly for variations in local state activity, and secondly for why these differences should pose such problems to central government. Therefore we briefly outline the reasons for the development of local state institutions, and the reasons why their policy variations should lead to local–central state tensions.

Uneven Development and the Local State

One question usually unasked by those looking at local–central government conflict, is why local state institutions exist at all, especially given the periodic problems they seem to cause central governments. To answer this we will draw on the concept of uneven development (see Duncan and Goodwin, 1988; Duncan, Goodwin and Halford, 1988 for more detail.) The uneven development of places, both economically and spatially, is painfully obvious: witness the dramatic restructuring of geographic space in recent years which has produced a regional crisis, inner-city decline, urban sprawl and deconcentration, and the 'two nations' of north and south (see Chapter 6; Massey, 1984).

Uneven development, however, does not simply mean spatial variation in physical and social phenomena. Rather, socio-economic processes are themselves uneven, thus dramatically increasing the disparities in pre-existing social and natural systems. Thus geographies – that is spatial variations – are a systematic expression of the very constitution and structure of capitalism. Consequently, social and physical environments are continually developed, abandoned and changed (see Harvey, 1982, 1985; Smith, 1984). These processes are not accidental, and the current geographical restructuring is only the most recent symptom of capitalism as an unevenly developing system.

Such uneven development is most mature and dynamic in capitalist societies, and it is also in capitalist countries that states and state institutions are particularly well developed. These two tendencies are not unrelated. State institutions are invaluable in the management and organisation of the increasingly large-scale, differentiated and changing societies typical of capitalism. But this very differentiation makes successful intervention a problem. To be effective state institutions need to be established at local, sub-national levels. For there is no reason why geographical variation should be confined to national state boundaries. If anything nation states are becoming less important in managing and specifying change, as supra-national states like the European Community (EC) or alternative organisations like multi-national corporations enlarge their authority. Indeed national states themselves are variable, ranging from the USSR and China to Hong Kong and the Maldive Islands. Dominant groups will need appropriately scaled state institutions in order to manage and organise highly differentiated social systems: hence the whole range of local state institutions, from secretive unelected local offices of central departments, through elected local and city governments, to elected executive regional assemblies like the Lander in West Germany or the individual states of the USA.

For local intervention to make sense, there must be local autonomy in implementing policy or even in formulating it. As centrally planned economies have found to their cost it is impractical and inefficient, if not impossible, for the centre alone to try to determine local responses to uneven development. The precise way of providing water supply in South Wales or managing labour reproduction in the old Durham coalfield cannot be wholly reduced to national guidelines or procedures. At the very least these must be adapted to take account of local conditions.

But this local autonomy may, by the same token, become a hostage to fortune. The uneven development of societies also means that class structures and other social relations are constituted spatially, sometimes in rather specific ways. Social groups and interests dominant locally may well be different from those dominant nationally, and their policies may also differ.

Local state autonomy gives such groups leverage; they can use state power to further their own interests and develop their own local interpretations of policy. As Miliband (1969) argues, local states become both agent and obstacle for national states.

Thus in managing society, local state institutions also interpret it. We label this the interpretive role of local states. Particular policies may be developed which are inappropriate, or even hostile, to those preferred by the centre. Society may be interpreted differently – unemployment may be seen as the result of structural tendencies within capitalism, rather than springing from individual limitations. The run-down of particular industries in certain places will not be accepted as natural, or inevitable, and local campaigns against closure may be mounted. During the miners' strike in 1984–5, for instance, some local governments on the Left gave the strikers considerable moral and material support. Others on the Right supported the Government, refusing to allow money to be collected for the miners on their premises. Both sets of local state institutions were supporting their own favoured interpretation of how society should be restructured. Local autonomy can thus be a double-edged sword, as locally constituted groups seek to use local state institutions to further their own interests and interpretations in opposition to those of the centre.

If the sword seems a little blunt, given the power of the centre, it is considerably sharpened by the development of representative democracy and universal franchise. Under such a system local state actions and the leverage exerted upon them by local interests are strengthened, and indeed sanctioned. With electoral legitimacy it is almost right and proper that locally constituted interests should promote their own preferred policies. Hence the local state also has a representative role: local states, and especially local government, are not only used by those dominant at the centre to manage uneven development, they also represent specifically local interests. Locally derived policies become legitimated through the ballot-box. Thus different groups are represented, and different interpretations of how society works are presented, through the local state. So far so good. But it is one thing to establish theoretical linkages between uneven development and local–central state conflict; it is quite another to indicate how this works in practice. We will turn briefly to this task now before detailing the latest manifestation of this conflict.

When trying to explain important policy variations, and challenges to the accepted policies of the centre, it is tempting to see the local economy as a crucial factor. Clearly, work experiences play a large role in constructing and defining political attitudes, while uneven development has produced a particular spatial division of labour which allocates both work and workers in a specific geographical way (see Massey, 1984). The Left has been especially ready to link radicalism at work to radicalism in local politics, using examples such as: 'Red Clydeside' during and immediately after the First World War, based on Glasgow's shipbuilding and engineering industries; the 'Little Moscows' of the Welsh, Scottish and northern coalfields in the inter-war period whose councillors gave their streets names like Engels Terrace and Lenin Avenue; Poplar in East London, whose challenge to the centre in the 1920s, now enshrined in the dictionary as Poplarism, was based on support from dock and transport workers; and Clay Cross, centred on the north Derbyshire coalfield.

Yet we must resist this assumption, and the economism it entails, for there are as many non-radical coal, engineering and shipbuilding areas as there are radical ones, while challenging forms of local politics have emerged from traditionally conservative areas (see Howkins, 1985; Dickens *et al.*, 1985, on the example of radical politics in rural agricultural regions). Spatially distinct patterns of production will always be combined with, and mediated through, spatially distinct social practices arising outside work in civil society, such as those based around gender, race and religion (see Cooke, 1983; Urry, 1981). Often the local politics arising from these combinations will be sustained culturally through people's ideas of what their locality is, or should be, even if this turns out to be just as much an 'imagined community' of localism as anything real in social, material or economic terms (see Anderson, 1983, on the imagined community of the nation).

The varied political effects of distinct combinations of these sets of relations is strikingly evident in Britain's current political geography. With regard to local government, many challenges to the Conservative administrations have come from places where manufacturing activity has collapsed and where the labour organisations of the workplace have been in decline. Often local government plays a key role in sustaining or promoting the oppositional cultures of these areas. Sometimes this is achieved through an appeal to a local 'imagined community' of radicalism, which has often outlived the material collapse of an area's traditional industries – as in South Wales, Sheffield and Liverpool. Sometimes it is achieved through building entirely new political coalitions in civil society, to replace those lost with industrial decline. This has been especially marked in London, where the radicalism of the 'new urban left' (see Gyford, 1985) has been based on coalitions between white-collar unions and civil organisations built up outside work to represent various disadvantaged groups, particularly women, blacks and sexual minorities. This coalition used local state institutions – especially local government – directly to challenge national legislation and implement several alternative local policies. National government reacted to these challenges by reducing the political autonomy of elected local government, and removing its powers to non-elected local state institutions insulated from these locally based coalitions.

Thus particular local policies arise through the uneven development of a whole range of economic, social, cultural and political relations. What is crucial is the ways in which they are combined in particular places and the ways in which this combination is expressed politically through the local state (see Duncan and Goodwin, 1988, and Duncan, Goodwin and Halford, 1988, for specific examples). This heterogeneity, and the plurality of social combinations and conflicts that result, is crucial to the distinctiveness of the local state and to its continuing threat to the centre; occasionally these differentiated social processes combine so as to produce distinctive policies which force a response from the centre, and bring to the surface the underlying tensions within local–central relations. This is what has happened over the past decade or so, and we now examine the details of this latest 'local government crisis'.

The Current Local Government Crisis

We have established how the crucial contradictory roles of the local state, those of interpretation and representation, are activated and sustained through uneven development. We also outlined how this uneven spatial and social development combines in particular places to produce policy variation within the local state. And we suggested that occasionally, at specific conjunctures, local–central conflict would result as national government attempts to control both the interpretive and representative roles of local government. Such a situation has arisen recently.

Since the 1979 election, local government and its relations to central government have become major areas of political conflict in Britain. This is because the Conservatives' political project involves introducing the values of the market-place into all areas of social and economic life. For the Government, free markets are both economically efficient and socially just. But their project depends on a paradox. The purifying winds of market efficiency depend on state action, both to remove obstacles and to create the appropriate social context for the introduction of 'Victorian values'. This immediately places the local state at the centre of the political stage and heightens the tensions of local–central relations. For local state institutions, and local government in particular, are both agent and obstacle in practice. They are an obstacle to the Conservative Government in that they provide collective welfare services, spend public money and promote alternatives to centrally preferred policies. They are an agent because they can also be used by the centre as experimental institutions in promoting new sets of social relations at the local level. Hence the centre's desire to control the actions of local state institutions.

The current tension between central and local government initially emerged in the mid-1970s following the oil crisis of 1973 and the subsequent economic depression. The Labour government attempted to combat this by controlling inflation through reducing public spending and containing real wage levels. Conditions attached to a loan from the International Monetary Fund in 1976 reinforced these as the twin principles of government policy. Inevitably the implications for local government expenditure were severe, and through the introductions of cash limits and monetary control the centre tightened overall financial limits. However, this form of intervention remained at the very general level of local government expenditure as a whole, and in particular concerned total levels of public borrowing and central grant. If the political will and political support were there, local governments could still go their own way by raising rate revenue to finance expenditure.

This changed in 1979 when the Conservative Government introduced a legislative path which led to direct and overt policy control over individual local authorities. They attempted to control both the interpretive and representative roles of local government by restricting the ability of local government to interpret social relations in alternative ways, and reducing their effectiveness at representing local interests. This necessitated controlling exactly what individual authorities could and could not do, rather than imposing general cash limits.

Centralising Local Government Finance

The Government began by strengthening central financial controls through a new block grant system introduced in the 1980 Local Government, Planning and Land Act, which replaced the Rate Support Grant as a mechanism for determining central grants to local authorities (see Duncan and Goodwin, 1988). Under the earlier system local spending patterns were taken as an index of need, and this underlay the distribution of the largest part of the central grant. These were replaced by Grant Related Expenditure Assessments (GREA), determined centrally according to the Department of the Environment's calculations of local need. The block grant is the balance of the GREA figure after the locally raised rate fund contribution is deducted – but the latter is assumed from a 'grant related poundage', also determined centrally. Furthermore, 'overspenders' which exceeded GREA levels were penalised through tapered grant reductions. Along with these controls on current spending, the Act also imposed ceilings on local authority capital expenditure. In addition, by 1981–2 central grants covered only 55 per cent of local government expenditure, compared with 63 per cent in 1975–6, even though total local expenditure had declined by 15 per cent in real terms since then.

Overall expenditure and central grant were both brought quickly under tighter control, and several other measures were introduced to centralise local government finance still further. What gradually became clear was that the Conservatives, fired with visions of restructuring society and needing to tighten control over the alternative actions of some local authorities, were placing the accent less on total spending and more on precisely how the money was being used.

Thus intricate manipulations took place to determine which authorities would be penalised, under a new system known as 'hold-back'. In July 1981 GREA was ignored and authorities were told simply to cut their 1981–2 expenditure by 5.6 per cent from the 1978–9 level in real terms – the so-called 'volume target'. In September 1981 GREA was reintroduced, and only authorities transgressing both limits were penalised. Not surprisingly these were mainly Labour-held authorities, mostly in London.

But still some councils refused to accept financial control, and levied supplementary rates to raise more money. The 1981 and 1982 local elections brought to power radical Labour administrations in Greater London, Merseyside and the West Midlands, and strengthened Labour control of the other large metropolitan authorities. All were now determined to maintain expenditure in order to finance their policy commitments, including heavily subsidised public transport. A further round of legislation appeared, with the introduction of the Local Government Finance Bill in November 1981 which proposed to curb local government autonomy through four measures. Firstly, the Department of the Environment would be able to set a ceiling on the rates that any individual authority could levy. Since this removed the convention that local government could set its own level of local taxation, a sop to local autonomy was proposed, allowing a supplementary rate to be levied after a referendum. The Bill also legislated retrospectively for the 'hold-back' penalties, gave the centre power to reduce the grant half-way through the financial year (known as 'super hold-back'), and introduced a new body, the Audit Commission, to supervise the auditing of local government expenditure.

The legislation was universally condemned by Government supporters and opponents alike, one Conservative MP telling his Party's Environment Secretary that 'When you go into a dung-heap you can expect to come out smelling of muck' (*The Guardian*, 25 November 1982). The government was forced to abandon the Bill, and introduced new legislation in January 1982, withdrawing the rate ceiling but also the right to levy a supplementary rate. Even this suffered major changes in its passage through Parliament, most notably the dropping of 'super hold-back'. In its final form the 1982 Local Government Finance Act abolished supplementary rates, imposed further central control of the Block Grant system, allowing the Secretary of State to make adjustments to the total distribution during the financial year, and set up the Audit Commission with centrally determined membership and functions.

By 1983 there was widespread confusion over the complicated system of central control through both volume targets and GREA, and some councils were able to increase their spending. On the one hand low-spending Conservative shires which fell under the GREA limit could increase spending, and break volume targets without penalty. On the other, some councils were now so penalised for 'overspending' that their block grant was completely lost, so removing any further penalty. Other authorities were juggling rate rises against penalties and still managing to pursue 'high-spending' policies which maintained service provision. An initial attempt to tighten control was made in December 1982, when exemption from penalty was removed from those councils which broke the volume limit, even if they remained below GREA. This provoked a furious response from Conservative councils and calculations were redrawn and reworked. In fact, the Government constantly juggled with block grants, target levels and penalty systems over the next few years in order to exclude some authorities (usually Conservative) yet catch others (mostly Labour).

In July 1985 the whole edifice collapsed under the weight of its own technical and political contradictions, when the Government was forced to announce that it would scrap targets and penalties in favour of using GREA levels alone. The previous year the new Audit Commission had blamed the complex and confusing financial system for local rate increases, rather than local government irresponsibility. And soon after targets and penalties were scrapped, the Commission's Director stated that the Government's attempts at financial centralisation had led to 'more waste, more inefficiency and less accountability' (*The Guardian*, 26 April 1986). In addition, the new Minister for the Environment, according to reports, 'could no longer accept the basic intellectual justification for the government's attempts since 1979 to control local authority current spending' (*The Guardian*, 7 May 1986). He later described the system of grants, controls and penalties as 'a maze in a fog, surrounded by a swamp' (*The Guardian*, 5 December 1987). But despite the increasing inefficiency of these attempts at centralised financial controls, the Conservative Government had managed effectively to destabilise the local government opposition through new and more direct legislation – that concerning rate-capping and abolition.

Before discussing these measures, it is worth noting that the Conservatives' own monetarist logic supports the view that financial penalties were primarily a political and not an economic weapon. The lodestone of academic monetarism is control of public borrowing, but by 1982–3 local government borrowing was a mere 4.1 per cent of the total Public Sector Borrowing Requirement (PSBR). Spending income from rates involves no borrowing at all, and between 1974–5 and 1981–2 local government expenditure fell by 15 per cent in real terms. If anything, central spending is out of control: it increased by 14 per cent over the same period. Even if overall macroeconomic controls are necessary on local taxation and expenditure, this hardly necessitates the Government's almost compulsive interest in individual council budgets. Rather this seems to be a form of political control over oppositional authorities. As such, this was allied to the introduction of detailed controls over particular policy areas. Legislation was passed curtailing local autonomy in the fields of housing (see Chapter 12), transport (see Chapter 11), health care (see Chapter 13), education (Howell, 1987), water, planning, local economic policy and civil defence (Duncan and Goodwin, 1988). Local government was pushed, or even compelled, by central legislation to carry out Conservative policy in what had traditionally been local government concerns. Thus councils were compelled to sell council houses, or not subsidise public transport, irrespective of a local political mandate to do just the opposite. Together these measures represented a Draconian attempt to nullify the representative and interpretive powers of local government. But for selected local authorities the worst was yet to come: even the revised financial measures and policy controls proved too general, and the Government began to look for more specific controls.

Destroying Local Government Autonomy: Rate-capping and Abolition

The Government began to move against specific individual authorities and the broad swathe of controlling measures became more and more finely targeted. Detailed financial control was introduced through the Rates Act of April 1984, generally known as 'rate-capping'. This followed legislation for Scotland, passed in 1981 and 1982, which had allowed the Government to control both local authority expenditure and taxation there and so see off the threat of a revolt in Scotland (which resolutely voted Labour) based in local authority strongholds. The Rates Act adopted the so-called 'Scottish Solution', and allowed the Government to set a top limit on the rate levels of local authorities judged by the centre to be 'excessive' spenders. It also gave general reserve powers, by which all councils' spending and rates could be controlled through an appropriate parliamentary order.

That the Government had taken a big policy leap from block grant penalties to rate-capping is shown up well by the words of Tom King, the local government Minister. In trying to defend the former system to Parliament he said of local authorities:

> It is their choice between services, and their choice (as) to the rate levels that they decide to impose. That is the freedom and discretion that exists in local government... the local councillors (have) responsibility for the final rating decisions and expenditure of their own local authority. That is the basis on which the local government and central government partnership exists. We each have our responsibility to our own electorates.   (8 July 1980, quoted in Stewart, 1984).

But in trying to justify the latter system, King was saying three years later that, 'Parliament would have to approve what would be the valid rate for each of these high spending councils. Any other rate would not be valid and could not be collected' (*The Guardian*, 27 May 1983). So much for partnership and local electoral accountability!

As usual the centre's financial arguments were shaky. Local government spending, and certainly its borrowing, was not out of control, and any increase in rates could almost all be attributed to reduced central grant and increased central penalties. Rates are no part of public borrowing, and selective rate-capping would only reduce aggregate taxation by less than 0.5 per cent. Moreover, limiting the rates of the eighteen authorities chosen for rate-capping in 1984 only reduced local government expenditure by £198 million in 1985–6, compared with a centrally defined 'overspend' of £900 million for 1984–5. Under the pressure of trying to defend the indefensible in the House of Lords, Lord Belstead, Conservative Environment Spokesman, later let the political cat out of the financial bag when he said, 'A number of local labour councils are now in the hands of extremists. Their influence and numbers are growing and there is no will or ability among the national leadership to curb them. What if the present irresponsible behaviour of the few spreads to 60, 80 or 100 authorities?' (*The Guardian*, 10 April 1984). For the other side the message was equally clear: 'The move is regarded by many left-wing council leaders as the ultimate weapon in the hands of central government to combat attempts by local authorities to uphold promises to their own electors in defiance of Whitehall and Westminster (*The Guardian*, 2 July 1983). In both political camps rate-capping was recognised as a means of controlling and curbing the interpretive and representative roles of selected 'extreme' local authorities by financially limiting their range and level of service provision. As Edward Heath, a former Conservative Prime Minister, told the Commons, 'I came into this House in 1950, having fought an election on Mr Churchill's theme that we were to set the people free. It was not that we would set the people free to do what we tell them' (*The Guardian*, 18 January 1984).

But this was still not enough. In a scheme hastily conceived by Margaret Thatcher just before the 1983 general election, the Cabinet decided to abolish the Greater London Council and the six other Metropolitan County Councils. These were the large 'strategic' authorities, set up in 1965 and 1974 respectively to deliver services to the rapidly expanding conurbations. They were the largest local authorities in England and Wales, in terms of population size and spending power. After the local elections of May 1981 all were Labour controlled, and most of them were in the forefront of local opposition to the Tory Government, using their large budgets to promote policies such as cheap public transport, alternative local economic strategies and police accountability. The proposed legislation would transfer their functions to a bewildering array of joint boards, regional authorities, district councils, regional quangos and central government. Abolition was set for 1 April 1986, so that this byzantine structure could be legislated for and lowered into place. Accordingly the Government decided to suspend the elections due in these authorities in May 1985, and to replace the elected councillors with those nominated by district authorities for the final year.

The Government defended these moves on both financial and technical grounds. In the course of the legislative process they lost both these arguments as independent consultants pointed to the cost and complications of abolition. Again the real motive was revealed by an unguarded government spokesman. Norman Tebbit claimed that London was:

... in the hands of Marxists bent on revolution. The Labour party is the party of division. In its present form it represents a threat to the democratic values and institutions on which our parliamentary system is based. The GLC is typical of this new, modern, divisive form of socialism. It must be defeated. So we shall abolish the GLC. (*The Guardian*, 15 and 18 March 1983).

The Government were also forced by the House of Lords to prolong the life of the elected authorities by one year rather than substitute nominated councillors. This was widely seen as the most damaging parliamentary defeat suffered by the Government in its entire term of office and it indicates the strength of opposition to the Government's local government legislation. But as with the other Acts we have discussed, which all needed withdrawal or significant amendment, the Abolition legislation survived its stormy passage and the strategic authorities were duly abolished on 1 April 1986. Instead of merely controlling the representative role of local authorities through financial and administrative restrictions, the Government had removed it entirely from the leading tier of local government in the country.

The Local Government Problem Won't Go Away

Uneven development necessitates some measure of local autonomy; elections provide some measure of local political legitimacy; and the result is that local government cannot simply be formed into a mere agent of central government. If this measure of legitimised autonomy is problematical – as it appears to be for a Government attempting to impose radical reform on British society – then clearly there will be a local government problem. The Government had hoped that rate-capping and abolition would deal with the most immediate aspects of this problem: the actions of those Labour-controlled urban authorities which persisted in demonstrating that there was an alternative to Conservative retrenchment. In a narrow sense it was successful, as offending 'extremists' have been abolished and/or forced to reduce planned expenditure by 25–30 per cent. But apart from these twenty or so highly visible authorities the wider problem still remains – how to control the interpretive and representative roles of elected local government in order to promote a particular version of social and economic change.

The Thatcher administrations approached this problem, of removing policy and power from the orbit of elected local authorities, in two main ways. First, central legislation has extended quasi-market principles of allocation into local service provision, lessening the scope for political choices by local authorities which now have to operate within strict financial limits and provide services in competition with private companies. Second, the powers of elected authorities have been gradually removed to various non-elected bodies, operating both at the local and regional level (see Duncan and Goodwin, 1988).

More legislation is in the pipeline to facilitate these processes. Following its embarrassing public relations defeats over abolition and rate-capping, the Government plans to restrict the scope allowed to local authorities for advertising and publicity campaigns. It also seeks to force authorities to put their services out to tender, so running service delivery along private sector lines of economy rather than public sector lines of need. The Conservatives also plan to restructure local government finance, replacing a property tax with a poll tax, nationalising non-domestic rate levels and changing the basis for distributing central grant. This involves replacing the 'rates' with a 'community charge' levied on individuals rather than on property. A 'community charge-cap' will replace rate-capping, in order to specify maximum spending levels. Theoretically, the new charge is supposed to increase the 'accountability' of local authorities and local elections. But the electors will not be able to choose to spend above a centrally prescribed limit, and the imposition of a uniform business rate will lower the amount of spending decided and voted upon locally to around 20 per cent. Central government will control the remaining 80 per cent of local expenditure. Thus, any increase in local expenditure beyond that considered necessary by central government will have to be financed disproportionately by local residents.

In addition to this increased central control, the Conservative Government plans to replace a slightly progressive tax with a generally regressive one. The Green Paper itself admitted that low-spending authorities with high domestic rateable values (usually Conservative controlled) will gain income, whereas high spending authorities with low domestic rateable values (usually Labour controlled) will lose. Moreover, within particular authorities the poorer wards, and poorer households, will be hardest hit, while the richer areas will tend to gain. The regressive nature of the new tax will thus be spatially and socially selective. It is difficult to disagree with Leach who notes that although the rhetoric of local accountability runs through the 'poll-tax' proposals 'the reality is increased central control' based on the assumption 'that central government can and should determine what local authorities spend' (1987: 12). And premised on this tighter financial control is of course a greater ability to determine the scale and scope of local policy alternatives.

Other legislation limits local authority competence in the fields of housing, education and local economic policy. Again two main strands within this can be discerned: the introduction of quasi-markets, and the removal of powers to non-elected bodies. With regard to the former, the Education Bill allows schools to opt out of local authority control, and new housing legislation allows council tenants to transfer their tenancies to a landlord in the private sector. These measures do not represent the introduction of a free market as such. Instead, they weaken the influence of local authorities, irrespective of whether local electors support the changes. This reduces the representative role of the local state. In addition, the fact that removing these services from the public sector is seen as introducing a 'free market' helps to win the political argument for the centre, and hence alters the interpretive role of the local state as well. Moreover, the Inner London Education Authority (ILEA) is to be abolished, and responsibility for education in central London transferred to the borough councils – which, as ILEA has an almost built-in Labour majority, will facilitate the opting out of schools in this part of London, and weaken the provision of adult education, youth services, nursery schools and special educational services.

Local authority control over council housing will also be weakened through the introduction of Housing Action Trusts, appointed bodies which will take over the running of public housing in selected inner-city areas. Likewise, new Urban Development Corporations have been set up to regenerate inner-city areas along private sector lines, control again being taken from elected local authorities. Indeed the whole thrust of the Conservatives' inner-city initiatives, announced in March 1988, is to give the private sector responsibility for urban regeneration at the expense of local authorities. In addition to the extension of appointed Urban Development Corporations, the Government announced new means of transferring grants to the private sector which by-pass the relevant local authorities, and new rules to force councils to sell publicly owned land (*The Guardian*, 7/8 March 1988).

The introduction of new unelected institutions such as Housing Action Trusts and the extension of others such as Urban Development Corporations, complete a threefold movement of power away from local elected institutions under the Thatcher governments. First, the existing regional state has acquired new powers in the fields of health, water and transport (Saunders, 1983, 1985). Second, various new unelected boards, quangos and institutions have been set up at the regional level, often to replace functions of the abolished metropolitan authorities (Duncan and Goodwin, 1988). And third, the Government is now increasingly introducing these unelected bodies locally, where they operate alongside the councils which they have replaced (Stoker, 1988).

These latest proposals have attracted condemnation from politicians, professionals and political commentators alike. Edward Heath, the former Conservative Prime Minister, called the new education proposals 'divisive', claiming them to be a confidence trick 'fatal to the education of a large number of children' (*The Guardian*, 2 December 1987). The new poll tax proposals have been opposed on many grounds, by numerous groups and institutions. The National Council for Civil Liberties said the system would 'erode privacy to an unprecedented degree', and the Child Poverty Action Group claimed the Bill 'penalises those on low incomes and will only lead to a more divided Britain'. Local government associations have also shown considerable concern. Even the Conservative-controlled Association of District Councils expressed reservations, claiming that the legislation has 'many areas that will require a great deal of attention', while more predictably the Labour-controlled Association of Metropolitan Authorities stated that 'The poll-tax will rob the poor to reward the rich, will need an army of snoopers, and cost at least twice as much to administer as rates'. (See *The Guardian*, 5 December 1987). Moreover, the Government's recent reaffirmation that local authorities are to be replaced by the private sector as the main means of stimulating inner-city revival has already been condemned by the Confederation of British Industry, whose members are supposed to be the chief beneficiaries of the scheme. The Confederation's director-general said: 'Local authorities cannot be by-passed – they are there and in many respects are very efficient and effective... we're not going to get there by either depriving them of resources... penalising them for spending money they ought to be spending... or worse still, holding them up to public ridicule...' (*The Guardian*, 9 December 1987).

In spite of such opposition, the Government will continue to by-pass and ridicule local authorities. It needs to do so in order to control their interpretive and representative roles. Through its interpretive role, local government is a participant and not just an object in the struggle to change British society, actively promoting alternative views of how society should work. Through its representative role it puts forward the views of those who may be hostile, or even opposed, to the ways in which central government proposes to restructure social and economic life. When these roles threaten, or make uncomfortable, the Conservatives' project of 'social realism', the centre is forced into an effort to neutralise the opposition – hence the current 'crisis' of local government.

The new legislation on local government finance, housing, education and inner-city regeneration promises to keep local government at the forefront of contemporary political conflict. Moreover, the large urban authorities which have been rate-capped will soon be using most of their capital expenditure to meet rescheduled debts and deferred payment schemes, which they set up to overcome centrally imposed financial limits. Service delivery will decline still further and local opposition will have to be faced as well as that from the centre. Far from receding, the local government problem promises to increase in scope and intensity. But, as we have argued, this situation is neither unexpected nor accidental. Local government is a major site of public spending and collective service provision – both inimical to the Conservatives' vision of economic 'recovery' and hence social restructuring. The local government crisis is essentially an attempt to still the voices of alternative interpretation and oppositional representation which arise through uneven social and economic development.

6
Deindustrialisation and State Intervention: Keynesianism, Thatcherism and the Regions

Ron Martin

Deindustrialisation: The Development of a National Problem

Few aspects of the British economy have attracted as much attention and debate over the past decade as the 'deindustrialisation' of the nation's manufacturing base. The term 'deindustrialisation' has acquired several different meanings and connotations (see for example: Blackaby, 1981; Martin and Rowthorn, 1986; Rowthorn and Wells, 1987). Yet whatever specific definition or explanation of deindustrialisation is adopted, the underlying conclusion is that since the mid-1960s, and especially since the early 1970s, there has been a progressive and debilitating decline in the relative and absolute contribution of manufacturing output, investment, exports and employment to the national economy. This is by no means unique to Britain, but in no other advanced capitalist economy has the scale of decline been so intense. In the same way that Britain was the first country to industrialise, so it has been the first to deindustrialise.

From Relative to Absolute Decline

In one sense, however, 'deindustrialisation' is merely a new term for an old problem. After all, the weak performance of Britain's industrial base has been a recurring source of political concern since the 1880s, when Britain's long-standing domination of world manufacturing production and trade was challenged by the more rapidly

87

growing economies of the United States and Germany (Royal Commission on the Depression of Trade and Industry, 1886). Between 1870 and 1913 Britain's share of world industrial production declined from 34 to 14 per cent. Economic historians now view this loss of industrial supremacy in the last quarter of the nineteenth century as marking the 'British climacteric', and some trace it to particular institutional and social features of Britain's landscape, such as the strength of trade unions, the overseas orientation of London's financial sector, or the country's 'humanistic snobbery' and anti-scientism (Lewis, 1978: 133).

The problem resurfaced in the 1920s and 1930s, when repeated deep recession, renewed international competition and adverse domestic financial and exchange rate policies combined to exacerbate the underlying inefficiencies and outmoded production methods of the traditional export industries, and led to a further loss in Britain's share of world trade and to severe structural problems of excess capacity and surplus labour. Because of the geographical concentration of the industries affected, particularly coal, iron and steel, shipbuilding and textiles, sectoral collapse became synonymous with the collapse of specific regions, especially central Scotland, the North-east and South Wales. Simultaneously, the South East and the West Midlands were already leading the development of the new engineering and consumer goods sectors that the structurally depressed areas seemed unable to attract or generate on the scale necessary to redress the decline of their staple industries. This spatial polarisation dramatically exposed the long-overdue need for economic restructuring and workforce redeployment, but equally rendered the task all the more difficult to achieve. Indeed, the plight of the 'depressed areas' challenged the prevailing political-economic orthodoxy of *laissez-faire*, and helped to stimulate the emergence in the 1930s of a more pragmatic interventionist policy stance (Alford, 1975; Parsons, 1986).

For two decades after the Second World War, however, rapid economic growth shielded society from the regional industrial problems inherited from the inter-war era, and disguised the poor competitive performance of manufacturing. Post-war reconstruction, the rapid expansion of world markets, and the adoption of Keynesian policies based on a commitment to full employment and the maintenance of aggregate demand, all formed part of a particularly favourable 'accumulation regime' (Martin, 1988a) that helped to fuel an unprecedented rate of economic growth. Between the early 1950s and early 1970s, output, productivity and real wages in British manufacturing doubled or more than doubled. Such was the general buoyancy of the economy that although Britain's growth still continued to lag behind that of other major industrial countries, although the international competitiveness of British industry continued to decline, and although unemployment rates in the depressed areas continued to average twice those in the more dynamic south of the country, these problems were regarded as marginal in an otherwise prosperous and fully employed society.

Yet even before this long post-war boom ended in the early 1970s, a process of deindustrialisation was already underway. Whereas in the early 1950s the surplus on manufacturing trade amounted to 10 per cent of GDP, by the late 1960s this had been halved to 5 per cent. Furthermore, industrial employment had also begun to decline. Employment in British industry peaked in 1966 at 9.5 million, of which manufacturing accounted for 8.4 million. By 1973 these numbers had fallen to 8.4 and 7.7 million respectively (Table 6.1). However, it was during the economic slowdown of 1973–9, and then the deep recession of 1979–81, that the full scale of the deindustrialisation problem became apparent. Between 1973 and 1981, output in manufacturing declined by 22 per cent, productivity growth ceased, the pre-tax corporate profit rate fell from 10 per cent to 4 per cent,

Table 6.1   The decline of industrial employment, 1966–88

	Number of employees in millions (Mid-year estimates)				
	1966	1973	1979	1981	1988
Manufacturing	8.4	7.7	7.1	6.1	5.0
Production industries[1]	9.5	8.4	7.8	6.8	5.4
Services	11.2	12.0	13.3	13.1	14.8
Total employees	22.8	22.2	22.6	21.4	21.6
Total labour force[2]	25.0	25.0	26.0	26.1	27.5

Notes: 1 Manufacturing plus mining, fuels, energy production and water supply, but excluding construction.
2 Includes self-employed, unemployed, and members of the armed forces.
Source: Department of Employment.

investment (which had peaked in 1971) fell by 23 per cent in real terms, and employment slumped to 6.1 million. Since 1981, as the aggregate economy has recovered, output in manufacturing has climbed back almost to its 1973 level and labour productivity has grown at more than 4 per cent per annum. But the downward-trending surplus on manufacturing trade has continued to decline, turning into a first-time deficit of £4.5 billion in 1983 and deteriorating to a deficit of £9.5 billion by 1987. Similarly, the workforce in manufacturing has continued to contract, and by mid-1988 was down to 5 million (5.4 million in production industries as a whole). Thus, in just over two decades, deindustrialisation has destroyed 4.1 million production jobs (3.4 million of these within manufacturing), and the numbers now employed in this sector are less than they were at the turn of the century.

The Geographical and Political Consequences

This deindustrialisation has proved problematic for several reasons. First, although not in principle disastrous, the loss of so many jobs has generated acute difficulties of labour market adjustment. The huge decline in manufacturing employment has taken place rapidly, while the labour force itself has simultaneously expanded by 2.5 million, so that although the service sector has created some 3.6 million new jobs since 1966 this growth has not absorbed both the influx of new entrants to the labour force and those workers expelled from industry. And to compound the difficulties of adjustment, while the shake-out of labour by industry has consisted mainly of male employees, much of the growth of service employment has been for female workers.

Second, the problem of workforce adaptation and reabsorption has been exacerbated by the uneven decline of manufacturing. During the first phase, 1966–73, the decline in manufacturing employment was concentrated in the manufacturing heartland, that is the Midlands, the North West and Yorkshire-Humberside, and in the South East (Table 6.2): here deindustrialisation was overwhelmingly a feature of the large industrial conurbations. In contrast Wales and East Anglia continued to enjoy residual industrialisation. But by the end of the 1970s, the rate of employment loss in the South East had slowed relative to the manufacturing heartland, employment grew in East Anglia, the East Midlands and the South West,

Table 6.2   The changing regional impact of deindustrialisation in Britain

	Change in Numbers of Employees (Mid-year to Mid-year)				
	Per cent Manufacturing			Absolute (000s) 1966–87	
	1966–73	1973–79	1979–87	Manufacturing	Services
South East	− 12.3	− 9.7	− 29.3	− 1042	+ 1419
East Anglia	+ 16.7	+ 2.0	+ 5.8	+ 45	+ 239
South West	0.0	+ 3.3	− 17.1	− 65	+ 319
East Midlands	− 2.8	+ 2.0	− 18.6	− 138	+ 356
West Midlands	− 10.3	− 9.0	− 29.3	− 500	+ 335
Yorkshire–Humberside	− 10.3	− 8.2	− 37.4	− 417	+ 248
North West	− 11.3	− 12.5	− 38.2	− 651	+ 156
North	− 3.3	− 8.1	− 36.3	− 200	+ 166
Wales	+ 3.8	− 4.3	− 32.4	− 104	+ 82
Scotland	− 8.5	− 9.0	− 36.3	− 341	+ 248
Great Britain	− 8.3	− 7.4	− 29.7	− 3413	+ 3575

Source: Department of Employment

and decline had extended to Wales and the Northern region. Then, after 1979, as the pace of deindustrialisation quickened, so industrial rationalisation and job loss affected every region of the country save East Anglia. However, this recent spatial generalisation of decline has also been uneven, in that the south-eastern regions of Britain, comprising the South East outside London, the South West, the East Midlands and of course East Anglia, have experienced a noticeably less intense and less destructive rate of employment contraction than northern regions. As a result of all this, the social and economic costs of deindustrialisation have varied considerably between different geographical areas.

Furthermore, although services are commonly regarded as the primary source of compensating job growth, service employment expansion has also been distinctly uneven. Those regions and areas that have experienced the greatest losses of manufacturing jobs have gained the least in terms of new service job growth, whereas those least devastated by deindustrialisation have so far benefited most from new employment gains in services and related activities (Table 6.2; see also Martin and Rowthorn, 1986; Martin, 1988b). Thus two decades of deindustrialisation have helped to sharpen and extend the socio-economic divides between the north and south of Britain (Martin, 1988c), and between the heavily urbanised and more rural parts of the country (Fothergill and Gudgin, 1982).

Deindustrialisation has also had far-reaching consequences for the politics of state intervention. The industrial crisis of the 1970s, involving the combination of stagnant output, negligible productivity growth, acute balance of payments problems, escalating wage inflation, and a major wave of industrial unrest, was instrumental in bringing about the breakdown and eventual political abandonment of the post-war Keynesian model of economic management. In the 1970s Keynesianism seemed unable either to promote industrial and economic recovery or to reduce endemic inflation. In contrast to the buoyant 'swinging sixties', an atmosphere of disillusionment and discontent pervaded the 'stagnant seventies': the economy was in decline, there seemed no cure for the 'British disease' (Allen, 1976) and the country appeared to have become ungovernable. Not only had deindustrialisation helped to undermine the Keynesian consensus, many observers felt that this very consensus itself had progressively undermined the country's manufacturing base. The policy vacuum created by this failure and mounting critique of Keynesian interventionism in its turn paved the way for the successful ascendancy in 1979 of Margaret Thatcher's 'New Conservatism' (see Chapter 1), which favoured a neo-liberal, free-market 'enterprise politics' as the best – indeed the 'only' – way of restoring economic growth and industrial competitiveness.

The Thatcher Government has claimed that its strategy has been successful in reviving British industry. In some respects this claim is justified: profitability in manufacturing has recovered considerably, and the rates of growth of output and productivity since 1981 have been the highest for two decades. But in terms of the continued fall in manufacturing's trade balance and employed labour force, 'Thatcherism' has not stemmed the pace of deindustrialisation: two-thirds of the fall in manufacturing employment since 1966, some 2.2 million of the total decline of 3.5 million, has occurred since 1979. Not surprisingly, therefore, a major debate has raged between the Government and its Keynesian critics over the real extent and nature of the recent industrial 'recovery' (this debate is assessed by Coates and Hillard, 1986, 1987). In the remainder of this chapter I shall argue that although quite different in policy orientation, both

Keynesianism and its successor 'Thatcherism' have each contributed to the deindustrialisation process, and to the growing regional inequalities that have developed as a consequence.

Keynesian Interventionism: The Post-war State and Industrial Decline

The main thrust of the New Conservative or New Right attack on the Keynesian state has been that it promoted the growth of an oversized public ('non-market') sector that squeezed the private ('market') sector of the economy of financial and human resources. These arguments have usually been allied to the claim that the growth of public spending, especially on the welfare state, together with associated increases in taxation, impaired industrial performance by reducing both the individual's incentive to work and the corporate sector's capacity to invest.

But although the share of public spending in GNP certainly increased substantially during the post-war period, from 32 per cent in 1950 to 47 per cent in 1976, there is little conclusive support for the assertion that this expansion of the public sector, a feature hardly confined to Britain (Heald, 1983), has caused industrial decline. For the performance of British industry relative to her major trading partners began to deteriorate as early as the 1880s, that is at least half a century before the public sector began to grow appreciably. And it was precisely during the early post-war expansion of the public sector that Britain's economy grew rapidly, suggesting that for a while at least the former may actually have been beneficial for the latter. The blame for Britain's economic and industrial decline cannot be attributed directly or solely to the growth of the state sector (Hall, 1986). Rather, the main causes of Britain's poor relative industrial performance and rapid deindustrialisation are to be found in the consistent failure of British manufacturing to modernise and innovate sufficiently, and thus to respond to the changing imperatives of international production and competition. This failure in turn can be traced to long-standing peculiarities and rigidities of Britain's institutional structures, market forms, and socio-cultural organisation (see for example: Wiener, 1981; Fine and Harris, 1985; Kennedy, 1987).

However, the post-war state cannot be completely absolved of responsibility for industrial and regional decline. There remains the vital question of whether the economic and industrial policies undertaken by the Keynesian state eventually contributed to deindustrialisation, and why more active steps were not taken to promote modernisation and renewal of the nation's manufacturing base. One argument has been that British industry has suffered from the inconsistency and changeability (even reversibility) of the policies pursued by successive governments, an inconsistency alleged to have derived in large part from the 'adversarial' nature of British politics (Grant, 1982). But in my view, the shortcomings of post-war policy in relation to industrial performance stemmed from three more fundamental features of Keynesianism as it was developed and practised in Britain (for accounts of this development, see: Schott, 1982; Bleaney, 1985): the preoccupation with short-run macroeconomic demand management and the neglect of structural and long-term factors in economic growth; the rather *ad hoc* and 'armslength' approach to industrial intervention; and the redistributive rather than developmental focus of regional policy.

The Limitations of Demand Management

The emphasis on the short run arose from the liberal collectivist nature of Keynes's own analysis of the inherent instability of industrial accumulation, an analysis which led him to advocate limited forms of regulatory state intervention while leaving the essentially market-based capitalistic structure of the economy intact (Cutler *et al.*, 1986). Although a potentially contradictory position, it nevertheless enabled both major political parties, Labour and Conservative, to assimilate his recommendations within their own different philosophical rationalisations of the post-war policy concensus. The objective of Keynesian state intervention, then, was not large-scale public ownership of industry or planned direction of private investment decisions and economic development, but the intermittent use of expansionary fiscal measures and public infrastructural investment schemes to provide occasional counter-cyclical nudges when the economy fell away from full employment.

This basic principle underpinned economic policy-making in postwar Britain from the 1940s to the mid-1970s, but it became increasingly difficult to maintain in practice because, as a form of economic management, it neither took into account, nor contained any mechanisms for influencing, the structural and supply-side characteristics of the socio-economy. For a while Keynesian demand management seemed to fulfil its promise of steady growth and full employment without any need for direct intervention in the affairs of industry or labour. But by the early 1960s some of the consequences of the neglect of the supply structure of the economy were becoming apparent: the maintenance of full employment growth increasingly carried with it two problems: inflation, and recurrent balance of payments crises. Hence Keynesian-based expansionism became transmuted into a policy regime of alternating 'go' and 'stop' cycles of demand stimulation followed by subsequent deflationary reining back. Another result was the introduction of incomes policies designed to control the inflation process directly, a device first used in 1961 and then repeatedly throughout the 1960s and 1970s, though with little overall success.

Two of the structural factors behind this inflation problem were to some extent the by-products of the Keynesian policy settlement itself. The first was the progressive concentration and centralisation of industrial capital (between 1950 and 1970 the share of the largest 100 firms in manufacturing net output doubled, while merger activity increased sevenfold), the associated rise of multi-plant and multi-regional firms, and the spread of mass production methods, the latter aided in part by the state's commitment to maintain mass consumption demand. Second, these developments in turn helped to stimulate a corresponding growth of union power and of industry-wide, multi-regional, systems of collective and comparability wage bargaining. When combined with full employment these conditions gave organised labour an unprecedented opportunity to push up real wages faster than the advance in productivity, thereby eroding industrial competitiveness, cutting corporate profitability, and thence dampening the rate of investment in new, efficiency-raising capital. To compound the impact of this vicious circle on both industrial decline and the effectiveness of demand management, industrial investment increasingly went overseas, so that by the mid-1970s the value of production by British business abroad was more than double total direct exports, and five times the foreign production (relative to exports) of key competitors such as Germany and Japan.

In addition, a third structural problem carried major implications for the viability and impact of counter-cyclical economic policy: the uneven industrial and economic geography of the country. Keynes's only consideration of the implications of uneven regional development for macro-economic demand stabilisation was his advocacy, in the late 1930s, of the dispersal of government armaments spending to the depressed industrial north of Britain in order to prevent the emergence at the 'centre' (i.e. in the south) of inflationary bottlenecks that would frustrate the national rearmament effort (Keynes, 1937). Otherwise he largely ignored the spatial structure of the economy in his macroeconomic analyses, and this was also a feature of post-war counter-cyclical policy, except briefly and in a limited way under Harold Wilson's Labour Government between 1964 and 1970, when an attempt was made to link regional economic development to national economic planning.

In practice, however, the uneven industrial and economic structure of the post-war British space economy meant that deflationary and reflationary measures had different effects in different regions. For example, the public spending cuts imposed in various post-war deflations frequently fell on the investment programmes of the nationalised industries, with highly localised effects on communities within the less dynamic northern regions and Assisted Areas where these industries were concentrated. On the other hand, many public spending programmes (for example on infrastructure and public procurement) benefited the South East disproportionately, with consequential cumulative positive multiplier effects in the region. Furthermore, because of the differential economic buoyancy of the southern and northern parts of Britain, attempts to stimulate national growth tended to generate inflation in the tight, high-wage labour markets of the South East and West Midlands well before the full utilisation of labour and industrial capacity was reached in the higher unemployment regions that made up the Assisted Areas. The uneven geography of growth therefore imparted an inherent inflationary bias to the national economy, and thus contributed to the periodic deflationary interventions that characterised the 'stop-go' policy syndrome. Certainly the South East and West Midlands were the source of damaging inflationary pressures which not only contributed to the deteriorating cost-competitiveness of manufacturing in the conurbations within these regions themselves, but also inevitably impinged on industrial performance across the remainder of the space economy.

Thus although Keynesian expansionism may well have fostered

an environment conducive to industrial and regional growth, of itself it did little to ensure or inspire industrial modernisation and redevelopment. Moreover, by ignoring crucial structural and spatial dimensions of the industrial economy, demand management helped to fuel a secular inflation problem which it was ill-equipped to control and which eventually contributed to the deindustrialisation process. Only in conjunction with an activist programme of industrial intervention could Keynesian macroeconomic regulation have begun to address the underlying problems of Britain's industrial base. Yet in this realm too there were serious shortcomings.

Industrial and Regional Policy: Managing Decline

Most studies of the industrial policies implemented between 1945 and 1979 conclude that their impact was limited. One reason was the lack of financial resources devoted to the task. As late as 1961 the British state spent less than £50 million on industrial and employment measures, compared to £270 million on agriculture (Grove, 1967), and only by the mid-1970s was Britain spending the same percentage of GDP on industrial assistance as France and Germany. A second reason was the misguided focus of policy priorities, involving an overemphasis on bailing out and supporting declining industries and firms at the expense of selective and strategic promotion of new and advanced sectors. And thirdly, industrial policy arguably depended too much on voluntarism and consensualism, whereas a more activist and *dirigiste* approach was required, similar to that adopted in Germany or France. The problem was not that industrial policy was too interventionist, as the Thatcherites claim, but that it provided too little too late.

Up until the early 1960s the two most significant elements of industrial intervention were nationalisation and regional industrial policy, both introduced by the 1945–51 Labour Government. However, nationalisation did not confer the control over the 'commanding heights' of industry that many of its protagonists hoped for. In the case of coal, iron and steel, and shipbuilding, for example, the policy task became progressively one of managing structurally declining sectors, and of attempting to reconcile the need to rationalise capacity and manpower with the adverse effects on those localities dependent on such industries. By far the most disappointing nationalisation, however, was that of the Bank of England in 1945, an institution which could have been used as a key instrument to steer investment finance into industrial and regional redevelopment, but which instead was allowed to remain virtually as independent from government, and as antithetical to the needs of industry, as it had been before the war (Morgan, 1984). In terms of regional policy, the framework that emerged from the 1945 Distribution of Industry Act and which shaped policy right through into the 1970s (and even into the 1980s), was basically Keynesian in orientation: the 'regional problem' was seen not as one of production but as one of localised unemployment arising from spatially mal-distributed 'demand', and thus was to be solved by redistributing industry from the prosperous 'south' to the lagging Development Areas using various location grants and controls (Parsons, 1986).

The only real concerted attempt to develop a *dirigiste* industrial policy occurred under the 1964–70 Labour Government which established several interventionist bodies: a Department of Economic Affairs (to develop national and regional planning), a Ministry of Technology (to foster research and development and promote advanced industries such as computers, telecommunications and machine tools), a National Incomes and Prices Board (to encourage productivity agreements between industry and labour), and an Industrial Reorganisation Corporation (to activate mergers and modernisation in the private sector). Several new instruments were also added to regional policy, and spending on regional industrial assistance was increased tenfold over the period. The aim was to modernise British industry by reforging it in the 'white heat' of new technology, to take it 'by the scruff of the neck and drag it kicking and screaming into the twentieth century' (Harold Wilson, quoted in Fry, 1975: 14).

The need for a modernisation strategy could not have been more urgent, but Labour's programme did not achieve much, and some of its policy initiatives actually contributed to deindustrialisation. The IRC (Industrial Reorganisation Corporation), for example, sought to raise industrial efficiency and rationalise overcapacity by spawning yet more big firms. It thereby encouraged the decline of production and jobs in the major conurbations, and reinforced the concentration of branch plant production activities in the northern regions on the one hand, and of corporate headquarters and research and development functions in the south and east on the other (Massey and Meegan, 1979). Thus in pursuing its modernisation objectives, the IRC reinforced the emerging regional inequalities and new spatial divisions of labour that were associated with deindustrialisation. Similarly, the expansion of regional industrial policy had ambiguous results. The number of assisted industrial moves from the south and midlands to the designated development areas increased substantially between 1964 and 1970. Although this undoubtedly brought much-needed employment to the depressed north and west, it increased the dependence of these areas on branch plant activity and their vulnerability to external corporate restructuring and disinvestment decisions. In addition, this spatial decentralisation of industry deprived the 'source' regions of the South East and West Midlands of investment just when they themselves were beginning to experience major industrial job losses. The problem was that the very conditions on which regional policy had been predicated, namely expanding pools of footloose industrial investment and employment in the 'source' growth regions, were now fading: from this period on, regional policy increasingly assumed the dubious function of redistributing a diminishing total of industrial jobs.

Over the ensuing decade, as economic and industrial growth ground to a halt, industrial intervention, both under the Conservative Government of 1970–4 and under Labour between 1974 and 1979, became progressively concerned with managing decline. Increasing sums were devoted to automatic regional grants in the development areas, but much of this aid subsidised large capital-intensive projects that generated few new jobs. Even if some of the more optimistic estimates of the employment impact of regional policy during the 1970s are accepted (e.g. Moore, Tyler and Rhodes, 1986), it did not check the rising tide of deindustrialisation in the assisted areas, particularly in Wales and the Northern region (see Table 6.2). Alongside these regional grants, greater sums were also spent on selective industrial aid, yet the bulk of these went to support failing unprofitable firms in declining sectors rather than to foster new high-tech activities. The Conservatives assisted various major companies, including Rolls Royce and Cammell Laird, and Labour followed with massive subsidies to Ferranti, Albert Herbert, Chrysler, Rolls Royce and British Leyland, among others. Indeed, half of the initial £1 billion capitalisation of the National Enterprise Board set up by Labour in 1975 as part of its 'new industrial strategy' and as a successor to the IRC, went to British Leyland and Rolls Royce (Fleming, 1980).

In sum, three points can be made concerning the development and impact of industrial policy up to 1979. Firstly, before the early 1960s industrial policy was not implemented on any significant scale, and its subsequent emergence was then as much the product of the growing problems associated with Keynesian economic management as of a (belated) recognition of the structural weaknesses of British industry. Secondly, although industrial policy cushioned the impact of deindustrialisation, it had marginal impact on the two key problems underlying manufacturing, namely low levels of productivity and an inadequate rate of structural modernisation focused on new industries with long-term growth prospects: post-war industrial policy was 'limited to a peripheral role of tidying up the edges of the economy, rather than providing any central thrust to alter and improve industry's performance and that of the economy as a whole' (Mottershead, 1978: 483).

Thirdly, in expenditure terms, the single most important element of industrial intervention was regional policy, but this was used more to change the location of industry rather than to stimulate new investment and industrial modernisation in the old manufacturing regions (Martin and Hodge, 1983). Successive governments and industry itself preferred this form of policy precisely because it was voluntary, automatic, and non-discriminatory between different firms or sectors (Grant, 1982). This emphasis on automaticity and non-selectivity severely limited the extent to which the British state could use this form of industrial intervention to direct industrial reorganisation and regional development. During the 1970s this shortcoming became increasingly apparent alongside the expansion of another, ostensibly non-spatial, form of government policy that actually had highly selective regional effects: namely the build-up of government spending on military-related research and development, advanced defence equipment and the aerospace sector, which all overwhelmingly favoured and further enhanced high-technology activities in the south and east (K. Morgan, 1986). As the 1970s drew to a close, then, little had been done to resolve the national industrial problem, and the north and west of Britain in particular were poorly placed to withstand the next phase of deindustrialisation that followed the advent of Thatcherism.

The Thatcher Era: Enterprise Politics and the Great Shake-out of Manufacturing

The Conservatives were elected into power in 1979 on a manifesto in which they claimed that they would rebuild the economy and reverse Britain's economic and industrial decline (Conservative Party, 1979). They have approached this task on two main fronts. The primary objective has been to control endemic and escalating inflation. The latter, they argue, was the direct result of the growth of excessive state activism and collectivism over the post-war period, two features which had interfered with the natural economic process of 'creative destruction' and cumulatively eroded the flexibility of the economy to respond to market forces. Their second objective, then, has been to revive free-market competitive capitalism as the basis of economic growth and wealth generation (see Martin, 1986).

To achieve these linked aims, the Thatcher Government has reversed and rejected many of the policies and orthodoxies associated with the post-war Keynesian state (a process that, in the realm of macroeconomic strategy, had begun under Labour in 1976). Thus it has abandoned demand management and the 'illusory' goal of full employment in favour of restrictive monetary policies to control inflation. It has also sought to 'roll back' the size and functions of the state, and to 'deregulate' the supply-side of the economy so as to give the maximum scope to competition, efficiency and individual enterprise. The intention has been not only to push through a major sea change in economic intervention and a new economic order, but also to promote a corresponding social and political reorganisation, a change in attitudes away from collectivism and dependence on the state and towards self reliance and individualism. More than under any other post-war government, rhetoric and ideology – prosecuted in the form of such slogans as 'popular capitalism', 'enterprise culture', 'getting the state off the backs of industry and the people' and 'individual freedom' – have become central elements of state policy (see Chapter 1).

Deindustrialisation in a Deflationary Environment

While this Thatcherite programme of 'free-market Conservatism' has been developed, British industry has experienced probably the most intense phase of contraction and restructuring of its history. Whereas the 1970s were characterised by the 'great slowdown' of the industrial economy, the 1980s have witnessed the 'great shake-out' of industrial labour and capital. Between 1979 and 1987 some 2.4 million jobs disappeared from the production sector, trade union membership fell by 2.75 million (most of this within industry: see Chapter 8), some 70,000 industrial companies went into liquidation, and the flow of industrial investment overseas rose sharply to new record levels. Obviously this enormous wave of rationalisation cannot be entirely attributed to the Conservatives' economic and industrial policies. Whatever government had been in power, employment and output would have fallen during the severe economic recession in the early 1980s. And given the relative weakness and inefficiency of Britain's industrial sector in the 1970s, the slump here was always likely to be much deeper than elsewhere. Nevertheless, it is now widely agreed, even by some monetarist as well as Keynesian economists, that the specific policies adopted from 1979 added considerably to the great shake-out, possibly accounting for as much as half of the decline in industrial employment, output and investment between 1979 and 1981.

For despite the fact that the Thatcher Government came to power at a time when the capitalist world was moving into recession, it introduced new money supply, public spending and PSBR targets which were highly deflationary (see Hall, 1986: 102–7). Even though these targets were exceeded in practice, the actual fiscal regime imposed in Britain was nevertheless four times more restrictive than any other country in the Organization for Economic Co-operation and Development (OECD) (Riddell, 1983: 90–1). Two effects of this tightness of monetary policy in the latter part of 1979 were the 30 per cent rise in the exchange rate and the jump in interest rates from 12 to 17 per cent (MacInnes, 1987: 65). Together these dramatically increased the costs and reduced the competitiveness of industry precisely when domestic and international demand were falling, thereby intensifying rather than cushioning the impact of recession. For the first time since 1945 a government had deliberately refused to implement expansionary fiscal measures to support industry and employment during a cyclical downswing. The exchange rate rises alone cost ICI, one of the country's leading industrial companies, £500 million in 1981 (Leys, 1985), and the international competitiveness of UK manufacturing declined by almost half in the first eighteen months of the Thatcher Government. Between 1979 and 1981 manufacturing output fell by 17 per cent, employment by 1.2 million or 16 per cent, and capital investment by a third (Figure 6.1).

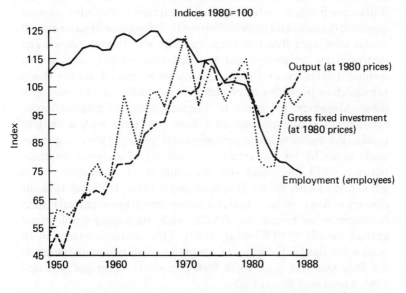

Indices 1980=100

Figure. 6.1   Employment, output and investment in the UK manufacturing sector, 1950–87

Note: Employment measured at mid-year; output and investment measured as annual totals.

Sources: CSO, *Economic Trends* (Annual Supplements) and Department of Employment, *Employment Gazette*.

Although possibly surprised by the scale of the 1979–81 slump, the Government argued that the severity of the fall in industrial employment was inevitable, long overdue, and essential, because unproductive labour and capital had been protected by years of collectivistic politics and state support. Thus sharp recession was actually seen as beneficial, for it had triggered the restructuring of hitherto unadaptable industry (Stapleton, 1981). Any additional depressive impact arising from the Government's own deflationary measures was discounted as being only a temporary side-effect. And in any case, it was assumed, the effects of the deflationary squeeze would fall where they were most needed, on the least efficient firms, workers and regions. What mattered was that industry would emerge 'leaner and fitter' to form the basis of sustained economic renewal.

But though British manufacturing is now unquestionably leaner and fitter, as measured by increased productivity and profitability, it is also much smaller when measured in terms of its ability to meet domestic demand and its contribution to the balance of payments. It would now seem that too much capacity was slimmed down and destroyed by the slump, and that deflation weeded out not only inefficient firms but also many that simply happened to have short-run cash flow problems and which were not inefficient in a long-term sense. Moreover, for many of Britain's principal manufacturers, rationalisation and restructuring were associated with a shift of production and new investment abroad (Cowling, 1986), an exodus made easier by the Government's abolition of exchange controls. Between 1979 and 1983 the net outflow of investment funds amounted to more than £23 billion; and between 1979 and 1986 the country's forty largest manufacturing companies reduced their employment in Britain by 415,000 while increasing employment abroad by 125,000 (Wintour, 1987). This internationalisation of production has been a major factor in the collapse of employment in the West Midlands and North West regions (Gaffikin and Nickson, 1984; Lloyd and Shutt, 1985).

While the Government sees the outflow of capital as a sign of strength and recovery, and as a valuable source of invisible *rentier* earnings, it has ignored the consequential loss of valuable visible export trade. Also, while the Government's 'tight money' policies have reduced inflation, the cost has been a continuing regime of high interest rates and a recurring overvaluation of sterling, both of which have frustrated rather than promoted the recovery of manufacturing competitiveness and exports. As a consequence, home-based manufacturing production has not kept pace with the rapid post-recession growth in domestic demand, fed by rising real incomes and particularly the explosion of consumer credit (which more than doubled between 1982 and 1988), and so huge flows of imports have been sucked in. Not until 1986 did manufacturing output climb back to its 1979 level, by which time the volume of manufactured imports had risen by more than a third, and a serious and deteriorating visible trade deficit had become established as a growing burden on the revenues earned from oil exports and invisibles. Even in the face of this mounting trade gap the Government has remained adamant that the 'problems that continue to beset British industry do not amount to a crisis and do not require an action plan' (Under-Secretary for Trade and Industry, quoted in *Financial Times*, 3 December 1985). A more accurate description of the Government's approach, however, would be that of a progressive retreat from manufacturing industry.

The Abandonment of Manufacturing

This disengagement from industry has two main dimensions. On the one hand, given its belief that past industrial policy has been invariably inefficient, the Government has reduced its support to industry by selling off many nationalised industries and public companies, and cutting grants and assistance to the private sector. On the other hand, as the contribution of manufacturing to the balance of payments has continued to contract so the focus of government policy has shifted to service sector activities, and from regional industrial aid to urban and general enterprise initiatives. Whether these policy changes can be regarded as marking a shift to a less interventionist stance is debateable; rather, the form and direction of intervention have altered.

Without doubt the most significant component of Margaret Thatcher's industrial policy has been the reprivatisation programme, some details of which are examined elsewhere (see Chapter 7). In its first term of office, the Government channelled large sums of money into the same unprofitable public businesses that had attracted the Conservatives' disapprobation during the 1974–9 Labour administration. British Leyland, the British Steel Corporation and British Shipbuilders all received substantial infusions of capital, as did several other private firms. As a result the Department of Industry's expenditure rose from £1 billion in 1978–9 to £2 billion in 1981–2. Initially, then, 'it looked as if the nation's most prominent critic of "lame ducks" had become, like its predecessors, another patron of handicapped waterfowl' (Hall, 1986: 112).

However, the Thatcher strategy was quite different from that of previous governments in two main respects. Firstly, specially chosen industrialists, renowned for their managerial ruthlessness, were brought in to reorganise the nationalised industries and make them profitable irrespective of the costs in terms of job losses, disinvestment of capital, or opposition from workers and the unions. Since 1979 more than 500,000 jobs have been lost as part of the reorganisation and rationalisation schemes imposed in steel, coal, shipbuilding, the national airline, the motor industry and the railways. Secondly, since 1983 the Government has embarked on a programme of selling off more and more of state-owned industries and companies, usually the most profitable activities or those whose financial debts have been cancelled in order to make them attractive to private sector investors (as in the case of Rolls Royce in 1988). Apart from the contribution of this reprivatisation policy to the goal of reducing public spending and the economic role of the state, it has also been advanced on the grounds that it increases competition – a highly dubious argument since state monopolies have simply become private sector ones – and as an overtly political and ideological attack on the wage-bargaining position and 'unique disruptive capability' of public sector unions.

No less significant is the restructuring of industrial aid to the private sector. The overriding objective has been to make economies. Since 1979 total spending on industrial aid has declined by a quarter in real terms. A second objective has been to redirect the focus of support. At one level there has been a move away from regional industrial assistance towards research and development. In real terms expenditure on regional industrial aid has declined by £160 million or by 25 per cent under the Thatcher governments, while funding for innovation and technological development in microelectronics, fibre optics, information technology and related fields has more than doubled, though at £250 million a year in current prices this still falls far short of what Britain's main competitors spend. At another level both regional assistance and support for high-tech and innovative industry have been subordinated to, and incorporated into, a so-called all-embracing 'enterprise initiative', the central focus of which is the promotion of small firms and new businesses, the key symbols of the new enterprise politics.

This new enterprise initiative is intended to signal the end of industrial policy as conventionally understood:

> Is this an 'industrial policy'? The phrase itself is unfortunate, because it appears to concentrate on industry rather than consider all the factors which affect the ability of industry and commerce to create wealth; it also carries the flavour of the DTI taking responsibility for the fortunes of individual industries and companies. It will be obvious that neither is

consistent with the philosophy of this [Government]. . . But the Government have a coherent set of policies towards industry and commerce. That set of policies is better described as an enterprise strategy than an industrial policy. . . The Enterprise Initiative will provide the most comprehensive self-help package offered to business. . . (Department of Trade and Industry, 1988: 41).

All this is obviously consistent with the Government's philosophy of free market competition and self-help, and with its reaction against sectoral intervention.

But it also reveals the Government's seemingly uncritical acceptance of some sort of 'post-industrial' vision of the British economy, in which manufacturing is no longer the basis of the growth dynamic and services are the source of future wealth and employment. It is indisputable that service activities will play an increasingly important role in generating wealth and jobs: indeed services already account for the bulk of GDP and total employment. However, this in no way lessens the need for a dynamic and internationally strong manufacturing sector; nor can services be relied upon to function as an *automatic* replacement for manufacturing output and exports:

> Services cannot substitute for manufacturing. . . New industries and new products require a long time scale. Lost capacity will take time to restore. Lost markets at home and abroad will take time to regain. Recovery from the present base is not just a matter of improvement. You cannot improve what has gone. (House of Lords Select Committee on Overseas Trade, 1985)

Services are unlikely to bridge the trade gap that now exists in manufacturing, simply because many services cannot be traded internationally. The House of Lords Select Committee on Overseas Trade estimated that because of the higher value added in manufacturing, each 1 per cent fall in manufacturing exports requires a 3 per cent rise in service exports to maintain the *same* level of economic activity. This seems unlikely when Britain's share of world invisible exports has 'fallen in the last twenty years in percentage terms by *more* than the share of world trade taken by our manufactured exports'. (Aldington, 1986: 8).

The Thatcher Government seems unpersuaded by such concerns, and instead points to the expanding financial sector and the country's role in international money markets as examples of leading services that generate considerable wealth and invisible export earnings; and to the buoyancy of the South East region, where these sectors are concentrated, as evidence of the prosperity that a service-based, enterprise economy can bring. The extent to which Britain can further expand its already large share of world trade in these particular services, and how far the specific experience of London and the South East can be replicated in or diffused to other parts of the country must, however, be open to debate.

Uneven Redevelopment and its Implications

In fact the recovery of the South East has highlighted two basic problems of the Thatcherite 'free enterprise' strategy. The first is that the Government's policies have not reduced spatial socio-economic inequalities; rather, these inequalities have increased dramatically (see Martin, 1988c). Admittedly, regional disparities would probably have widened anyway in response to the underlying recesssion of the early 1980s. But the Government's policies have been far from geographically neutral in their effects: instead they have intensified the squeeze on the manufacturing regions while enhancing the business climate and opportunities for financial and related services already focused in London and the South East. The Government apparently finds this quite acceptable; not only was the deindustrialisation of northern Britain inevitable, given the region's greater dependence on manufacturing, it was also necessary because it was there that the post-war rigidities and inefficiencies responsible for industrial and economic decline were most concentrated, and where therefore the processes of shake-out and slim-down were most needed.

In some respects this view is unexceptional: the rationalisation and restructuring of the 'old' economy of the industrial north were long-overdue and long-neglected priorities, and perhaps only a government utterly committed to exposing the industrial base to the rigours of monetary discipline and international competition was capable of setting in motion the modernisation that previous administrations had repeatedly failed to take seriously. But this approach is far less convincing in its assumption that the economic revivial of the northern regions will best be achieved by relying on the 'democracy of market forces' and minimal state support that are alleged to have promoted the rapid recovery of southern Britain (Atkinson 1986). The reality is that the south and east has been much more favourably placed to recover from deindustrialisation, in part because of its more suitable inherited economic structure, but also because the economy of this area of Britain is substantially underwritten by the state.

This latter point is not acknowledged by most Thatcherites, but one leading Conservative, Michael Heseltine, does appear to be conscious of the limitations of the 'market view':

> The South East is developing faster than the rest of Britain: the North more slowly. What is too little understood is that much of the success of the South East is not just attributable to market forces. It is also a product of government decision – or lack of it. For decades the South has been the most subsidised part of Britain... The centres of public and private power have shifted to London because we have built in a dynamic for centralisation in the South. There is of course an economic market place with its own logic and momentum. But added to that market place is the discretion of government which dictates the location of prosperity, of people, of investment... [R]egional incentives... are tiny... when compared with the real subsidies amounting to billions of pounds a year which are likely to concentrate wealth in the South. No one talks about them, the counter-regional subsidies, the subsidies to centralism, which are determined by government (Heseltine, 1988: 7–8).

Some of these 'counter-regional subsidies', such as the system of tax allowances, public transport subsidies, government defence procurement, state-funded infrastructural investment, and the government's involvement in financial and money markets, obviously predate Thatcherism. But since 1979, many policy measures have actually increased this spatial bias in state support and further encouraged the concentration of wealth and jobs in the south. Thus the Government's reductions in personal taxes, its new social capital spending programmes (on roads, railways and airports), its various schemes for new and expanding small businesses, and even its deregulation of financial markets, these all have tended to accelerate the agglomeration of economic activity in the south. This is not to ignore the urban and regional aid received by the north of Britain, but if that aid is now intended to inculcate and promote a sense of 'self-help', the fact that it is far outweighed by the state's counter-regional subsidies to the south renders the meaning of the 'enterprise economy' somewhat vacuous. Furthermore, the 'self-reliance' of the northern part of Britain is not enhanced by the Government's *laissez faire* agnosticism towards hostile foreign takeovers of major companies based there (such as Nestlé's recent acquisition of Rowntree's in the North East), takeovers that involve the loss of important indigenous employers and locally controlled jobs.

The second problem is that the uneven recovery has fuelled the emergence of inflationary 'overheating' in the south of Britain, akin to that which arose during the height of the Keynesian era in the early 1960s. The recovery of employment has been concentrated in the south: since 1983, the number of employees in employment in the southern half of the country (the South East, East Anglia, South West and East Midlands) has risen by 662,000 (6.2 per cent), as compared to an increase of only 237,000 (2.3 per cent) in the northern regions. Also it is in the south that the 1980s' wave of small business creation ('enterprise culture') and the boom in share ownership ('popular capitalism') have been focused. Above all it is in the south, and especially in the South East, where earnings and personal incomes have grown fastest, 25 per cent more than in the north, and where a major wave of house price inflation has more than trebled property values since 1979. And it is from this geographical area that the national 'booms' in mortgage debt and consumer credit have emanated.

The Government sees this mounting congestion and inflationary pressure in the south as the products of economic success. Most leading Thatcherites also believe that market forces will automatically diffuse that success to the rest of the country 'because the workings of the market mean that industrialists are forced further and further north to take business opportunities' (Lord Young, quoted in *Business*, 1987). While some employers and employees are being attracted to the less costly and less congested north, there are no compelling reasons to believe that this market-led dispersion will be sufficient on its own to close the north–south gap in growth and employment that has widened during the Thatcher era. Unfortunately, only a few Conservatives (such as Michael Heseltine and Leon Brittan) recognise this and accept the case for increased state intervention to redevelop the northern regions. The irony is that the 'overheating' of the south, itself a product of Thatcherism, now appears to be hindering the Government's deflationary strategy; and to the extent that retaliatory anti-inflation action by the Government, for example the raising of interest rates, dampens activity it does so as much in the slower-growing north as in the buoyant south, and thereby does little to reduce the imbalance between these two broad regions of the country.

Deindustrialisation and the State: A Concluding Comment

My argument here has been that while certainly not the main cause of Britain's rapid and intense deindustrialisation over the past two decades, the state has not been an innocent bystander in the drama. I have sought to trace the impact of state intervention on deindustrialisation in terms of the two dominant economic-political ideologies within which government policies have evolved, namely Keynesianism and Thatcherism. Throughout the post-war period the two main political parties have maintained different underlying attitudes towards state intervention in industry. Although the Conservatives have consistently stressed the need for a profitable and competitive industrial base, they have always been reticent about employing large-scale intervention to secure those goals. Labour has been much more interventionist in orientation, as demonstrated by its commitment to nationalisation, but also noticeably reluctant to intervene to increase the profitability of the private sector. With its demand management, social welfare provision and regional policy, post-war Keynesianism offered a middle way between liberal capitalism and state socialism, a framework for state activism that was acceptable to both political parties. One of the unfortunate side-effects of that 'policy settlement', however, was that the issue of industrial strategy was never properly addressed, or at least not until it was already too late to remedy the decline of British manufacturing.

The Conservatives' decisive withdrawal from the Keynesian consensus has enabled them to revive their long-standing historical predilection for free market capitalism and economic Darwinism. For them the continued shrinkage of British manufacturing over the 1980s represents not so much a problem as a passing phase on the natural trajectory of economic development, a trajectory dictated by the forces of competition and the logic of the market-place and which cannot be planned or directed by the state. Their reforms of economic and industrial policy, designed to create the 'self-help' economy, have taken Britain back towards the nineteenth-century tradition of *laissez-faire*, back to an era when that tradition itself began to be questioned precisely because British industry seemed incapable of independently responding to the rising tide of international competition. As for the Labour Party, they still seem wedded to a discredited Keynesianism, to nationalisation, and to a belief that Britain can be re-industrialised. If the latter means the revival of manufacturing employment, then this seems an unrealistic goal. But if it means restoring manufacturing's balance of trade and increasing its technological dynamism, then these are vital aims. So far, however, the Labour Party has failed to present the electorate with a viable strategy for achieving what Thatcherism itself has still to accomplish. Likewise, neither of the two main political parties has a convincing policy for rectifying the widening of regional disparities that has accompanied two decades of deindustrialisation, even though those disparities continue to pose an important constraint on the performance of the national economy.

7
Rewriting History and Reshaping Geography: the Nationalised Industries and the Political Economy of Thatcherism

Ray Hudson

Introduction

The final years of the Second World War and, in particular, those of the immediate post-war period seemingly promised a better future for most people in the United Kingdom. A radical post-war settlement was negotiated which centred around a commitment to a 'high and stable' level of employment and the creation of a welfare state. Furthermore, a crucial element in this settlement between capital, labour and the state involved the nationalisation of economically and politically significant industries such as coal, electricity and transport. In some senses these were indeed the decisive 'commanding heights' of the economy, providing goods and services that were vital to profitable production in other industries.

The newly nationalised industries symbolised the post-war settlement and the new consensus and compromise between capital and labour, mediated through the extension of state involvement via these innovatory forms of public ownership. And of these, it was perhaps coal mining that bore the deepest symbolic significance (Beynon and McMylor, 1985: 40). It was precisely for these reasons that some forty years later, as part of an attempt to redefine the political parameters of economy and society in the United Kingdom, Margaret Thatcher's Government launched a savage attack on the nationalised industries and set in motion a denationalisation programme of unprecedented proportions.

The contrast between the political climate in the 1940s and 1980s can be exemplified with respect to events at one colliery, now closed: Horden, in County Durham. On Vesting Day, 1 January 1947, the Lodge Secretary of the National Union of Mineworkers (NUM) there, Josiah Winter, buried a hatchet in the base of a flagpole in the colliery grounds, so symbolically breaking with the past. In 1985 the Lodge Secretary remarked that 'the Coal Board have dug it up again' (see Beynon *et al.*, 1985: 1–2). There could be no clearer statement of the sense in which another decisive break with the past is being constructed. In the remainder of this chapter I want to explore more generally why the Thatcher Governments have 'dug up the axe' and wielded it in a savage assault on the nationalised industries, exploring the reasons for this and the diverse effects it has had upon them rather than those upon the newly privatised companies. Because of the historical geography of the nationalised industries, such policies were bound to have strongly locationally differentiated effects (see Table 7.1)[1] Before this, however, it is

Table 7.1   Employment in selected industries, 1978–84 (thousands)

	Coal mining		Iron and steel		Shipbuilding and repair	
	1978	1984	1978	1984	1978	1984
South East	5.4	3.6	7.6	8.6	39.5	14.6
East Anglia	n.a.	n.a.	0.2	0.9	3.7	2.8
South West	n.a.	n.a.	2.3	1.5	19.9	20.2
West Midlands	23.1	19.2	43.7	22.5	3.2	0.5
East Midlands	68.0	57.9	18.9	7.3	1.8	0.5
Yorkshire–Humberside	79.4	66.1	64.4	34.1	5.4	2.6
North West	11.7	8.6	6.3	6.5	9.5	2.9
North	44.8	31.3	33.8	13.7	47.6	20.9
Scotland	26.4	16.9	25.2	12.5	40.7	22.2
Wales	36.1	28.5	60.2	25.4	1.2	0.7
Great Britain	295.0	232.0	262.6	133.0	172.5	87.7

Source: Department of Employment, 1978 and 1984, *Annual censi of Employment*: Note that data are not available from this source beyond 1984.

necessary to discuss nationalised industries in the pre-Thatcher era
to provide a context for the changes wrought after 1979.

Nationalisation Policies in an Era of Consensus Politics, 1947–79[2]

Over the three or so decades between the first post-war nationalisations and the election of Margaret Thatcher's first government in
1979, a broad consensus gradually developed between Conservative
and Labour central governments on the need for selective nationalisation, and as to the manner in which and criteria by which
nationalised industries were to operate. In many cases, too, a
considerable consensus emerged between managers and senior trade
union officials, as the latter were drawn into the day-to-day running
of nationalised industries via the creation of consultative and
participatory arrangements. Thatcherite policies towards the nationalised industries must be seen against this history of a considerable
measure of cross-party agreement and management–labour collaboration, for it was this consensus, both specifically within the
nationalised industries and more generally, that the Thatcher
Government deliberately set out to shatter after the 1979 general
election.

This shared perception emerged despite deep ideological differences that were especially sharp in the 1940s and 1950s. Then, as
now, Conservatives expressed a belief in the market as the most
efficacious mechanism for moulding the trajectory of national
economic development while Labour then, unlike now, was committed to seizing the 'commanding heights' of the economy and
transferring them to public ownership. This common view developed, in a sense, out of necessity, from a pragmatic recognition by
Conservatives that it was the least of the available evils that
presented itself to them in government in the 1950s. The industries
that were wholly or partly nationalised were correctly regarded as
vital to national economic performance, but in some respects could
scarcely be described as the 'commanding heights' of the economy.
In particular, on the occasion of their various nationalisations they
were technically backward, with long histories of inadequate investment, unable to match productivity norms in other major capitalist
states. Manufacturing capital in the United Kingdom in general,
therefore, did not oppose the state taking direct responsibility for

these industries, not least because most of them promised scant prospect of profit (for exceptions, see Brown 1962).

In these circumstances, industries such as coal, electricity and steel presented a paradox to manufacturing capitals in the United Kingdom. They required their outputs to be cheaply and efficiently produced within the United Kingdom (since sources of cheap imports were either lacking or were precluded by balance-of-payments considerations) to help guarantee their own competitive position and profits, yet individual capitalist enterprises would not invest in them because of the low expected rates of return. Nationalisation offered a mechanism for resolving this paradox. Capitals in the United Kingdom were not opposed to it, either because of their reliance upon the outputs of these industries or because of the generous compensation they received if their property was taken into public ownership. Although there were certain party political differences between Conservative and Labour governments, they had a shared interest in underpinning the competitive position of manufacturing activities within the national territory. This had a direct effect on their room for manoeuvre in state policy formation via its impacts on national output, national economic growth rates, taxation yields, the balance of trade and so on. Clearly, governments had rather different goals, at later points in time, in partly or wholly nationalising industries such as aircraft, shipbuilding and repair, and motor vehicles, as these produce commodities for final consumption rather than inputs to the production processes of private manufacturing capitals. Concerns such as national security and defence capability (aircraft, ships), the impact on national output and exports (motor vehicles) or reducing locationally concentrated job losses in politically sensitive localities (motor vehicles, ships) informed governmental sanction of other nationalisation decisions. Finally, the organised labour movement had a long-standing commitment to public ownership as a way of furthering the interests of workers in industries that were nationalised. Nationalisation was seen as offering opportunities for better wages and working conditions, more security of employment, and more scope for the involvement of trade unions in the running of these industries. Nationalisation also provided a mechanism to influence government policies intended to shape the trajectories of local, regional and national economic development. The extent to which nationalisation allowed these goals to be attained even before 1979 is, however, very questionable. It was only too evident by then that it had already become a mechanism for centralisation, concentration, rationalisation and massive locationally concentrated job-shedding in the 1960s and 1970s.

In fact the overall extent of nationalisation in the United Kingdom was always fairly restricted. As Urry (1981: 136) points out, it never involved more than 'a fairly small part of British industry (10–15% of assets, 8% of employment) . . .' but this 'fairly small part' was highly unionised and very heavily locationally concentrated, much of it in the political heartlands of Labour Party support. It is important to stress this because it both helps explain the absence of opposition to earlier rounds of closures in nationalised industries,[3] and points to the essentially *political* motivation that underlay the selective assault on the nationalised industries from 1979. But more immediately relevant here is the point that the limited extent of successive nationalisations reflects the fact that *this* political solution to the organisation of particular industries was – and could be – only adopted in those cases where the interests of the relevant sections of capital, labour and the state were seen substantially to overlap, even if they were not wholly coincident. This created the space for the formation of a power bloc around governments committed to pushing through nationalisation measures, in some cases enthusiastically, in others reluctantly.

Precisely because only a few industries, or parts of industries, have been nationalised, demarcating the boundary between the private and public sectors in the 'mixed economy' in this way has had profound implications for the future management of these industries – implications that came to be accepted by governments of both parties and, indeed, by significant fractions of the workforces and trade unions within them. Since the goals specified for the nationalised industries were to underpin the competitiveness of private manufacturing capital or to compete directly with private capital, and in these ways 'strengthen' the national economy, they had to be operated in relation to the same 'efficiency/profitability' criteria as 'normal' private capitalist enterprises. This was made explicit and public in 1961 when rate-of-return-on-investment criteria were introduced for the nationalised industries, criteria that were subsequently further strengthened well before 1979.

The key point, then, is that profitability criteria for the nationalised industries are a lot older than Thatcherism. In this sense, there is a strong thread of continuity between the pre-Thatcherite and Thatcherite periods, with the seeds of Thatcherite policies towards the nationalised industries sown at least two decades earlier. What is undeniable is that after 1979 this emphasis upon profitability was strengthened and reworked in an intensified form by successive Thatcher governments (for example, by Draconian cuts in the External Financial Limits of the nationalised industries, reducing their scope for borrowing to fund their operations). By redefining the parameters within which nationalised industries had to operate, with the magnitude of the quantitative changes reflecting a qualitative change in the dominant political viewpoint, successive Thatcher governments ensured that the only way that nationalised industries could strive towards their new financial targets was by cutting capacity, output and jobs and sharply raising labour productivity in those factories, plants and mines that remained. Moreover, they selectively changed senior management personnel, to break the old 'cosy' relations between managers and trade unions officials, appointing individuals such as Graham Day, Walter Marshall and Ian McGregor who were in tune with governmental rhetoric about the centrality of the market.

Nationalisation, Privatisation and the Politics of Thatcherism, 1979–87

Since 1979, then, there has been a decisive change in the *political* environment in which nationalised industries operate in the UK. The debate about redrawing the boundaries between public and private sectors and, to a lesser extent, about the criteria to be used in managing nationalised industries has taken a new turn. The election of Margaret Thatcher's Government in 1979 ushered in an era in which political priorities were focused – *inter alia* – upon cutting public expenditure, rolling back the boundaries of the state and encouraging privatisation, and radically reducing the perceived power and redefining the role of trade unions. These objectives were central to its programme to break the mould of the post-war settlement and the class compromises around which it was built. This, and the nationalised industries in particular, were now seen as a major barrier to capital accumulation in the United Kingdom and to accumulation by United Kingdom capitals (though dismantling the post-war settlement bore considerable risks for some sections of capital as well as labour). The market, above all the international market, was to be vigorously promoted as *the* mechanism for restructuring nationalised industries and class relations in the United Kingdom. It was not so much the case that the market replaced the state as the principal means of determining capacity, output and employment in these industries; rather, the Thatcher Government redefined the politics of production in such a way as to shape the market in a very different way and create the space for it to operate as part of its alternative, 'New Right' strategy.

The pursuit of profit therefore became the central and sole preoccupation within the nationalised industries, for two sorts of reasons. Firstly, once nationalised industries, or parts of them, became sufficiently profitable, they could be sold off to the private sector, simultaneously cutting public expenditure and reducing the scope of the public sector while helping attain other political goals of the Government. For example, the considerable proceeds of privatisation sales – some £11.0 billion over the period 1979–86 – enabled the Government partly to fund its regressively redistributive tax-cutting policies while privatisation became central to the Government's (largely unrealised) plans for more widespread share ownership and the growth of 'popular capitalism' (Hudson and Williams, 1989). Secondly, the pursuit of profit within the nationalised industries has necessitated savage reductions in employment and led to the redefinition of conditions and terms of employment for those retaining their jobs. These changes have helped both alter and weaken trade unions in three ways: through loss of members; through encouraging divisions between workers (within and between plants and industries) as they seek competitive or individualised solutions to the threat of redundancy; and through demonstrating that unions are unable to prevent these changes coming about. Moreover, the costs of unemployment and deteriorating conditions of employment are largely experienced in areas which are solidly within a Labourist tradition. There is a minimal political cost, or even arguably a political benefit, attached to such changes for a Conservative Government that is, in the words of its Prime Minister, committed to 'ending socialism'. Although in some cases – most notably the British Steel Corporations's (BSC) Ravenscraig works in Scotland – electoral and party political considerations have taken precedence over the logic of the market (for a time at least), such rare exceptions sharply highlight the more general trend towards market and profitability determination of changes in the nationalised industries, regardless of the localised human and social costs that this entails.

In understanding why this is so, it is crucial to appreciate the changes in the international political and economic environment that have made this switch in policy possible. For by the late 1970s the United Kingdom economy was no longer *necessarily* dependent upon domestic production of commodities such as coal and steel. Other options existed, via sourcing from imports, as international market conditions changed dramatically. World markets were awash with cheap coal and steel as a consequence of massive global over-capacity and over-production. Guaranteeing production within the United Kingdom via nationalisation was, therefore, no longer necessary, at least not to the same degree. The potential long-run dangers of dependency upon imports of key commodities were ignored in favour of the short-term economic gains and longer-term political ones of switching to imports. This is perhaps most clear in the case of coal and electricity generation (though it is by no means confined to these industries). In the 1940s and 1950s some 95 per cent of the United Kingdom's primary energy demands were met by domestically produced coal, the vast majority of it from deep-mines. In the 1980s there is a glut of cheap coal on the world market and coal must compete with natural gas, oil and nuclear power as sources of electricity generation. Similarly in the case of bulk steel, massive global over-capacity allows steel users the option of cheap imports rather than steel produced in the United Kingdom. Consequently, the remains of the nationalised coal and steel industries are powerfully squeezed by the pressures of the international market. The existence of these alternative sources of supply via imports has changed the arena of debate within the United Kingdom as the threat of foreign competition has been used to secure changes in domestic production. But it would be wrong to believe that this has all come about as the result of the invisible hand of the market, for this reworking of the connections between production in the United Kingdom and the international market is part of a deliberate political strategy. The broader strategy of internationalisation as the Thatcherite solution to the United Kingdom's economic problems has both facilitated the outflow of capital, by removing exchange controls in 1979, and encouraged foreign direct investment in the

United Kingdom. This aspect of the strategy has also had direct impacts on nationalised industries. The most celebrated example of this is Nissan's car assembly plant at Washington New Town (Holloway, 1987), which will have direct consequences for British Leyland (BL) and, in turn, for the (for the moment) nationalised steel industry.

Such changes in cars, coal and steel, then, involve both a redrawing of the private–public sector boundary and changes in the nationalised rump of these industries. Such changes are most appropriately seen as part of a *political* strategy to dismember key public sector industries rather than as an *economic* strategy for reorganising crucial branches of industry. This political strategy was developed in the period before 1979, when the Conservatives were in opposition and reflecting upon the defeats inflicted on Edward Heath's Government in 1972 and 1974 by the miners and their trade union allies. This had a profound effect upon them. It bred a determination to ensure that no future Conservative Government suffered a repetition of this humiliating experience at the hands of the miners or any other powerful group of workers, especially in the public sector.

The Conservative Shadow Cabinet began work on a strategy to achieve this objective. Lord Carrington, Energy Minister under Heath, was charged with providing a detailed analysis of the lessons to be drawn from the events of the early 1970s. The resultant report focused upon the enormous potential power available to workers in key industries, if organised in strong trade unions. It drew particular attention to the effects of advanced technology in the fuel and power industry, the economic dependence of modern society upon electricity and the central role played by coal in the United Kingdom economy. The report noted that armed forces personnel lacked the skills needed to run modern power stations; therefore a power workers' strike could be totally decisive (see Beynon and McMylor, 1985: 34–6). The key proposition advanced was that the balance of power in society was uneasily weighted between the state and small, strategically located groups of workers, and the political problem facing any future Conservative government would be how to deal with this situation.

Against this sombre background, Margaret Thatcher pressed Nicholas Ridley to produce a further strategic document. It was widely leaked in 1978 (see *The Economist*, 27 May 1978) and starkly spelled out the intentions of any future Conservative Government in a sophisticated political strategy for tackling the issues raised by Carrington. It addressed itself to the prospective 'political threat' within a critical industry, supported by the 'full force of communist disrupters'. It set out a five-point strategy that is fundamental in an understanding of subsequent Conservative Government policies towards the nationalised industries:

1. Return on capital figures should be rigged so that an above-average wage claim can be paid to the 'vulnerable' industries.
2. The eventual battle should be on ground chosen by the Tories, in a field they think could be won (railways, British Leyland, the Civil Service or steel).
3. Every precaution should be taken against a challenge in electricity or gas. Anyway, redundancies in those industries are unlikely to be required. The group believes that the most likely battleground will be the coal industry. They would like a Thatcher government to *a*) build up maximum coal-stocks, particularly in the power stations; *b*) make contingency plans for the import of coal; *c*) encourage the recruitment of non-union lorry drivers by haulage companies to help move coal where necessary; *d*) introduce dual coal/oil-firing in all power stations as quickly as possible.
4. The group believes that the greatest deterrent to any strike would 'be to cut off the money supply to the strikers, and make the union finance them'.
5. There should be a large, mobile squad of police equipped and prepared to uphold the law against violent picketing. 'Good non-union drivers should be recruited to cross picket lines with police protection.'

The extent to which this report has been followed as a blueprint for the Thatcher Governments is crucial in understanding the sequence and timing of the 1980 strike in the steel industry, the Government's retreat from confrontation with the miners in 1981, and the 1984–5 strike in the coal-mining industry (see Beynon and McMylor, 1985). These were critical moments in the Government's political strategy to cut down both the nationalised industries and the basis of powerful trade union opposition within them to its political strategy. The axe had been dug up again.[4]

Reworking Work in the Nationalised and Newly Privatised Industries

The very scale of job-shedding from the nationalised industries in the context of high levels of national unemployment and particularly high levels of unemployment in localities and regions heavily dependent upon nationalised industries has produced considerable pressure to accept 'new' working conditions and terms of employment. Again, this process had begun before the election of the Thatcher Government, with the clearest illustration being the changes set in motion by Michael Edwardes at BL after his appointment in 1977 as chairman. These changes were pushed to their final conclusion after the 1979 election with powerful Government support. More generally, driving through such radical changes in the nationalised industries has been crucial to that Government's broader strategy. These could then be held up to the private sector as exemplification of the sorts of changes that it would need to secure in order to become or remain internationally competitive via reasserting managers' 'right to manage'.

It was no coincidence, therefore, that the nationalised steel industry, a soft target because of its fragmented and weak trade unions, became the first to experience the full weight of the new Government's policies towards the nationalised industries. Already in disarray before 1979 because of the abandonment of the major expansion programme announced in 1973, the BSC embarked on a further programme of capacity closures and job reductions after the 1980 steel strike, with the steel unions in no position to oppose it. In part these cuts were a consequence of the Government pushing through a series of 'Phoenix' mergers between 1981 and 1986, which redefined the public–private sector divide in steel even more sharply around a 'private sector/profitable special steels' and 'public sector/ less profitable or unprofitable bulk steels' axis (Hudson and Sadler, 1987a). Essentially this involved a series of mergers between BSC and international engineering conglomerates such as Guest Keen Nettlefold (GKN) and Tube Investments (TI) to form new jointly owned companies, each dominant in one product range and market segment within the United Kingdom. Such mergers have often been heavily subsidised via public expenditure. They have enabled companies such as GKN and TI to prosecute their strategies of diversification but restricted BSC to the intensely globally competitive and much less profitable bulk steel market.

In these circumstances, BSC has sought to achieve profitability via increasing its competitiveness and labour productivity. It has done so, not so much by investment in new technology and means of production as by cutting its core workforce, imposing greater managerial control over its remaining core workforce to secure its more flexible deployment, and increasing the use of sub-contracted and casual labour. This has perhaps reached its most extreme expression (to date) in the terms and conditions of casual employment at BSC's 44-inch pipe mill at Hartlepool (Hudson and Sadler, 1985b: 34–5).

Rather different strategies have been followed in the coal mining and shipbuilding industries. In shipbuilding, for example, the Government strategy has not been to reserve segments of the market for particular companies but rather deliberately to create competition between yards within British Shipbuilders (BS). In these circumstances the pressures upon workers to accept changed working conditions and practices to try and guarantee a higher rate of productivity in 'their' yard are intense. But such inter-plant competition is perhaps most intense, savage and divisive when part of a formerly nationalised industry is privatised and deliberately set in competition against the remaining yards in the nationalised industry (see Hudson, 1986b: 201–2). In these ways workers have been seemingly inexorably drawn into accepting the competitive solution that lies at the heart of the Thatcherite project, via vying with one another through the medium of labour productivity within the arena of the market.

British Coal (BC) has also been faced with pressures to increase labour productivity. In contrast to British Shipbuilders, its strategy has involved the selective introduction of new technical conditions of production into different coalfields, collieries and faces within collieries, especially via the introduction of MINOS, the Mine Operating System (Winterton, 1985) with the intention of increasingly automating production and tightening managerial control over labour. This process of differential investment is again one that pre-dates the rise of Thatcherism by many years (Hudson, 1988: chs 6 and 7). Nevertheless, these processes were given a new twist in the post–1979 setting of Government directives to BC to become profitable in the context of substantial global over-production of coking and steam coals, a drive to expand domestic open-cast production as part of a more general privatisation strategy, and a clear Government commitment to break the power of the NUM. Consequently, new fixed capital investment in MINOS, heavy duty faces and so on, is being increasingly tied to collieries where workers will agree to increased flexibility and new working conditions, and this both reflects and reinforces divisions between miners within collieries, between collieries and between coalfields. The emergence of the Union of Democratic Mineworkers (UDM), assiduously encouraged by the Government during the 1984–5 strike, has added a fresh dimension to this process. BC can now threaten to deal only with the UDM if the NUM refuses to countenance changed working conditions, especially in new collieries. This is further driving a wedge between NUM areas as for some the choice of new working conditions in an NUM pit is preferable to these conditions in a UDM pit or to no pit at all, while others in the NUM, notably its President, Arthur Scargill, refuse to have anything to do with either flexible working or the UDM. In this way different areas within the NUM are played off – or maybe play themselves off – against one another while the struggle between the UDM and NUM continues.[5] This helps create the space for BC to be able to redefine working conditions and productivity norms in its remaining deep mines and to argue that it *must* do so in the face of competition from cheap imports *and* open-cast output from within the United Kingdom. Moreover, it can do so in some circumstances with at least the grudging compliance or tacit support of groups of miners and sections of coal mining trade unions. In this way the political economy of Thatcherism connects changes in international energy markets with changes in the labour process in energy production within the United Kingdom in a way that further reinforces its own already-powerful, perhaps even hegemonic, position.

And What of the Future?

It is difficult to dispute the conclusion that '*politically* privatisation has succeeded beyond the Government's wildest dreams' (de Jonquieres, 1987, my emphasis). It would be equally unwise to believe that the process has reached an end – notwithstanding the débâcle of the British Petroleum (BP) flotation in the wake of the 1987 stock market crash – or that the Conservatives under Margaret Thatcher will not win a fourth general election early in the 1990s. Consequently, the public sector will in all probability continue to shrink. There is no evidence that the Thatcher Government sees any reason to deviate from its conviction that, wherever possible, privatisation is preferable to continuing the long march to find a satisfactory way of managing public sector industries.

How will this affect the nationalised industries? It is possible to make some reasoned forecasts, for in many ways their future has already been clearly mapped out as regards cars, coal, electricity and steel. It is clear that BSC is to be privatised in the near future. In a situation of gross global over-capacity in bulk steel production, this would result in two, maybe three, of the current 'big five' BSC complexes being closed: the most likely candidates for closure would be Ravenscraig and Teesside (for reasons that are explained in Hudson and Sadler, 1989). Those remaining would be wholly sourced with imported coking coals. Likewise, privatisation of the Central Electricity Generating Board (CEGB) will have further deleterious consequences for deep-mined coal production in the United Kingdom, irrespective of whether or not BC is privatised. The requirement that the larger of the two newly privatised electricity-generating companies – to all intents and purposes the rump of the CEGB – retain the high-cost nuclear stations will only intensify the pressures to seek out cheaper sources of fuel for its non-nuclear stations. In a situation where the newly privatised electicity companies are no longer contractually constrained to purchase coal mined in the United Kingdom, they would undoubtedly sharply increase their consumption of imported coal, perhaps to around 20 million tonnes a year in the short run. This will have two effects within the United Kingdom. Firstly, it will increase pressure for expanded open-cast output, both by BC and/or via an extension of private mines. By the end of 1987 it was clear that the Secretary of State for the Environment, Nicholas Ridley, was intent on driving a coach and horses through his own Planning Inspectors' recommendations so as to make this possible. Secondly, the combined pressures of greatly increased cheaper imports and domestic open-cast output will lead to a decimation of the remaining deep mines. It is quite conceivable that within a decade there may be only four or five major deep-mining complexes (possibly sufficiently profitable to have been privatised themselves), within the United Kingdom, each producing 8 to 10 million tonnes of coal a year. These will be located in parts of the Midlands and Yorkshire, and deep mining, though not open cast, will have disappeared from the former peripheral coalfields of north-east England, Scotland and Wales.

In other nationalised industries the Thatcherite strategy for encouraging the internationalisation of production via inward direct foreign investment will have severe effects. This will become most marked in motor vehicle production as Nissan's Washington plant continues to expand and other Japanese producers establish them- selves (such as Honda at Swindon). The effect of this will be to intensify pressures on existing motor vehicle producers – including BL – to meet their productivity norms via job-shedding, reorganisa- tion of working practices, and intensification of work on the line. There will certainly be knock-on effects into component suppliers and the by-then wholly privatised steel industry as the effects of changes in one sector ripple and reverberate through others.

Clearly these changes will have momentous impacts on the future geography and patterns of industrial production and employment in the United Kingdom. Not least, they imply further massive location- ally concentrated job losses in areas which the Thatcher Govern- ment sees as bastions of Labour support, locked into old collectivist attitudes, and unlikely to vote for it. Indeed it is clear that, in terms of electoral calculation, it has no need of votes in these areas, though it cannot be seen to be wholly indifferent to their fate, not least by some of the members of its own party. Consequently, it has made policy responses to unemployment in these areas but its policies to encourage new employment there are more notable for their intended ideological effect in promoting the virtues of the 'enterprise culture' than for their effects in lowering unemployment there (Hudson and Sadler, 1987b).

No doubt there will be some who, having read this far, will conclude that this is far too gloomy and pessimistic a scenario. They might, for example, argue that in fact the Thatcher Government will collapse in the web of its own contradictory policies and be replaced by a Labour Government strongly committed to the nationalised industries, to higher levels of national employment and to more active regional and urban policies to reduce intra-national dif- ferences in social and economic conditions. Maybe; though I doubt it. For the experiences of the 1940s and 1960s strongly indicate that for this to happen much stronger interventionist policies would need to be pursued than has previously been the case, centred on *control* of private capital. But the ground for such policies, never very firmly established in the United Kingdom has, for the foreseeable future, been cut away since 1979 by the removal of restrictions on capital export and the massive net disinvestment by capitals from manufacturing in the United Kingdom. It is by no means clear what there would be left to nationalise by – say – 1990, even in the unlikely event of a Labour Government wishing to embark on this course of action. Nor is there any reason to believe that the Labour Party would adopt radically different policies to those of Margaret Thatcher with regard to existing nationalised industries. For as one commentator has perceptively remarked (de Jonquieres, 1987, emphasis added): 'Labour has moved a long way from its previous insistence on sweeping state control of the "commanding heights" of the economy... The Government's approach to privatization may still be far from commanding universal approval. But Labour's change of attitude is *eloquent testimony* to the *extent to which the policy has shifted not only the frontiers of the state, but also the terms of the political debate*'. It is this last point that is the crucial one. It reveals how the Labour Party has been comprehensively out-manoeuvred by the Conservatives in the 1980s to the point where it is confronted in a political arena in which it sees no *electoral* choice but to mimic Thatcherite policies over the nationalised industries (and more besides). In this sense the legacy of Thatcherism will outlive not only Margaret Thatcher but also future Conservative Governments.[6]

Notes

1. I shall, however, have very little to say on the effects of these policies as a proximate cause of deindustrialisation, of locationally concentrated employment loss and the social and economic consequences of this. Some of these issues are discussed in Chapter 6 and in Hudson 1985; 1986a and b; 1988; Beynon, Hudson and Sadler 1986; Hudson and Sadler, 1985a.
2. To regard this period as a homogeneous one, uniformly characterised by consensus is, of course, a considerable over-simplification (see Hudson, 1988). It is regarded as such here in order to contrast it with what came after 1979.
3. It was crucial in the 1960s in preventing public opposition to massive cutbacks in coal mining. Labour local authorities and the mining trade

unions in these areas did not wish to embarrass 'their' Government while it, in turn, promised alternative jobs via its new regional planning and policy measures. The fact that it did not deliver these jobs was another matter. Again, in the 1970s another Labour Government temporarily reprieved steel plants located in areas of strong political support for it, and produced new proposals intended to create alternative jobs there (see Hudson, 1988, Chapters 6 and 8).

4. The contrast between the Government's assiduous adherence to the strategy set out in 1978, and the trade union movement's failure to take it seriously, is a striking one. As a result, the Government only took on the unions at a time and on terrain of its choosing, its meticulous preparation for confrontation contrasting sharply with the unions' lack of preparation. For discussion of aspects of this, see Chapters 8 and 14.

5. The re-election of Arthur Scargill and his reiterated opposition to the 'new realism' suggests that the divisions within the NUM and between it and the UDM are unlikely to disappear in the foreseeable future.

6. This paper in part draws on research carried out as part of the ESRC's 'Changing Urban and Regional System' initiative. It also draws on research commissioned by Cleveland County Council, Easington District Council and Sheffield City Council. This work and much else that is drawn on in this paper draws on research carried out with Huw Beynon and David Sadler. Their efforts are gratefully acknowledged but the usual disclaimers apply.

8
The Changing Geography of Trade Unions

Doreen Massey and Joe Painter

Introduction

Recent years have been tough for the trade unions. Headline after headline has proclaimed their imminent demise, their irrelevance to changing occupational and industrial structures and to supposedly transformed ideologies. They have come under political onslaught. Given all of this, they have survived remarkably well.

The emerging evidence of a stabilisation in their position, at least in numerical terms, itself says something about the causes of the problems. Trade union membership has not declined because of some autonomous ideological shift away from unionism, or more generally away from collectivism and towards individualism (Gallie, 1987). On the contrary, there is some evidence that those who remain in trade unions today are more consciously trade unionist than previously. Given the political climate, being a trade union member is possibly more of a political statement than it was when, in the then major sectors of the economy, taking up trade union membership was almost a reflex action.

The bulk of the recent decline in trade union membership has resulted from a straightforward loss of jobs, a process concentrated in the more unionised sectors, and from people going out of union membership when moving jobs to sectors where unions have been less successful in gaining an organisational foothold (Gallie, 1987). These two processes are associated mainly with the massive recession in the early eighties and with very long term structural changes in the economy, particularly changes in the labour process and in the occupational structure of the workforce. To these problems can be added an extraordinarily hostile government bent on attack. With hindsight, the first factor (the recession) seems to have been the cause of all the headlines, but it will probably be the other two phenomena (the long-term 'structural changes' and the political onslaught) which ultimately will be seen to have posed the bigger challenges. We shall look at these in the sections which follow.

Table 8.1 shows the clear shift from growth to decline in total membership of all unions between the 1970s and 1980s. This has not been reversed. But the real collapse took place in the recession years between 1980 and 1983, which fits at aggregate level with Gallie's findings. Since then, when manufacturing in particular suffered very badly, the year-on-year losses have been reduced. Furthermore, the most recent results confirm a far better performance for a range of unions even than in the middle of the decade. The GMB (General, Municipal, Boilermakers and Allied Trades Union), for example, gained over 2,000 members in the last quarter of 1987, while the Union of Shop, Distributive and Allied Workers (USDAW), the

Table 8.1   Changes in trade union membership, 1974–85

Year	Total number of members	Union members as a percentage of the workforce[2]	Percentage change in membership over previous year
1974	11.8	46.6	+ 2.7
1975	12.2	47.9	+ 3.6
1975[1]	12.0	47.2	
1976	12.4	48.5	+ 3.0
1977	12.8	50.1	+ 3.7
1978	13.1	50.7	+ 2.1
1979	13.3	51.1	+ 1.3
1980	12.9	49.5	− 2.6
1981	12.1	46.6	− 6.5
1982	11.6	44.8	− 4.2
1983	11.2	41.6	− 3.1
1984	11.0	39.9	− 2.2
1985	10.7	38.4	− 2.5

Figures relate to December of each year, to the UK and all trade unions.
Notes: 1   In 1975, 31 organisations were no longer considered to be trade unions. There are thus two sets of figures for 1975, one with these organisations included and one with them excluded.
2   Includes unemployed.
Source: Central Statistical Office, 1988.

National and Local Government Officers' Association (NALGO) and the Union of Construction, Allied Trades and Technicians (UCATT) all showed membership gains of between 1.1 and 2.3 per cent in 1987 as a whole (see Table 8.2).

But if the unions have survived (just) the worst of the recession, they nevertheless face major challenges from various (related) sources.

The recession of the early 1980s was arguably an accentuation of many structural economic changes which had been underway for some time. They have involved: major shifts between sectors of the

Table 8.2   Membership of the twenty largest TUC unions 1985–7

Union	1987	1986	1985	% change 1986–7	% change 1985–6
TGWU	1 348 712	1 377 944	1 434 005	−2.1	−3.9
AEU	815 072	857 559	974 904	−5.0	−12.0
GMB	803 319	814 084	839 920	−1.3	−3.1
NALGO	759 780	750 430	752 131	+1.1	−0.2
MSF	653 000			+3.5	
ASTMS	*	390 000	390 000		0.0
TASS	*	241 000	251 254		−4.1
NUPE	650 930	657 633	663 776	−1.0	−0.9
USDAW	387 207	381 984	385 455	+1.4	−1.0
EETPU	329 914	336 115	347 635	−1.9	−3.3
UCATT	255 883	249 485	248 693	+2.7	+0.3
COHSE	207 841	212 312	212 980	−2.1	−0.3
UCW	197 758	191 959	194 244	+3.0	−1.2
SOGAT	193 838	199 594	205 916	−2.9	−3.1
NUT	178 294	184 455	207 651	−3.3	−11.3
BIFU	165 839	158 746	157 468	+4.5	+0.8
NCU	151 407	155 643	161 315	−2.7	−3.5
CPSA	149 484	150 514	146 537	−0.7	+2.7
NGA	124 638	125 587	126 074	−0.8	−0.4
NAS/UWT	120 544	123 945	127 612	−2.7	−2.9
NUCAPS	118 740			+0.2	
SCPS	*	88 738			
CSU	*	29 768			
NUR	117 594	125 000	130 261	−5.9	−4.0
TUC	9 126 911	9 243 297	9 585 529	−1.3	−3.6

* merged unions
Source: *Financial Times* 1987, *Financial Times* 1988a.

Key to table

TGWU	Transport and General Workers' Union
AEU	Amalgamated Engineering Union
GMB	General, Municipal, Boilermakers
NALGO	National and Local Government Officers
MSF	Manufacturing, Science, Finance
ASTMS	Association of Salaried, Technical and Managerial Staff
TASS	Technical and Supervisory Section
NUPE	National Union of Public Employees
USDAW	Union of Shop, Distributive and Allied Workers
EETPU	Electrical, Electronic, Telecommunication and Plumbing Union
UCATT	Union of Construction, Allied Trades and Technicians
COHSE	Confederation of Health Service Employees
UCW	Union of Communication Workers
SOGAT	Society of Graphical and Allied Trades
NUT	National Union of Teachers
BIFU	Banking, Insurance and Finance Union
NCU	National Communications Union
CPSA	Civil and Public Servants Asociation
NGA	National Graphical Association
NAS/UWT	National Association of Schoolmasters/Union of Women Teachers
NUCAPS	National Union of Civil and Public Servants
SCPS	Society of Civil and Public Servants
CSU	Civil Service Union
NUR	National Union of Railwaymen

economy; changes in the work process leading to changes in the occupational structure of the workforce; a transformation in the gender composition of the employed population; and a growth of part-time work.

The current Government's onslaught has been launched against this background. In this chapter we shall look mainly at the sectoral shifts and at some elements of the political attack. In both, 'geography' has been an important part of what has been going on.

The Challenge of a Changing Structure

There were definite geographical bases to the trade union movement in Britain in the immediate post-war years. The pattern largely reflected the geography of industry and a particular industrial structure. This was a trade union movement based on a capitalism which was overwhelmingly urban, and where different parts of the country retained their individual industrial specialisms.

During the period of post-war growth, through to the end of the 1950s, the broad outline of this geography was largely reinforced. But since then it has changed quite radically: while some unions have grown rapidly in new regions, there has also been a massive decline in many areas of former strength.

The new geography of union membership is more widely-distributed, both overall and within individual unions. The heartlands of the trade union movement have declined relatively and absolutely. There has been decentralisation to new areas. The growth of new sectors in the economy has produced threats and opportunities for trade unions. It has enabled the development of new, more widely dispersed trade unions, and it has seen the rise of non-unionism in particular areas, industries and sections of the workforce. This in turn suggests the emergence of new potential trade unionists.

The Decline of the Heartlands[1]

In the immediate post-war years trade union membership in Britain was concentrated in the cities and in particular regions of industrial concentration. Many individual unions, especially those organised in specific industries, were overwhelmingly based in just one or two parts of the country. In 1951, for example, nearly half of NUTGW's (National Union of Tailors and Garment Workers) membership was in London, Leeds and Manchester, and half of NUFLAT's (National Union of Footwear, Leather and Allied Trades) members in the shoe industry were in the East Midlands. Some unions were even more geographically concentrated: the Association of Textile Workers (ATW) was exclusively confined to North West England, and the NUM (National Union of Mineworkers) was synonymous with the coalfields.

These are all unions which organised in specific industrial sectors, and their geography mirrored that of the industries in which they were based. But other unions, even though they might spread across much of manufacturing industry, were still overwhelmingly concentrated in the main industrial areas of nineteenth and early twentieth century British capitalism. The AEU (Amalgamated Engineering Union) and its forebears is a classic example. In this earlier period half its members were in five areas: London, Lancashire, Birmingham–Coventry, South Wales and the Glasgow–Paisley area.

We refer to these geographical bases as the unions' 'heartlands'. They varied between unions. In some areas a single union might organise most trade unionists – the coal and textile areas are the most obvious examples. Elsewhere the heartlands of the different unions overlapped to form bases of trade unionism more generally, especially in the cities. Since the 1960s these various heartlands have been seriously eroded. In part, this loss reflects the decline in total membership of unions which were almost entirely confined to particular areas, but it is also the result of differential patterns of loss and gain. Most notably the old bases of membership in these unions have seen the greatest proportional reduction, although the timing has varied considerably between unions.

Fig. 8.1 shows the geography of loss and gain over thirty years for

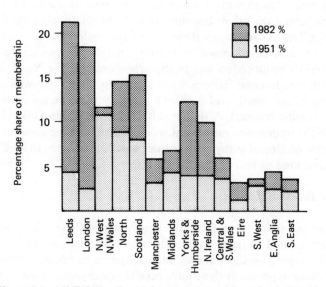

Figure 8.1   NUTGW – change in percentage share of membership, 1951–82

Note: Areas are not the same size and may not conform to accepted definitions of name of region as union membership areas have been used. Membership areas with the same name among unions may not be of a similar geographic size, as the definition of the area varies among unions.

the garment workers; and the same tendency to a flattening-out of variations in membership between different areas is repeated in many other unions. In the AEU, for instance, the shift in balance has been quite dramatic. In 1951, 3,500 more members of the then AUEW were in the old base areas than in the rest of the country. However, by 1979 the situation was reversed and the areas which had once been the union's periphery had 120,000 more members than the old heartlands. Moreover, this shift was dramatically reinforced through differential patterns of decline after 1979. Between 1979 and 1981, total membership of the AUEW fell by 17 per cent, but the decline in the heartland area was 22 per cent.

Not all unions were so geographically concentrated in the early post-war years. Membership of general unions, such as the then GMWU (General and Municipal Workers' Union), and unions in sectors more directly related to population distribution (mainly service sector unions such as USDAW), was much more widely dispersed, though with a numerical bias towards the cities which strengthened the urban concentration of the union movement as a whole. Trends even within these unions are reinforcing the tendency towards a more dispersed geography. In 1961, 28 per cent of the GMWU's membership was in the urban areas of the North West and its London and Eastern region, and only 20 per cent was in the whole of the North and Scotland. By 1979 these magnitudes had been almost reversed. A similar shift happened within USDAW.

So the trade union movement is confronted with the absolute and relative decline of many of its former bases of strength. In itself this is some kind of loss of identity, of history.

Why Has It Happened?

To some extent the shifts in the geography of these unions reflect organisational changes within the unions themselves. There have been mergers, amalgamations, and changes in recruitment strategy. But more importantly there have been major changes in the sectoral composition, technology and geographical organisation of industry itself.

There seem to be three crucial components of these changes:

1. *The decline of older industries*:   First there has been straightforward industrial decline as the deindustrialisation of Britian has spread through successive generations of industry (see Chapter 6).

Among the first to decline were old labour-intensive and characteristically female-employing consumer goods industries. Increasing imports and a wider international reorganisation of production had dramatic effects on the clothing, shoe and textile industries and consequently on NUTGW, NUFLAT and the ATW.

The decline of other industries, for instance engineering, began in the 1960s and 1970s, taking with it sizeable chunks of unions such as the AUEW. Finally, deindustrialisation has also affected the geography and internal composition of the more general unions. The decline of the EETPU (Electrical, Electronic, Telecommunication and Plumbing Union) in Merseyside, Humberside, South Wales and London between 1974 and 1983 is related to the fall in membership in the older manufacturing sections of the union. Similarly, the decline of the then GMWU in London, especially in the 1960s is associated with the steady destruction of that city's manufacturing base.

2. *The search for cheaper labour*: There have also been geographical shifts in response to intensifying competition. Within Britain, a differential pattern of change has seen the net decline of the major conurbations and net gains in the smaller towns and the peripheral areas.

The changing geography of the NUTGW clearly shows this process. Figure 8.2 tracks the changing balance between the NUTGW's original geographical base and the rest of the country from the early 1950s to the early 1980s. The old base shows continuous decline but, before 1979, there was absolute growth in membership in other regions. The clothing industry, trapped between low-cost imports and rising competition for labour in its established locations, relocated elsewhere – the North, Scotland, parts of Yorkshire and Humberside, Northern Ireland, the South West, East Anglia and the outer South East – in search of cheaper labour.

Similar kinds of spatial restructuring have occurred in other industries, particularly in engineering. Here though, the processes and their timing have been different. Figure 8.3 plots the course of events for the AUEW. Total membership grew until 1979, as did both the centre and the periphery of the unions' geography up to 1971. Only since 1971 has growth in the periphery been at the expense of the old heartlands. But actual movement *has* occurred not only to find cheaper labour, but also to escape well-organised

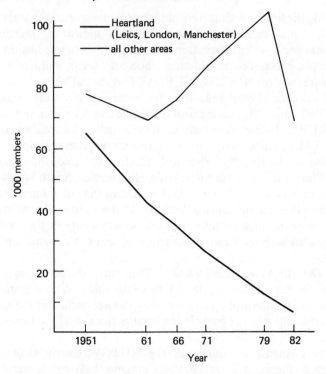

Figure 8.2   Changing geographical base of NUTGW membership, 1951–82

labour. The numerical strength of the heartlands has been associated with an organisational strength which itself has become part of the reason for its own relative decline.

3. *Changes in the production process*:   There have also been considerable changes in the technology of production. The introduction of automated and computerised equipment has often reduced the numbers of skilled manual workers while increasing the numbers both of technicians and of relatively unskilled 'machine minders'. This process has been yet another to affect detrimentally the older 'craft' unions within manufacturing.

Increased automation has helped managers to introduce new forms of production organisation. Working practices common in Japanese industry are used as models. The need to cut costs and

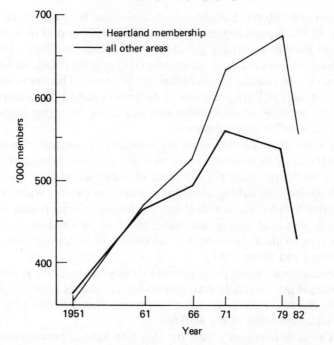

Figure 8.3   AUEW membership for England, Wales and Scotland,
1951–82

respond rapidly to changing product markets has led to efforts to
increase the functional, numerical and time flexibility of workforces.
Quality circles and workplace councils have been established in a
few plants. These developments, if they become widespread, could
weaken workplace trade unionism, by bypassing traditional forms
of union organisation like shop stewards' committees, and by
emphasising the role of the individual and the small team rather than
the collective workforce.

New practices may be introduced in the context of investment on
greenfield sites, in some cases by foreign (including Japanese)
companies. Such changes may be associated with the introduction of
single-union agreements. The Japanese car manufacturer Nissan
started production at its Sunderland plant in July 1986 after
reaching a single-union agreement with the AEU. There are just two
grades of shop-floor workers at the plant, compared with the heavily

demarcated plants characteristic of traditional British manufacturing. In fact reports suggest that no more than 7 per cent of workers at the plant have actually joined the AEU (*Financial Times*, 1988b).

Such changes may also be introduced in existing plants, although they may be resisted by established trade unions. This happened in the disputes at Ford and General Motors in early 1988, where the unions managed to reduce what they saw as the damaging effects of the changes for their members.

Finally, these developments are sometimes associated with locational change or investment on a new site, particularly in an area or to a workforce with a lower level of unionisation. For instance companies establishing electronics plants in South Wales have actively avoided areas with strong traditions of unionisation associated with coal mining, and have preferred un-unionised women workers to their more heavily unionised male counterparts (K. Morgan and Sayer, 1984).

Indeed, once again, geographical mobility can make life easier for management, especially where technological change implies potentially disruptive changes in the work process, skill definitions and the social composition of the workforce.

This is clear not only from the changing balance between unions representing different types of workers, but also in the changing membership composition even of individual unions. Within the GMB there has been a dramatic rise in female membership. Feminisation often reflects the downgrading of skills. And in the GMB it has been greatest in those areas, particularly Development Areas, to which there has been decentralisation. Since the 1960s the proportion of women members in the North, Scotland and South Wales has risen faster than anywhere else. But more importantly feminisation also reflects changes in sectoral composition within the union (from shipbuilding to local government and food and drink for instance). The point is that together they have brought about significant changes in both the internal composition and the geography of the union.

The Growth of New Sectors

Shifts in the wider sectoral structure of the economy are reflected in the aggregate figures for unionisation in different sectors. Over a period of ten years, the best-unionised sectors of the economy have

Table 8.3   Employment change and union density by industry

Sector	Change in employment 1976–86	Union density 1984
		%
Banking, insurance and finance	+ 709 000	43
Business and other services	+ 383 000	21
Hotels and catering	+ 211 000	21
Wholesale distribution	+ 162 000	32
Energy and water	− 61 000	88
Transport	− 123 000	85
Metals and mineral products	− 290 000	68
Vehicles and transport equipment	− 322 000	81
Metal goods and mechanical engineering	− 493 000	55

Union density measures the proportion of the relevant workforce belonging to a trade union
Source: Labour Research Department 1987

seen the largest reductions in employment (Table 8.3). As well as the relative growth and decline as people join and leave the workforce, people changing jobs (for example from transport to wholesale distribution, a not-impossible move) are likely to be going from more to less unionised sectors.

Sectoral changes in the economy have also seen the growth of new unions, in particular the white collar unions both within and outside the public sector. Both the initial geography of these unions and subsequent developments have reinforced the changes outlined in the previous sections.

Take first the public sector unions. By their very nature most of them have been spread across the country. Moreover their growth has been associated with a shift in the balance of their membership from the conurbations to surrounding regions. For NALGO, between 1951 and 1983 the gains in membership outside the London, West Midlands and North West conurbations were greater than those within them (see Figure 8.4). For NUPE (National Union of Public Employees) regional membership data, which is only available for dates after 1970, shows a similar pattern. Between 1971 and 1983 the share of membership in the unions' 'periphery' of the North, South West and Wales increased from less than 7 per cent to over 20 per cent.

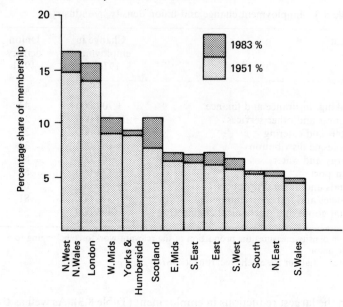

Figure 8.4   NALGO – change in percentage share of membership, 1951–82

There are a number of reasons for the changing geography of the public sector unions. First, there are important geographical differences in union traditions. In the case of NUPE's health service membership, union officials pointed out that it is generally more accepted and expected for nurses, for instance, to join a union in Scotland than it is in some other areas. A second factor, which promotes dispersion, is the general decentralisation of population from conurbations. Third, there have been significant changes in the allocation formulae applied by central government in distributing resources among regions, involving greater emphasis on public services in 'problem' peripheral regions.

Taken together, the increase in membership of the public sector unions (between 1951 and 1983 NALGO and NUPE together grew by over a million, over half this increase occurring after 1970) and the increasingly dispersed nature of the unions highlights their growing weight in the new geography of the trade union movement as a whole. More recent figures indicate that the combined memberships of NALGO, NUPE and the other major health union, COHSE (Confederation of Health Service Employees) grew by 6 per cent between 1976 and 1986, ten years which have otherwise been very difficult for the unions.

White collar unions in the private sector were more concentrated than those in the public sector, but not as concentrated as the craft or industrial unions. These unions too have become more evenly distributed. For the then AUEW-TASS (Technical, Administrative and Supervisory Section) between 1951 and 1982 the proportion of the membership in London and Manchester declined, and although that for the West Midlands increased, so did the proportional share for the South West and South Wales, Northern Ireland and Southern England.

Similarly, the membership of the old ASTMS (Association of Scientific, Technical and Managerial Staff – since merged with TASS to form MSF – Manufacturing Science Finance) became more dispersed. Whereas the proportion of membership in the West Midlands declined over the early 1980s, the decline in the West, the North and central Eastern areas was smaller and there were gains in East Anglia and Northern Ireland. The recent decline in membership in London, as in the West Midlands, is related to the collapse of industry. Ironically, however, one characteristic of Britain's changing role in the world economy is the strength of financial services. MSF's membership in this sector is growing and has to some extent compensated for the union's London losses in manufacturing.

These rapid changes in sectoral structures and labour processes have been accompanied by changes in the workforce. An increasing proportion of workers are women – the feminisation mentioned earlier – especially women working part-time (see also Chapter 10). A crude sectoral analysis of the changing workforce illuminates these trends. Firstly, manufacturing has collapsed: 7.9 million people were employed in manufacturing in Great Britain in 1971, but by December 1986 this figure had fallen to 5.1 million (Central Statistical Office, 1987; Department of Employment, 1988). By far the largest proportion – some 93 per cent – of manufacturing employment remains full-time, and the proportion of jobs held by women has stayed virtually static, at just under 30 per cent.

By contrast, service sector employment has risen steadily, from 11.3 million in 1971 to 14.3 million in December 1986. A much greater proportion of jobs are now part-time: 32.1 per cent in 1986, compared to 23.5 per cent in 1971. The proportion of jobs done by women has risen from 49.5 per cent to 54.6 per cent over this period and, of the 7.8 million women employed in services in 1986, 49.1 per cent were part-time; the corresponding proportion in 1971 was 39.2 per cent (Central Statistical Office, 1987; Department of Employment, 1988). These figures conceal important differences between public and private sector services, but the broad picture is of a declining manufacturing sector providing full-time jobs, mostly for men, and a growing service sector providing some full-time jobs for men and a mixture of full- and part-time jobs for women (see also Chapters 6 and 10).

These changes have posed challenges and offered opportunities to the trade unions. By and large, trade unionism has in the past been male-dominated. Women workers have been less well unionised than their male counterparts, and positions of power in unions, even in those like NUPE with large female memberships, have tended to be occupied by men.

The increase in part-time and temporary working is also a source of new challenges for trade unions. Because part-timers tend to spend less time at work than full-time colleagues (not as obvious as it seems, since 'part-time work' may involve full-time hours but only part-time rights) they have less contact with each other and with their potential union. The strength of collective organisation is thus already undermined by the nature of the employment contract. Temporary workers may also be less inclined than permanent workers to join a union, as they may not see their job as a long-term relationship requiring the support of traditional trade unionism.

The location of many new jobs away from old regions of union strength adds a geographical challenge to the others. With little local union or labour-movement culture to draw on, workers in expanding regions like the South East, East Anglia and the South West must develop from scratch a familiarity with the ideas and practices of trade unions.

Many unions are responding to these challenges. For example, the TGWU (Transport and General Workers' Union) has launched a 'Link-up' campaign to recruit part-time and temporary workers, while the GMB is actively trying to improve its appeal to women and minority groups through a vigorous equal opportunities policy. NUPE is also trying to give a higher priority to issues affecting women, and USDAW has launched a membership drive in the form of a national 'Reach-out' campaign and a local-level recruitment initiative in the badly unionised retail industry.

Whether these campaigns can be successful remains to be seen, particularly given the difficulties of organising in the growth sectors like leisure, tourism, financial services and high technology manufacturing (*The Independent*, 1988), but the unions have at least accepted the challenge.

The Political Attack

It is in this context that the Thatcher Governments have launched their attack on trade unions. Long-term 'structural' changes cannot be separated from the impact of the politics of the current Government. These structural changes are not immutable, nor is the Government's onslaught independent of the economic context in which it occurs. These economic and political developments are conditioned by each other.

Firstly, many of the policies of this Government have hastened the long-term changes described above. Its monetarism, and its prioritisation of finance over manufacturing, and of high-technology over traditional industries, have all reinforced the problems faced by the sectors in which unions have historically been strongest. The accentuated move towards service employment, especially in the private sector, has had parallel effects.

Secondly, a number of the Government's wider policies seem to be motivated as much by a desire to break up bases of union strength as by more explicitly expressed aims. The Government's dislike of local authorities is evident, and is based on a recognition of the ability of some Labour councils to become foci for mobilising opposition (see Chapter 5). But it is also true that the local public sector also represents some of the more coherent remaining bases of trade union influence and membership. The attack on local authorities, the resultant cutbacks in their services and in particular measures such as competitive tendering are also attacks on NUPE and NALGO. Similarly with the health service – the Government's intense dislike of COHSE and (again) NUPE is well known and is at least one element in the strategy of breaking up, by one means or another, public sector provision.

Thirdly, moreover, the Government seems to have been both

clearly aware of the long-term changes in the economy and acute .enough to focus its attacks and attention on key points within those changes. Furthermore, on a number of occasions the geographical dimension has been a key element in the situation.

This is neither new nor unique to this government. We saw examples earlier of companies using locational change and choice against trade unions, and in the 1960s and early 1970s when such decentralisation was at its height, regional policy helped facilitate such moves. Again, national energy strategy over decades has in part been conditioned by fear of the potential power of the NUM. And it was clearly seen as strategically important to keep the newly developing off-shore oil industry as free as possible from trade union power and influence.

Nonetheless the Thatcher Government has been particularly precise in its selection of targets. The degree of planning which went into the miners' strike, and the care with which the battle was selected and provoked, has been documented elsewhere (Beynon, 1985). This was a strategic attack on a crucially symbolic part of the trade union movement (see also Chapter 7) and was also an attack on one of the heartlands mentioned previously. The mining regions were not just highly unionised areas; they were, indeed still are, bases for an ideology and a way of life in many ways utterly opposed to Thatcherism. The one significant field where this was not true was Nottinghamshire and the potential for division which this provided, combined with differences in at least short-term economic futures, was fully exploited. It was an early demonstration of Margaret Thatcher's acute geographical sense!

This geographical sense is being demonstrated again with the attack on urban areas and their local authorities. After the coal-fields, the major urban areas are among the most important of the geographical bases of resistance. Moreover, while the membership of public sector unions has become more depressed in recent decades, they retain very large memberships in the big cities, and these unions are among the fastest growing in the country. In the general context of decline their proportionate numerical significance has increased enormously. Indeed, although figures to prove this point are impossible to come by, it seems likely that most trade unionists in many of the larger urban areas in this country are now in a fairly small number of increasingly strong, and often belligerent, public sector unions. In that context, inner-city policy, together with the policies on local government, education and health, can be interpreted as attacks on one of the few strengthening bases of trade unionism, sectorally and geographically.

There have been other instances of 'seizing the moment' (and the place) too. There seems little doubt that Government enthusiasm for certain forms of foreign inward investment in former Development Areas (the North East, Scotland, Wales) owes not a little to the perceived effect it might have on industrial relations in British industry more widely. Nissan's investment in the North East is an obvious example, and although it has certainly not produced an immediate revolution in the labour process and labour–management relations throughout the British car industry, it has had its imitators. More widely, Nissan's location in the North East, a region formerly renowned for its highly unionised sectors, shows just how far moods have been changed by years of high unemployment and sheer desperation for jobs. In the 1960s and early 1970s many firms decentralised to these so-called 'peripheral' regions in search of female labour, assuming that such labour would be both cheap and relatively uncontaminated by the trade union history of the region. On many occasions the male workforce of the region was avoided. This may now be less true as a result of the combination of continuing high unemployment, a new generation of male labour, and a new-found political confidence among elements of management. The way in which the British Government backed a US multinational (Ford) against British trade unions over the proposed investment in Dundee shows the importance attached to this particular element in the tussle over the future of trade unionism.

But most new investment is going into the outer-outer metropolitan area of the South East. And it is in this area, held up by the Government as the image of the future, that union densities are lowest and falling fastest among key sections of the workforce. One significant bundle of sectors here, though by no means the most important in terms of numbers, is grouped around 'high technology'. The relative decline in importance of big corporate research laboratories, in contrast to the increase in smaller detached outfits, the relative power of scientists and technologists in these labour markets (reinforced by nationally inadequate training and a high degree of concentration in one region), and a rhetoric (and sometimes a reality) of participation and control in smaller high technology units, have produced an atmosphere dominated by competitive individualism and utterly antipathetical to trade unionism. Conditions in a key growth sector are thus particularly difficult for trade unions. They were certainly made worse by the government's banning of trade unionism at GCHQ (Government Communications Headquarters) in the heart of the M4 corridor. With so much high-technology industry in the region dependent upon military expenditures, the point is unlikely to have been missed by those competing for government contracts.

As a final example, there is Docklands, a massive development crucial to the Government's strategy for Britain's place in the international division of labour of the twenty-first century – this time as a financial centre with London as one of the few world cities. Yet this development is in an area once highly unionised, an important base of the TGWU, and indeed one of the places where general unionism was born. Of course the new economic activities are not about employing the local people. Nonetheless some of them will be employed in a variety of mainly servicing capacities. And it has clearly been crucial to keep 'the unions' out. A ballot of staff on the privately-run Docklands Light Railway found a four-to-one majority of those voting in favour of union membership. Even so the company refused to award negotiating rights to any union unless an absolute majority of all staff voted in favour of unionisation. (Subsequently the union came back with a second ballot and won an overall majority of those eligible to vote).

Conclusion

Recession, longer-term economic changes, and an immediate political offensive (to which one might add a changing – in some cases radicalising – wider political climate), have presented immense challenges to British trade unionism. The problem posed by the recession was the sheer speed and intensity of change; the longer-term changes pose challenges of working out new ways of organising, in new sectors, among new groups in new places; and the political attack is over the very existence, and the *terms* of existence, of a meaningful trade union movement.

Geography has been integral to all this. At the broadest level, the geographical shifts imply a major change in local conditions of organisation. The new areas and regions are different from the old.

The 'heartlands' are not the bases that they were. By no means all the areas of numerical strength were areas of militancy, still less of political radicalism. The dominance of localities by single industries and single unions can as easily lead to paternalism and class complicity (and concepts of the economy of 'our region') and to the weakening of trade unionism, as to independent union strength. But some of them were the geographical heart, symbolically and organisationally, of the movement. In different ways this has been true of some of the coalfields, and of the complex of car-industry-related unions in the West Midlands. Different again have been the cities. Lane (1982) has written of the rich texture and diversity of the network of unions which made the cities so good for (certain forms of) organisation. And, inevitably, because they were home to so many of these unions, the cities have been hit particularly hard. As ever, the process has been differentiated. The Birmingham area remained relatively buoyant until the late 1970s when the manufacturing union base of many other cities had been rocking for years. Its present decline is very much a phenomenon of Thatcherism. If one city stands out as having suffered from declines in almost all these unions, it is London. The timing and rate of decline has varied between unions but the combined effect is startling. Moreover, the very process of change can itself present difficulties, as old established centres of organisation become more marginal, at least in numerical terms, to a union's strength, and new areas begin to assert their increased weight. What is more, the membership in the new areas is being built up, not in a post-war boom, but in a period of restructuring. Combine this with all the other changes that are going on within the unions – shifts in the balance between unions, shifts in the balance of skills and industries, and shifts in gender composition – and one can understand feelings of uncertainty, even a loss of identity. We may mourn or celebrate these changes, but they are certainly a lot to cope with.

Moreover, geographical shift has not just produced new problems for unions to deal with, and new conditions to organise in; it has also been actively used as a weapon against trade unions. The current use of greenfield sites as locations in which to restructure labour processes and industrial relations is just the latest phase in capital's use of 'geography' against labour.

Yet things are not entirely gloomy. In simple numerical terms the situation has stabilised since the recession. And other evidence, of a more qualitative and political nature, indicates that the union movement is not to be written off. The results of ballots on closed shops and on political funds have been positive. A report on pay deals pointed to the 'sheer resilience of collective organisation' and argued that no-strike and single-union deals had had little impact on the vast majority of pay negotiations (Incomes Data Services, 1987; see also Kelly, 1987). Indeed both IDS and Kelly note that some recent changes, such as strike-ballot legislation and certain forms of agreements about flexibility in the labour process, can be turned into strengths for trade unions. Certainly the 1988 Ford strike indicated, as the plants began to be affected across Europe, the potential vulnerability of tightly-integrated multi-plant networks operating on just-in-time systems, without the changes in culture and social relations needed to support those systems (Sayer, 1986).

It seems unlikely that there is anything irretrievably anti-union in the new growth areas. Defence of public sector services, with its links to consumers and its base in communities, often dominating the union movement in urban areas in the north, is one potential base of a different sort. There are interesting comparisons to be drawn and lessons to be learned, from the new areas of growth. While Scotland's Silicon Glen is renowned for its extremely low levels of unionism, electronics factories in South Wales are much more likely to be organised. There are differences between the industrial structures, to be sure, but there are more similarities, and the contrast in levels of unionism is instructive since it indicates that there is little that is inevitable. Although the old heartlands (in terms of location, sector and segment of the workforce) now seem in retrospect to have provided good conditions for organising, they did have to be built up in the first place.

Notes

1. This and the following two sections are based on a previous article by Doreen Massey and Nicholas Miles (1984).

9
The Politics of 'Race' and a New Segregationism

Susan J. Smith

Introduction

The study of 'racial segregation', both as a spatial pattern and as a socially constructed way of life, lies at the core of modern social geography. As an outcome of the biased operation of markets and institutions, the phenomenon has also been of interest to housing analysts and practitioners. In Britain, however, those concerned with the politics of 'race' have paid more attention to the economics of labour migration and the sociology of 'race relations' legislation than to the geography of settlement. This is curious, given politicians' own pre-occupation with 'racial segregation' as a 'problem' in supposedly 'multi-racial' societies.

This chapter attempts to draw the politics of 'race' – or more accurately, of racialisation[1] – into the geography of segregation, and to illustrate the importance of this combination for the political geography of contemporary Britain (referring mainly to England). I begin with some definitions and with a review of the relevance of 'racial segregation' in British political history. I then explain how, over a thirty-year period following the war of 1939–45, the practice of segregation emerged from an ideology of integrationism. Finally I argue that with the ascent of a distinctively British 'New Right', this *de facto* racial separatism is increasingly sustained by the resurgence of an implicitly segregationist ideology.

The Nature and Origins of 'Racial Segregation'

Twentieth-century genetics has proved beyond all doubt that there are no natural human 'races'. Racial categorisation (and, therefore, the racialisation of immigration, poverty, inequality and so on) is a political, economic and social process. The tendency to invest essentially phenotypic variation with symbolic significance, and for such variation to be aligned with economic and social inequality, is therefore just a starting point for investigation. 'Race' is not an explanatory variable, but rather the outcome of practices and ideologies which themselves require explaining.

It is common to refer to these practices and ideologies as racist. As an all-encompassing term referring to the changing criteria for identifying and dominating racialised groups, this broad definition of racism has been important. Most crucially, it has been the focus of a shift in academic inquiry (and, indeed, political action) away from 'problems' related to the behavioural preferences and cultural norms of the black populations and towards those structures and institutions of white society which create problems for black people[2] (in geography, see Jackson, 1987). For the purposes of this essay, however, it is necessary to be more specific. Following Fredrickson (1981), therefore, I shall restrict the term 'racism' to the doctrine of biological inequality. In this sense, racism, as *ideology*, provides a reservoir of imagery and a source of 'justifications' for those who believe, or wish others to believe, that phenotypic variation – often, but not always, indexed by colour – has some biologically rooted (and hierarchically ordered) social and behavioural significance. Racist *practices* apportion rewards, life chances and opportunities unequally between the groups so defined, thus reproducing racial categories and racialising inequality.

In practice, various criteria have been (and could be) invoked as principles of racial categorisation, including perceived pigmentation, physique, descent, historical or geographical origin, language and religion or other cultural traits. Racism, however, as defined above, is just one body of ideas informing the practices which draw on these perceptions to create 'races' and to sustain systematic inequalities in power and authority between them. 'Races' can be (erroneously) defined as a 'natural' source of human variety as much by appeal to cultural history or divine ordination as with reference to biology (Reeves, 1983). 'Nature, nurture and providence' can be invoked to similar effect in the process of racialisation, but they seek vindication from very different areas of scholarship (natural science, philosophy and theology, respectively).

Racism may, then, be seen as one of several interlocking racial ideologies, and as one of a range of practices sustaining racial inequality. This wider set of practices and ideologies may be linked with the project of 'white supremacy' which Fredrickson (1981: ch. xi) defines to encapsulate 'the attitudes, ideologies, and policies associated with the rise of blatant forms of white or European dominance over "non white populations"'. As such, this project works towards 'the restriction of meaningful citizenship rights to a privileged group characterised by its light pigmentation'. To this end racism coexists, and overlaps, with other racial ideologies, including some forms of nationalism (see Miles, 1987) and segregationism (which is the topic of this paper).[3]

Segregationism may be regarded as a system of beliefs which seeks justification for racial exclusivity *within* national boundaries, and which helps politicians justify not only overtly separatist practices, but also the inadvertently segregationist outcomes of ostensibly aracial policy. Properly conceptualised, therefore, 'racial segregation' may be seen as a practice which mediates the apportionment of material resources, while segregationism may be recognised as a racial ideology which infuses the organisation of meanings and legitimises some of the forces responsible for racial differentiation.[4]

The relevance of this conceptualisation of 'racial segregation' is most powerfully demonstrated by Cell (1982) and Fredrickson (1981). Although theirs are works of history rather than geography, and set in regions (South Africa and the American South) where 'racial' separatism is, or has been, legally enforced, they offer at least two generalisations that may be of relevance to contemporary Britain. First, their evidence points to the very fine line between *de facto* and *de jure* segregation. Segregation must be judged as much by what it means and expresses as by the precise legislative mechanisms that sustain it, and legislation underpinning 'racial segregation' need not always be formulated with explicit reference to racial categories.

Secondly, these authors show that segregationism is not the dying cry of supremacist doctrines ingrained in colonial history. It is, in fact, a relatively new concept in political and public life which gained little momentum until the early twentieth century. Even if legally enforced segregation is now a South African anomaly, history indicates that just as the content and practice of racism has changed, so too is segregationism a flexible and adaptable doctrine. Indeed, it seems that racial exclusivity may be less a legacy of the past and more a strategy for the future in advanced industrial economies. In this sense, in its *de facto* form, 'racial segregation' – as a practice and as ideology – may prove to be a particularly resilient instrument of 'white supremacy', even in Britain.

It is, nevertheless, tempting – and comforting – to regard this kind of generalisation as one limited to the experiences of South Africa and the American South. Rich (1986a and b), however, shows that the force of segregationism is not as tightly bounded in space as many would like to think. In the early 1900s British politicians were more than ready to be persuaded of the merits of racial separatism, and segregationism played a significant part in the development of policies of Colonial Trusteeship and Indirect Rule (at this time the process was variously legitimised with reference to its supposed relevance to black people's political advance, to the notion of environmental 'fitness', and to the health requirements of colonial officers).[5] Today, of course, the attitudes, ideologies and policies associated with 'racial segregation' in Britain differ dramatically from those associated with South Africa or the old American South. Britain has no history of domestic slavery, has never countenanced a *de jure* 'colour bar', and during the main period of migration and settlement was developing a welfare state designed to redistribute wealth according to need amongst the socially disadvantaged and economically deprived. Nevertheless, 'racial segregation' has been a consistent theme of this country's urban geography for more than forty years (see Peach, 1981). It has, moreover, equally consistently been an expression and a purveyor of racial inequality – in the labour market, in the housing system and in access to the wide range of opportunities, resources and life chances that are differentially, but systematically, apportioned over space (S. Smith, 1989; see also Brown, 1984; Cross, 1983, 1985; Johnson, 1987).

As a medium for the racialisation of inequality, residential segregation in modern Britain is not generally as intense as in South Africa or North America, it is not legally enforced, and it may simply be a transient phase in the adjustment of markets and institutions to the needs and demands of a recently established black population. On the other hand, these patterns may be an integral requirement of the current restructuring of the economy and of social policy, demanding more, not less, legitimacy from the institutions of the state. It is this possibility that I want to explore.

Integration versus Nationalism: Towards the Racialisation of Residential Space

As a practice and a way of life 'racial segregation' in Britain was established during three decades of labour and refugee migration – from the Caribbean, South Asia and East Africa – following the Second World War. Initially the residential clustering of New Commonwealth immigrants was a direct function of their marginal position in the economy. They provided a replacement or supplementary workforce for a range of traditional industries whose viability was extended because the availability of cheap labour allowed entrepreneurs to increase productivity without raising wages (Harris, 1987). Precise patterns of settlement varied, reflecting the interactions of housing systems and labour markets in different cities and regions (Ward, 1987). In relative terms, however, black people consistently found themselves spatially concentrated at the bottom of the housing ladder.

Low incomes, together with financial obligations to dependants overseas, immediately put black people at a disadvantage in the housing market. At a time, moreover, when central government may have been contemplating the use of housing as a form of immigration control – and would not, therefore, entertain any co-ordination of housing and immigration policy – the effects of economic marginalisation were reinforced in at least two ways. First, employers were not (unlike their continental counterparts) encouraged to take responsibility for housing their workers. Secondly, no penalties were levied on (and considerable sympathy was extended to) local authorities which, by imposing long local residence requirements, denied black immigrants their right – as British citizens and as low-income families – to queue for council housing (even as late as 1960 only about one per cent of black households lived in the public sector).

Given their weak position in the labour market, and in the absence of state- or employer-subsidised housing, black people had essentially two residential options. They could seek accommodation in the multi-occupied lodging houses of a declining privately rented sector, and so cluster within the so-called twilight zones of the major cities; or they could *buy* cheap housing, in areas blighted by short leases or scheduled for slum clearance – again located in the older inner urban rings (see Paris and Lambert, 1979).

It is relatively easy to show how the practice of segregation was initiated in post-war Britain. It is crucial, however, to recognise that in these post-war decades factors other than the differential apportionment of economic and welfare rights worked to reproduce 'racial segregation' and to sustain the inequalities it expressed. For during this time 'racial segregation' gained increasing prominence as a politically constructed problem. Ironically it was the very fear of replicating South Africa's spatially organised 'colour bar', together with panic over the future of North America's volatile urban ghettos, that first prompted British politicians to regard 'racial segregation' (as distinct from the more fundamental facets of social inequality embedded in this spatial form) as a problem worthy of legislators' attention (S. Smith, 1988). Defined as such, however, this new urban 'problem' helped legitimise a range of policy solutions which brought important political rewards, but had very little impact on the racially inequitable (racialised) division of residential space. The sequence of events involved may be summarised as follows (see Table 9.1 for a chronology of events referred to in this chapter).

For as much as a decade following the war, the residential clustering of 'colonial' immigrants, though perceived as problematic, was depicted by politicians as a passing phase of cultural adjustment and economic integration. In time, dispersal and assimi-

Table 9.1   Chronology of key political and policy developments relating to racial segregation in Britain

Date	Government/Prime Minister	Events relating to immigration, nationality and race relations	Housing/urban policy
1945	*Labour*/Attlee		Resumption of slum clearance
1948		British Nationality Act	
1951	*Conservative*/ Churchill		
1955	Eden		
1957	Macmillan		
1958		Notting Hill 'riots'	

Table 9.1 *cont.*

Date	Government/Prime Minister	Events relating to immigration, nationality and race relations	Housing/urban policy
1961		South Africa leaves Commonwealth; Britain applies to join the EEC	
1962		Commonwealth Immigration Act	
1963		Britain refused entry to EEC	
1963	Home		
1964	*Labour*/Wilson		
1965		Race Relations Act	
1966			Local Government Act
1968		Race Relations Act; Immigration Act; Kenyan Asian 'crisis'	
1969			Housing Act; Local Government Grants (Social Needs) Act
1970	*Conservative*/Heath		
1971		Immigration Act	Housing Act
1972		Ugandan Asian 'crisis'; Britain enters EEC	
1974	*Labour*/Wilson		Housing Act
1976	Callaghan	Race Relations Act	
1977			Housing (homeless persons) Act
1978			Inner Urban Areas Act
1979	*Conservative*/ Thatcher		
1980		Urban unrest (Bristol)	Housing Act
1981		British Nationality Act; Urban unrest (widespread)	
1985		Urban unrest	
1987		Immigration Bill	
1988			'Action for Cities'; Housing Bill

Source: after S. Smith (1989)

lation were expected to follow as a numerically small minority became absorbed into British institutions and society. Thus despite pressures from some quarters of government (exposed by Dean, 1988), *laissez-faire* was deemed the only viable strategy at a time when foreign policy was engaged in the delicate task of replacing Empire with Commonwealth, and in a climate of opinion in which Britain was assumed to lead the world in tolerance and understanding.

In 1958 this outwardly comfortable scene changed dramatically. The Notting Hill riots, sensationalised by the mass media, convinced the public that 'race relations' was not a problem limited to societies overseas; and the language of 'race' – as a corollary of immigration, indexed by colour – was drawn to the centre of British politics (the process is best documented in Miles, 1984). At the same time, Britain's European future became a much higher priority for foreign policy than did leadership in the Commonwealth, and as a corollary, British nationalism shrank from its global proportions to the more parochial, and separate, concerns of England, Scotland and Wales. This soon began to undermine the earlier ideal of a common Commonwealth identity, and as a politically constructed problem, 'racial segregation' had a crucial part to play in the transition.

First, by casting the 'problem' expressed at Notting Hill as a function of the numbers and spatial concentration of 'coloured colonial immigrants', politicians were able to package what had become a major public concern in a discrete, manageable way. The 'difficulty' was linked with immigration, but was portrayed neither as a consequence of the way in which capitalism works, nor as the product of racism or discrimination. Rather the spatial concentration of black families was itself identified both as a cause of environmental decay and as the harbinger of unfair competition for limited resources between 'black migrants' and 'white indigenes'. This was not regarded as a consequence of racism but rather as a *cause* of prejudice. As Eric Fletcher put it, 'overcrowding is causing colour prejudice. Colour prejudice is not spontaneous in this country – British people are friendly to coloured immigrants – but the degree of prejudice is growing as a result of these housing conditions' (Hansard, 22 November 1957, v. 578, c. 753).

Secondly, this conceptualisation of segregation as the locus of an emerging 'race relations' problem gave it an important role in governments' attempts to rescue national pride as the Empire crumbled and Europe seemed less than inviting (turning down Britain's first (1961) appeal for entry to the EEC in 1963). By 1968, the scene was set for Enoch Powell successfully to depict 'racial segregation' as a threat to what was, symbolically, the nation's greatest remaining resource – its territory. Powell spoke of the 'extending of the numbers and area of the immigrant' (television interview cited in Gordon and Klug, 1986: 19), of 'the transformation of whole areas . . . into alien territory' (Birmingham Speech, 20 April 1968), and of areas from which 'the people of England, who fondly imagine that this is their country and these are their hometowns, have been dislodged' (Eastbourne address, cited in M. Barker, 1981: 39). Such remarks cost Powell his career in the Heath government, but they also appeared to unleash a massive surge of racist – and, indeed, segregationist – sentiment amongst the general public. This helped stimulate the popular patriotism which swept the Conservatives to power in 1970; it was so successful in this respect that, in Bulpitt's (1986: 32) opinion, if Powell had not existed 'it may have been necessary to invent him'.

Once defined as a problem of numbers, location and territorial extent, the character of 'racial segregation' inevitably inspired 'solutions' whose stated aim was to diminish the visibility of black settlement. But while the supposed goal was social integration through residential dispersal, I shall argue that the policies invoked were exclusionary and separatist, and that, as a result, racial inequalities remained entrenched in the organisation of residential space.

The earliest, most sustained, and most potent legislation advanced in the name of integration was the imposition of immigration controls (restrictions that are commonly recognised to have had disproportionate applicability to *black* migrants). At the time it was introduced (in the Commonwealth Immigration Act of 1962) immigration control made no economic sense – indeed, Labour presented a strong argument against such legislation precisely because of its economic irrationality. Controls were justified, however, not on grounds of their economic rationality, but instead by an appeal to their role in the promotion of social stability. The stated aim for limiting immigration flowed from the assumption that, in the words of R. A. Butler, 'the greater the numbers coming into the country the larger will these communities become and the more difficult it will be to integrate them into our national life' (Hansard, 16 November

1961, v. 649, c. 694–5). In short, controls were introduced primarily 'to allow the government time to produce effective integration programs and to give the immigrants and the natives sufficient time to adjust to each other' (Freeman, 1979:56).

Not surprisingly, immigration controls had little obvious impact on the organisation of residential space. They did, however, strengthen Britain's bid to join Europe, by demonstrating the independence of the domestic labour market from that of the Commonwealth. Additionally, the failure of such controls to promote integration provided a convenient point for the Labour Party to relinquish its electorally unpopular opposition to control and adopt instead Roy Hattersley's dictum that 'without integration, limitation is inexcusable; without limitation, integration is impossible.' The sought-after panacea of dispersing the impact of migration was still to depend on immigration control, but its effectiveness was to be enhanced by Race Relations legislation. Labour's change of heart over the immigration question cast a shadow over the Party's willingness to legislate against discrimination, and the weak measures of the 1965 Race Relations Act (which did not outlaw discrimination in the housing market) must be regarded less as a move towards anti-racism than as part of an emerging bipartisan consensus 'to do little or nothing about growing racial problems within the country' (Ashford, 1981: 239). The measures invoked were certainly too weak to introduce radical new opportunities for the social and spatial mobility of black people, even after the Race Relations Act of 1968 made new provisions against direct discrimination in housing and employment.

In contrast to immigration controls and Race Relations legislation, housing policy offered considerable potential for affecting the organisation of residential space throughout the 1960s. Yet politicians, bent on dispersal and integration, seized on this only as a last resort. Even then, after a brief, and not very successful, attempt to achieve a dispersed settlement pattern amongst Ugandan Asian refugees (see Bristow, 1976), responsibility for dispersal in housing was devolved to the local authorities, with no clear guidelines for implementation. This is a further example of a bipartisan 'agreement' to peripheralise the race issue – both in legislative terms, and to lower tiers of government – as discussed by Bulpitt (1986). By this time, however, (i.e. 1975) although black people had gained entry to significant portions of the public rented sector (albeit in the least desirable tenancies) the 1969 Housing Act[6] had curtailed the supply of new stock, fiscal constraints were increasingly diminishing local authorities' autonomy, and in practice 'dispersal' offered little hope to black people seeking to improve their housing conditions (see Flett, 1979).

To summarise, for more than thirty years 'racial segregation' was cast by politicians across the political spectrum as a 'problem' relating to the numbers and location of black people, and as a violation of white Britons' rights and sensibilities. Political solutions therefore aimed to reduce the impact of this 'problem', ostensibly through dispersal and integration. In practice, such concerns served primarily to 'justify' racist (exclusionary) immigration laws, while racial inequalities remained embedded in the organisation of residential space. The ideology of integration had served as a smokescreen for policies which not only confirmed the salience of 'race' in political and public life, but also sustained segregation and exacerbated the relative deprivation of racialised minorities.

From Practice to Ideology: Segregationism and Britain's New Right

As a practice, 'racial segregation' has not diminished during the 1980s. Current trends in housing policy have enhanced the role of residential differentiation in the process of racial categorisation, and confirmed the tenacity of residential segregation as an expression of racial inequality. Nevertheless two things *have* changed in recent years, injecting an important new dimension into the politics of race in Britain. First, the spatially selective effect of economic restructuring in recent years has meant that patterns of segregation increasingly restrict (rather than simply reflect) black people's labour-market opportunities and their life chances in urban Britain. Secondly, the ideology of integration – which, in theory, at least, challenged the legitimacy of specifically 'racial' segregation – has lost its force, making way for doctrines which (albeit euphemistically) appear to validate rather than undermine the principle of racial separatism.

My earlier comments indicate that, in the post-war years, the practice of racial segregation could be regarded as a reflection in the housing system of black people's marginal position in the labour market. This generated inequalities that were exacerbated by immigrants' *de facto* exclusion from council housing as a welfare right, and by policies that were unable to tackle either the organisation of residential space or the forms of disadvantage this expressed. Today, however, the incidence of labour-shedding associated with technical and industrial change is disproportionately concentrated not only in the kinds of occupations where black people cluster, but also in the kinds of areas where black people are most likely to live (see Cross, 1985). Segregation must, therefore, increasingly be seen as a factor constraining black people's opportunities to participate fully in the economy and inhibiting their ability to benefit from the many social rights (to health care, education, and so on) whose quality and availability varies in space.

The organisation of residential space may, in short, be regarded as a component of the 'structural racism' which Cross (1983) argues is concentrating black people spatially, socially and economically into areas of decline. Cross (1986:87) argues that, under such circumstances, racial ideology must take a form less concerned to justify labour extraction (as it did during the major periods of labour migration from the New Commonwealth and Pakistan to Britain) than to legitimise the processes of 'separation, containment and control' which are now required to regulate the workforce under conditions of labour surplus. From this perspective, the demise of integrationism can hardly be viewed with surprise.

Nevertheless, the de-emphasis of integration in the legislative agenda is not in itself a cause for concern. It was always a diversion from the more fundamental problems of racism and discrimination which implicated residential segregation in the racialisation of disadvantage. Far from representing a period of post-colonial enlightenment, integrationism denied cultural minorities the right to live together without sacrificing the prospect of decent homes in pleasant neighbourhoods. It is not the abandonment of such a strategy that is disturbing, then, but rather the doctrines that have replaced it. For while integrationism was challenged across the political spectrum it was ultimately undermined less by the ideals of anti-racism advanced from the Left, than by the economic and political requirements of an emerging 'New Right'. I shall show that, as a consequence, the bases of racial differentiation have not been attacked by central government through a vigorous programme of legal sanctions, equal opportunities or affirmative action. Instead, the policy-relevance of 'race' (of racial disadvantage and discrimination) is increasingly questioned, while segregationist sentiments have been revived in the interests of political legitimacy and national pride.[7]

In accounting for these observations, I shall argue that just as racism (narrowly defined) was the dominant ideology informing the process of labour extraction, so a second racial ideology, segregationism, is increasingly invoked to help regulate the process of labour shedding, and to legitimise the spatial forms through which this is expressed. In this capacity, the significance of segregationism may reach beyond the labour market to penetrate other spheres of economic management and social policy, with wide-ranging consequences for the organisation of social life and the apportionment of civil rights. This can best be illustrated in a critique of that uneasy pairing of neo-liberal economics with neo-conservative authoritarianism which infuses a distinctively British 'New Right'. Focusing on each strand in turn, I show how the 'monetarist' policies of the former (oriented towards the theme of economic regeneration) combine with the belief systems of the latter (invoking national pride and tradition as the key to moral regeneration) to ensure, on the one hand, that the practice of racial segregation continues, and on the other hand, that its legitimacy is guaranteed.[8]

The Sanctity of the Market

Margaret Thatcher's electoral success originally hinged on a revival of neo-liberal economics (which is actually based on ideas drawn from the neo-classical Chicago school associated with Milton Friedman, and from the 'liberal' influence of Hayek in Austria, and on public choice theory as nurtured by London's Institute of Economic Affairs). A commitment to arrest economic decline by cutting public expenditure, reducing taxation and stimulating investment offered the electorate a tempting alternative to the corporate socialism of the 1970s (see Chapter 1). Despite its apparent popularity, this ostensibly 'aracial' package of economic policies also carried far-reaching and largely negative implications for the black population. The reasons are as follows.

Fundamentally, neo-liberalism deals with *individuals* (literally, or as families or firms), emphasising the principle of equal opportunities in the market-place and denying group characteristics any policy-relevant status in political or public life (except where they are associated with certain 'technical' forms of special need such as frailty or handicap). According to this reasoning, if housing inequality is a problem for black people, it would not tend to be depicted as the product of systematic discrimination or disadvantage, but rather as a symptom of imperfections in the housing market resulting from over-intervention by the state. From this perspective, inequality is racialised *only* in politics – as a divisive strategy invoked to win political gain – not in more fundamental aspects of the differential distribution of resources and life chances. 'Race' is not therefore recognised by the neo-liberal Right as a policy-relevant axis of inequality in mainstream decision-making, nor indeed as an authentic experiential basis on which to articulate resistance. In fact some politicians are increasingly suspicious of attempts to legislate against racial disadvantage, to act against racial discrimination or to pursue the aims of anti-racism.[9] 'Racial segregation' appears as a problem, therefore, not because of the incidence (or existence) of racism but because of the politicisation of social inequality around the issue of 'race relations'. (It is important to stress here that the principle of anti-racism also aspires to a society in which minorities are not racialised; the implications of neo-liberalism, however, appear to be that this can be achieved by ignoring rather than confronting the persistence of racism, racial discrimination and racial disadvantage.)

Neo-liberal economics therefore informs the argument that apparently systematic inequalities in the organisation of residential space are a consequence of over-intervention by the state, exploited by interest-group politics. This arrangement is expected to be challenged where markets are freed from political influence. With a shift in the organisation of provision for general housing needs away from a system relying on state subsidies in kind (through council housing) towards one resting on state subsidies in cash (through tax relief on mortgage interest) the inequalities expressed in residential segregation should, according to neo-liberal theory, begin to subside. Therefore, as the 'commodification' of housing gathers speed (which it has done since the 1980 Housing Act)[10] there is pressure to reconceptualise the problem traditionally labelled 'racial segregation' as a passing phase of market adjustment rather than as a product of racism institutionalised throughout the housing system.

In practice, however, there is evidence that this reasoning has failed, in that black households remain concentrated in the worst segments of the housing stock and in locations (within cities and regions) that have largely been by-passed by the process of industrial regeneration. This situation is not just a legacy of post-war interventionism, but is actively exacerbated through council house sales (the main vehicle for extending market penetration within the housing system during the 1980s). Because of their disadvantageous starting point (see S. Smith, 1987), and as a consequence of discriminatory lettings procedures (which are exposed, for example, by the Commission for Racial Equality, 1984; Henderson and Karn, 1984; D. Phillips, 1986) black council renters have not, on average, tended to live in properties desirable for purchase under the right-to-buy legislation. Their scope to translate rented homes into capital assets has been limited by their over-representation in flatted estates and in inner city locations (whereas most sales have been houses rather than flats, and in outer rather than inner locations). Black tenants may therefore effectively be trapped in the worst segments of a residualising local authority stock, with little scope to move to improve their living conditions or job prospects as the more attractive rented properties are sold to sitting tenants (a process examined by Ward, 1982).

Black owners, on the other hand, forced by low incomes and discrimination in the allocation of housing finance into the lower end of an increasingly differentiated owner-occupied market (through practices identified, for example, by Karn, 1983 and Stevens *et al.*, 1982) find themselves in the kinds of properties least able to store wealth and most demanding of financial investment for modernisation or repair. Black (especially Asian) owner-occupiers in the major cities (especially outside London) are disproportionately likely to live in dwellings whose use value is limited by physical deterioration and whose exchange value may be falling relative to other dwellings in the same city or region (Karn *et al.*, 1986).

There is little here to indicate that the ideals of neo-liberal economics have succeeded in ironing out the systematic racial inequalities that are embedded in the organisation of residential space. Nevertheless the concern for the 1990s is not simply that the practice of racial segregation is sustained by wider strategies of economic management and employment restructuring, but that, ideologically, this source of systematic inequality increasingly goes unchallenged. The reasons can only be appreciated by interrogating second strand of New Right thinking – neo-conservative authoritarianism.

The Quest for National Pride

In order to secure the popular legitimacy of 'aracial' mainstream policies in the face of the (ostensibly unintentional) inequitable outcomes they generate, governments have resurrected some key principles of traditional Tory authoritarianism. King (1987: 17) has observed that 'Conservatism is secondary to liberalism in New Right ideology because it arises primarily in response to the consequences of liberal economic policies'. Given trends in the labour market and in the housing system, these responses may increasingly be expected to promote or justify the practice of racial separatism. Below, I shall suggest that this is achieved first in the construction of a racially exclusive concept of nationalism, secondly in the expression of this supposedly natural 'cultural' boundary in the organisation of public life, and finally in the strategies of social control developed to contain black resistance to these material and ideological conditions.

One of the most significant recent developments in the politics of 'race' in Britain (albeit one which Thatcherism once attempted to dismiss) is the revival of 'one-nation' Conservatism. One-nation-hood carries assimilationist overtones, linking the strength of a nation to its unity and cohesion, and regarding common traditions or ways of life as the guarantors of national pride and public order. Rooted in Disraeli's assertion that the Tory party is a 'national party or it is nothing' (see Kavanagh, 1987: 190), a revival of one-nation Conservatism has not only stimulated a politically advantageous popular patriotism (see Murray, 1986), but has also created a social climate which portrays national unity as incompatible with, and superior to, multiculturalism. This political atmosphere exposes the crudely assimilationist implications of the early 1980s electoral slogan: 'Labour says he's black, Tories say he's British', and today a dual identity (black *and* British) is implicitly rejected in the structure of the Conservative Party which, in August 1987, aimed to replace its affiliated Asian and West Indian Associations with a 'one-nation' forum (*Daily Telegraph* 26 August 1987).

In practice, the Right has found some scope to incorporate the black communities into its conception of nationhood (appealing, for instance, to the virtues of entrepreneurship and the sanctity of family life that are often associated with Asians in Britain). For the most part, however, the supposed 'ideals' of one-nationhood are thwarted not only by the iniquitous consequences of 'colour blind' policy but also, and fundamentally, by the very definition of British nationality.

M. Barker (1981), Miles (1987) and Parekh (1986) have all exposed the racially exclusive underpinnings of British nationalism. Although the 1948 Nationality Act afforded black members of the Commonwealth full rights as British citizens, each Immigration Act since 1962 has undermined the eligibility of black people to take up these rights. This has prompted Miles (1987: 37) to argue that 'the intervention of the state to redetermine who had the right to live within the boundaries of the British nation-state was a concession to, and a legitimation of, racism'. This process culminated in the 1981 Nationality Act which brought the definition of citizenship into line with the rights of entry and settlement that are conferred by the immigration laws. This Act has played an important role in the re-establishment of national identity, replacing the expansionist connotations of Commonwealth embedded in the 1948 Act with a more parochial form of patriotism rooted in Britain alone. The irony of the 1981 Act, therefore, is that 'it is designed to define a sense of belonging and nationhood which is itself a manifestation of the sense of racial superiority created along with the Empire' (Dixon, 1983: 173).

The fact that the new definition of nationality theoretically embraces many black Britons is clouded by the number it *excludes*, and by its role in shifting the grounds of the immigration debate. Today the 'Hattersley dictum' is increasingly rejected in favour of concerns like those expressed by John Stokes about the damage immigration might wreak on 'the essential identity of this old historic nation' (Hansard, 10 March 1980, v. 980, c. 1092). Far from encouraging 'assimilation', the sentiments underpinning one-nation Conservatism rest on a nostalgic quest for patriotism rooted in a vision of national homogeneity which itself defines black people as outsiders (see Murray, 1986). The *rhetoric* is all-embracing (and this is what keeps 'race' at the margins of mainstream public policy), but the reality is divisive. Modern conservatism has therefore had to develop both ideological and practical strategies to cope with the force of black resistance.

At an ideological level, attempts to rationalise the lived experience of racial differentiation are best explored by M. Barker (1981). He shows how racial categories are tacitly (indeed, euphemistically) sustained in a revival of the traditional Conservative assumption that 'it is natural to form a bounded community, a nation, aware of its differences from other nations' (p. 21). From this uncontested starting point, 'cultural' diversity is defined to include both white exclusivity and black resistance, both of which persist because it is 'in our biology, our instincts, to defend our way of life, traditions and customs against outsiders – not because they are inferior, but because they are part of different cultures' (pp. 23–4). This kind of reasoning wins public sympathy for legislators struggling to deal with those social problems, especially in the 'inner city', which are deemed to persist because they are 'more difficult to deal with in a multi-cultural society' (Norman Tebbit, Hansard, 9 December 1985, v. 88, c. 1001). Through such imagery a concept of 'intrinsically different but more or less equal' has worked its way into political and popular discourse. Cultural identification has been conflated with racial categorisation, and a range of separatist and exclusionary practices in the labour market, the housing system and in the sphere of social policy can be 'justified' by appeal to choice, preference or special need. 'Racial segregation' may, from this perspective, continue to be regarded as a social problem, but it is also viewed as a display of cultural variety that might legitimately be expressed by white as well as black communities.

However, resistance to divisive and iniquitous practices cannot be contained simply through the niceties of 'cultural' diversity or the rhetoric of exclusivism. Where dissent threatens the legitimacy of the status quo – either through reasoned argument or popular protest – forms of control are required. To justify the orientation of such strategies, residential segregation among the black population must remain an important index of urban *malaise*. It has, therefore, become a short step from arguing that it is natural for people to form bounded communities to believing that it is also natural to be hostile to outsiders. It is, as Harvey Proctor argued in a speech to the Newham North-East Conservatives, 'as though multi-racialism had acted as a catalyst to the growth of crime by destroying the sense of community, solidarity and identity' (*The Guardian*, 11 November 1986). By referring to the instinctive origins of social conflict, legislators are able to construct the problem of race-related civil unrest in a way which diverts attention from economic and political inequality and towards the 'inherent' social instability of the 'multi-racial' inner city (see Fitzgerald, 1987; Solomos, 1986).

As a consequence, 'racial segregation' is not only depicted as an expression of cultural choice but has also become the yardstick of a supposed crisis of public order and moral decline in urban Britain. Crucially a territorial link has been forged between the presence of black people, the eruption of urban violence and the demise of popular morality. This has allowed the areas in which black people are most likely to live to become the focus for new, ostensibly demand-led forms of social control. These strategies prioritise 'containment of forms of black resistance against racial domination' (Solomos *et al.*, 1982: 15). As a consequence, during the 1980s, the quest for law and order has been exposed as a euphemistic reference to 'clamping down hard on black people in the inner cities' (Fitzgerald, 1987: 3), and modern urban policing is depicted as part of a move to 'control and contain the political struggles of the black and working class communities' (Bridges and Bunyan, 1983: 106) (see also Chapter 14).

It seems, then, that despite assimilationist rhetoric and a legacy of integrationist ideas, both in theory and in practice racial separatism now has greater force than ever before. This is true not only because of the uncritical, colour-blind implementation of neo-liberal economics but also, and increasingly, because of the 'success' of Tory authoritarianism in legitimising the forms of racial separatism that result. For the first time since the war, the practice of segregation is underpinned by a separatist ideology which affirms the salience of race yet denies the force of racial inequality.

Conclusion

Although the study of 'racial segregation' lies at the core of social geography, this analytical task has rarely been informed by the politics of race. Nevertheless this neglected dimension is crucial if we are to grasp the theoretical and practical significance of residential segregation for the politics of contemporary Britain.

I have suggested that, as a practice, 'racial segregation' developed from the economics of labour migration, in a political climate dominated by the ideology of integration (a sentiment widely shared across the political spectrum). This ideological preference grew from politicians' fears about South African Apartheid and the North American ghetto, but ironically its primary 'achievement' was to justify racist immigration controls. Like the Race Relations Acts which followed, these controls were supposed to facilitate residential dispersal. Yet housing policy – the one area of legislation that might have been effective in this respect – was largely ignored throughout the 1960s (i.e. during the height of state intervention in post-war Britain). The measures which were employed had scarcely any impact on the organisation of residential space, let alone on the inequalities this expressed.

By the late 1970s immigration was sufficiently curtailed, and state intervention so (politically and financially) contentious, that the impetus for integration was lost. As a practice, however, racial segregation retained its force. During the 1980s market processes have worked to sustain rather than alleviate racial inequality at the intra-urban scale. The housing system appears to be retaining black households not only in the poorer segments of the housing stock, but also in areas where labour is being shed in a spatially restructuring economy.

As these processes gathered momentum, the ideological vacuum left by the demise of integrationism was filled less by the principle of anti-racism than by a resurgence of segregationism. The conservative element of Britain's 'New Right' now offers an interpretation of racial segregation that, at best, conflates racial categorisation with cultural preference and at worst inserts the residential clustering of the black populations into the heart of a crusade for law, order and public morality. Either way the political climate is one which tacitly sustains the social reality of 'race' while denying the structures of racial inequality. This language of 'separate but equal' cannot challenge the material and ideological inequalities encapsulated in 'racial segregation'. As a practice, therefore, segregation remains an index of black people's limited access to some fundamental rights of citizenship; and as a symbol it expresses the force of 'white supremacy' in Britain.

Notes

1. I use this term to place emphasis on the *process* by which racial categories are politically and economically constructed on the basis of traits like skin pigmentation or lineage that are logically irrelevant to the conduct of politics or to the management of the economy.

2. There is some debate amongst activists as to the status of 'black' politics as a vehicle for resistance against racism. Nevertheless here the appellation 'black' refers to people of Asian and Afro-Caribbean origin or descent. This should not imply that such groups are culturally or politically homogeneous, but it does acknowledge that they face similar problems in a society where colour has become a means of excluding individuals from their rights as residents and citizens.

3. This is not a claim that racism, even when narrowly defined, is being displaced, or that its force in public life has weakened. There is no inexorable sequence of racial ideologies, though there may be temporal variations in the extent to which they overlap and reinforce one another.

4. This reasoning does not challenge the authenticity of culture as a principle of social organisation or a vehicle of resistance (except where this is used as a euphemism for 'race' and therefore as a principle of resource allocation or denial).

5. Frenkel and Western (1988) give a thought-provoking account of how residential segregation between 'natives' and colonial officers was officially encouraged through a misguided attempt to protect the latter from malaria.

6. This Act shifted the emphasis of housing policy away from comprehensive redevelopment and towards *in situ* urban renewal.

7. Although this section focuses on some failures of the present Conservative Government, it is worth emphasising that, when in power, neither Left nor Right has an unblemished record in defending the rights of immigrant or minority groups.

8. Much of this discussion is informed by the work of Barker (1981), Barry (1987), Elliot and McCrone (1987), Gordon and Klug (1986), Hindess (1987), Kavanagh (1987) and King (1987).

9. In July 1980, for instance, three back-bench MPs called for the abolition of the Commission for Racial Equality (CRE) and the repeal of Race Relations legislation (Hansard, 1980, v. 1175, c. 1767). Similar motions were debated at a Conservative Party conference in 1983.

10. Although owner occupation has been increasing steadily throughout the last half-century, a turning point occurred in 1980 with a Housing Act that gave public sector tenants the right to buy their homes (often with substantial discounts).

10
Women in Thatcher's Britain

Linda McDowell

Three terms of Conservative government have placed gender at the centre of the political agenda. At the simplest level there has been the demonstration effect of a Conservative government led by a woman. Woman have also been more likely than men to vote Conservative – about 4 per cent more likely in 1983 (Wilson, 1987), although the gender gap closed in 1987. The 1970s and 1980s have witnessed a decline in the proportion of women voting for Labour candidates, from 38 per cent in 1974 to under 25 per cent in 1987. But at a deeper level gender is now a central issue, although I am not arguing that Thatcher or Thatcherism is solely responsible for this centrality. The coincidence of wider social and economic changes in Britain, and at an international level, with a radical Right government committed to reduced welfare spending, has produced this centrality. British politics – and economic and social relations since 1979 – have been based on a fundamental contradiction between material changes that simultaneously challenge but also reinforce women's roles: as carers, providers and domestic labourers in the unwaged, private sphere of the home and the community; and as essential waged labourers, drawn in increasing numbers into capitalist wage re-lations. These material changes – primarily cuts in welfare provision and the expansion of waged work for women – have occurred hand-in-hand with the strengthening of an ideology based on women's role in the family and on women's dependence on men.

The 1980s have seen significant changes in the structure and gender composition of the waged labour force with high rates of unemployment, especially in the earlier part of the decade. There has been a decline in the number of men in full-time employment as there was for women until 1986 when the number of women employed full-time increased and almost reached its 1979 level again. There has also been a continuous increase in part-time employment, particularly for women, although it has not been sufficient to compensate for the overall loss of full-time jobs. The expansion of employment for women has, in fact, been a continuous trend since the 1950s, but women's proportionate share of the labour market has noticeably increased in the last decade because of the high rates of male unemployment from 1979. At the same time there has been no attempt to facilitate women's participation in waged work by substituting state provision for their domestic labour. Rather there have been cuts since 1979 in areas such as health care, nursery schools, after-school provision and care for elderly and dependent relatives. The net result for most women has been a significant increase in their overall workload and a decline in their standards of living.

The argument in this chapter is divided into several parts. First, I shall examine the impact of economic restructuring on the gender division of labour. Secondly, the consequences for women – both as workers and as carers – of the attacks on the welfare state since 1979 will be outlined. Thirdly, I want to show how Conservative policies have negotiated and created growing contradictions in women's position by simultaneously asserting a belief in individual liberty and a commitment to equal rights for women alongside a moral reassertion of the sanctity of the nuclear family. Finally, the implications of the contradiction for feminist politics and for women's participation in more conventional political structures will be outlined.

The deepening contradictions created by women's growing participation in waged labour and their continued responsibility for the tasks of social reproduction are not, of course, a new feature, nor solely a reflection or even consequence of Conservative policies since 1979. A feminist critique of the welfare state is now well established. For example, the Beveridge Report (1942) accepted women's traditional role in the family, arguing that *married* women's main task was to ensure continuity of care for men and children. The welfare state and the tax system still reflect the assumption of women's economic dependence on men. Throughout the 1950s and 1960s this view was implicit in the political consensus about the welfare state. What challenged traditional assumptions about gender roles was the development of a part-time job market for married women. There has been a radical shift in the extent to which married women, and in particular women with young children, work for wages. Between 1971 and 1981 the participation rate in waged labour for married women increased threefold whereas that for single women was almost unchanged. The increased burdens created for individual women by what became euphemistically known as their 'dual roles' made clear the limitations of the commitment to equality for women by parties of either political complexion. The Labour Governments of the 1970s were as strongly wedded to an ideology of 'family values' as the post-1979 Conservative administrations have been. However, Thatcherism's commitment to dismantling many of the key areas of the welfare state and the accompanying challenge to collectivist provision has starkly revealed the contradictions inherent in an economy increasingly based on the exploitation of women in the labour market, where they are constructed as secondary peripheral workers working for 'pin money', but continuing to rely on women's domestic and unwaged labour to sustain the relations of social reproduction. This uneasy contradiction currently exists in a climate that seems to deny the necessity of renegotiating traditional gender relations. The structures of inequality and subordination within the family and in the labour market appear to be remarkably resistant to change. In both areas the growing significance of women's labour remains unrecognised and concomitantly relatively unrewarded.

Women, Work and Economic Restructuring

Deindustrialisation has dramatically altered the structure of the British economy (see Chapter 6). The associated changes in employment – an increase in service sector jobs, the vast majority of these part-time, the introduction of new technology and restructured work processes – have had important consequences for the gender division of the British labour force. The decline of manufacturing has resulted in a loss of employment for men, particularly in the traditional heavy industries such as mining, iron and steel, shipbuilding and heavy engineering. Employment loss by men has been concentrated in the main in the North, North West, Wales and Scotland. Women, too, have lost manufacturing jobs in the regions.

Table 10.1 shows changes in the number of employees and their gender composition between 1971 and 1986. In this period there was

Table 10.1   Employment trends: Great Britain 1971–86 (millions)

June	1971	1976	1979	1981	1983	1984	1985	1986
Employees in employment	21.6	22.0	22.6	21.4	20.6	20.7	20.9	21.0
All male	13.4	13.1	13.2	12.3	11.7	11.6	11.7	11.6
All female	8.2	9.0	9.5	9.1	8.9	9.1	9.2	9.4
FT female	5.5	5.4	5.6	5.3	5.0	4.9	4.9	5.4
PT female	2.8	3.6	3.9	3.8	3.9	4.2	4.3	4.0
Total unemployed	0.7	1.2	1.2	2.3	2.9	2.9	3.1	3.2
Women as % of all employees:								
All women	38.0	40.9	42.0	42.5	43.2	44.0	44.0	44.8
FT women	25.5	24.5	24.8	24.8	24.3	23.7	23.4	25.7
PT women	13.0	16.4	17.3	17.8	18.9	20.3	20.6	19.0
Total working population*	24.6	25.5	24.8	26.1	26.9	26.4	26.8	27.3

Source: Department of Employment.
*includes self-employed and HM Forces

a marked growth of jobs regarded as particularly appropriate for women, in both public and private sector services. In the public sector there has been growth in part-time employment in areas such as education and the health service. Despite welfare cuts, employment has expanded, although with increased moves towards privatisation, services such as cleaning, catering and laundry are shifting from the public sector into the private sector. In the private sector there have been increases in employment in retailing, hotels and catering, leisure industries and personal services as well as in secretarial, clerical and data preparation and processing tasks in such areas as the business and finance sector. In the former types of private sector employment operations typically are labour intensive and under-capitalised and workers are often extremely badly paid.

The net result is a rise in the overall numbers of women in waged work and their increased concentration in services, disproportionately in part-time, low status and low paid employment. In

Table 10.2   The gender division of labour in manufacturing and the service
sector, 1986 (millions)

| | Men | | Women | | |
	Full-time	Part-time	Full-time	Part-time	All employees
All industries and services	10.9	0.8	5.5	4.1	21.1
Manufacturing	3.6	0.05	1.6	0.3	5.2
Services	6.5	0.7	4.0	3.7	14.2

Source: Department of Employment.

Table 10.2 the distribution of men and women between manufacturing and services is illustrated. Men are also working in increasing numbers in services. Indeed by 1986 there were almost two men in service employment for every one in manufacturing.

Women currently account for almost 50 per cent of all waged workers (47 per cent in 1988) and they may outnumber men in employment by the early 1990s. About two-thirds of all women at any one time work for wages, although the real figures may be higher than this as many workers who are recorded as 'economically inactive' in employment statistics often work on a casual part-time basis, for example as barmaids and in temporary child care or other forms of homework. For women who are 'officially' employed, domestic and family responsibilities are a key factor in hours of employment, as well as in workforce participation rates in general. Less than a quarter of women with children under five are employed compared with 80 per cent of women with children between eleven and fifteen years old. Married women are far more likely to be employed part-time than single or childless women, and this is even more so for married women with children. Highest participation rates are found among young, single women.

As well as influencing patterns of participation, it has been argued that women's domestic obligations have a significant impact on the types of employment women do, the attribution of skill designation to these jobs and the financial rewards (Cockburn, 1985; Game and Pringle, 1984; Phillips and Taylor, 1980). The supposed attributes of

femininity such as caring, sympathy, an interest in people, persistence, attention to detail and manual dexterity have been variously
employed to explain women's concentration in servicing and caring
jobs in the service sector, and in assembly work in the manufacturing
sector. Fig. 10.1 shows how women were distributed between
occupations in 1986.

Women typically are concentrated in relatively few occupations.
Many of these jobs are virtually exclusively women's preserves, such
as nursing. But gender segregation is marked in other occupations.
Half of all employed men work in occupations where the workforce
is 90 per cent male and half of all women in jobs where the
workforce is 70 per cent female. Women in particular work in
occupations where there is a heavy demand for part-time work.
Part-time employment increased by 2.3 million jobs between 1961

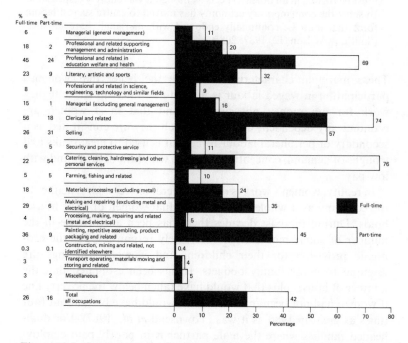

Figure 10.1   Percentage distribution of women by occupational grouping,
              Great Britain, 1986
Source: Equal Opportunities Commission (1986). *Women as Men in Britain: a
              Statistical Profile*, published by permission of the Controller of Her
              Majesty's Stationery Office.

and 1980 and by a further 0.5 million between 1981 and 1986. Almost half of all women in waged work are part-timers and almost all part-timers (86 per cent) are women.

Deindustrialisation has resulted in a form of economic restructuring that is reliant on a far higher proportion of temporary, casual part-time and contract workers – employment patterns that typify women's working careers. This shift in the nature of employment practices and the associated increase in women in the labour force has resulted in a fundamental gender restructuring of waged work. But the ideology – as opposed to the reality – of women's waged work has not altered:

> The irony is that the increase in such employment practices signals a vastly increased dependence on a wage labour force that, paradoxically, must be treated in all other respects as though it was entirely dispensable. In short the contemporary economy has moved to centre stage a labour force that must be continually endowed with marginal characteristics. (Smith, in Wilson, E., 1987: 208.)

These marginal characteristics include the belief that women's participation in waged labour is limited and interrupted, that they work for pin money not survival, and that most women are economically dependent on men. As such they are constituted as a secondary or peripheral labour force that is used to meet peaks and troughs of demand, concentrated in jobs with little security and with low pay.

In reality, women's work is not peripheral or secondary, neither to the economy as a whole, nor to individual women or their households. During the past decades there has been an increase in the number of single mothers who are solely responsible for the economic provision for their children, and women's earnings are essential to many family budgets. It has been estimated that the number of households that would have fallen below the poverty line if women had not been in waged work would have been about four times as great in 1986 as it was (Townsend *et al.*, 1987). For dual-headed families where the male partner is in poorly paid employment or is unemployed, women's earnings are vital.

One of the geographical consequences of the rise in women's participation rates has been a reduction in regional disparities in the proportion of women who work for wages. The decline in manufacturing jobs for women has been mainly in those regions where traditionally women's participation has been high, whereas the expansion has taken a spatially more even form. This reflects the growth of women's participation in 'consumer' service occupations that are distributed in relation to the population. Regional variations in industrial structure as a whole have become less marked since the 1950s but there are still disparities between the regions. However, detailed analyses of gender variations between regions by industry and by occupation need undertaking to reveal the extent to which women in different regions but in the same industry are actually doing different jobs.

The Welfare State and Women

Despite the rapid rise in the number of married women in the labour market, the welfare state and the tax system assume women's economic dependence on men and their continuing role as carers within the nuclear family. Since 1979 successive Conservative governments have relied on a rhetoric of the 'family' and a reassertion of 'Victorian values' to justify cuts in welfare spending. The 'family' evoked in Conservative social policy is based on a strict sexual division of labour where the paterfamilias is the main economic provider and the women is primarily a homemaker and mother. In particular, motherhood is being reasserted both as an ideal to aim for and as a full-time occupation (David, 1986).

The 'New Right' argues that previous state interference in the family has caused a range of so-called family problems, from teenage 'promiscuity', separation and divorce, to the growing numbers of single mothers. By reasserting women's primary caring role it is assumed that these problems will eventually disappear. The ideological centrality of the nuclear family is thus constantly re-invoked to justify cuts in welfare provision. In absolute terms, the level of spending on the welfare state has increased since 1979, mainly because of greater numbers dependent on social security and unemployment benefits and because of an expanding elderly population, reliant on pensions and heavy users of the National Health Service. However, in many areas there have been cuts in services, increases in charges, and growing reliance on private provision. These cuts have reduced the living standards of the poorest members of British society, many of whom are women, and increased the burdens of women caring for dependants.

A key area in which the ideology of caring as a 'labour of love' is clear is that of so-called 'community' care for elderly and disabled people. 'Community' of course usually implies women's labour. The political Right has successfully counterposed state and individual care in terms of propositions about moral responsibility. For example, in a speech made just before she became Prime Minister, Margaret Thatcher argued as follows:

> We know the immense sacrifices which people will make for the care of their own near and dear – for elderly relatives, disabled children and so on, and the immense part which voluntary effort even outside the confines of the family has played in these fields. Once you give people the idea that all this can be done by the state ... then you will begin to deprive human beings of one of the essential ingredients of humanity – personal moral responsibility.
>
> (M. Thatcher, 1978, quoted in Croft, 1986)

These sentiments – about state provision sapping the moral fibre of the nation – have been reiterated many times since 1978 in debates about the welfare state. However, as Finch and Groves (1983) have shown in an assessment of the role and costs of community care, relying on the unpaid domestic and voluntary labour of women is an inexpensive solution to the care of old people and of people with disabilities and terminal illnesses. Further cuts in essential support services for carers – in home helps, meals on wheels, in geriatric medicine, in general nursing services – have increased the amount of unpaid work for women as well as reducing their own waged employment prospects. For women not only form the majority of unpaid workers in this area, but also constitute the bulk of the low-paid workforce in state collective services for the old and ill; this is especially true of black and ethnic minority women.

The Audit Commission (1986) calculated that the state spends £6 billion a year on long-term care and support for the elderly, mentally ill and mentally and physically handicapped people, excluding the cost of acute hospital care and GP (general practitioner) services. About 1.5 million adults in England and Wales receive some form of care, often insufficient for their needs. The remainder is provided by relations and friends, usually women. The Family Policy Studies Centre has calculated that these unpaid carers, if remunerated at the average hourly rate for a local authority home help, would cost the state an additional £5.1 to £7.3 billion each year.

Changes in the social security and tax systems and in the structure of the economy, added to the rise in the number of single parents and an ageing female population, have resulted in the growing feminisation of poverty. There has been a widening of the structures of inequality in Britain in the 1980s, particularly between two-parent, two-wage-earner families on the one hand, and lone-parent families and families dependent on a single wage earner, whether male or female, on the other. Townsend *et al.* (1987) argue that the number of women in poverty has increased under successive Conservative administrations. They identified four distinct sub-groups of poor women. The first group consists of women who look after children or other dependents unpaid and have insufficient income passed on to them indirectly for that purpose. The second group is made up of women with low earnings in full-time or part-time employment who are members of households whose total income falls short of the poverty line; the third group is lone women with children and the fourth is elderly women living alone, many of them widows. There are now more than 3 million women in the latter two groups.

Several measures have exacerbated the financial plight of many of these women. The earnings-related formula for the annual uprating of pensions was abandoned in 1979 and the real value of the basic state pension has fallen. According to the Government's own figures in the 1985 Green Paper (Cmnd 9519, vol. 3, p. 36), the basic pension will have halved in value relative to earnings by 2033 (Townsend, *et al.*, 1987).

In the welfare field, some of the clearest evidence of the Right's assumptions about women's familial roles and their economic dependence within the household is to be found in the Social Security Act 1986, implemented in April 1988. The net result of measures in this Act is to increase women's insecurity. In the Green Paper that preceded the Act the emphasis was placed on increasing 'self-reliance' and 'personal independence' based on the assumed moral superiority of personal rather than collective responsibility. In fact, however, the act is based not on the presumption of *individual* responsibility but on *family* reponsibility. The provisions of the Act are based on greater reliance on means-tested benefits, calculated on the aggregation of household or family resources. This is both incompatible with a rhetoric of personal responsibility and also assumes an equitable division of resources between family members, which studies of family budgets have shown is not often the case (Pahl, 1983).

Specific changes that will increase women's dependence and the extent of inequalities between men and women include changes to pensions and maternity benefits and to women's eligibility for unemployment benefit. The universal maternity grant was replaced in 1987 by a means-tested benefit available only to those claiming income support or family credit. At the same time statutory maternity pay was introduced to be administered by employers, with a new qualification test that excludes large numbers of pregnant women. In addition in the 1986 White Paper on 'Building Businesses ... not Barriers' a proposal to weaken the right of part-time workers to reinstatement after maternity leave was included. In other ways, too, women's dependency is deepened by the Social Security Act 1986. Alterations to the State Earnings Related Pension Scheme will reduce its value for elderly widows. Similarly the introduction of the Social Fund and the abolition of special needs payments assume that women should be economically dependent on men, without regard to the actual financial circumstances of individual families. Women's eligibility for unemployment benefit has also been affected by the introduction of stringent conditions to establish a claimant's availability for work. These penalise, in particular, women with pre-school children who must demonstrate that they have already existing child-care arrangements before being entitled to benefit. In a situation of an absolute minimum of state provision for pre-school children and costly private alternatives, this requirement 'fails to grasp the reality of such women's lives' (David, 1986: 48). Women's right to child benefit payments has also been under attack in the last decade. Vigorous campaigns seem to have ensured that it is still paid directly to mothers rather than through men's wage packets, but in 1987 the commitment to maintain its real value relative to inflation was abolished and the planned April 1988 rise was reduced.

Proposed changes in the taxation system will also increase inequalities between men and women. In contrast with the USA, the tax system does not allow any child-care expenses to be deducted from taxable income and a recent ruling by the Inland Revenue that workplace nurseries are a fringe benefit that is taxable has increased their cost. The total number of places, anyway, is insignificant. There are also proposals to reform personal taxation to abolish the married man's tax allowance and replace it with a system of tansferable tax allowances. Although there are strong arguments against the present system, the proposed system will in fact *increase* married women's dependence as the avowed aim stated in the Green Paper 'The Reform of Personal Taxation' makes clear. The new legislation is to remove 'the present special incentive for two earner couples. Such positive discrimination is neither necessary nor economically desirable at a time of high unemployment, particularly among the young'. In other words, the clear answer to high rates of unemployment is for married women to stay at home. In the 1988 Budget a new proposal to tax married women as individuals from 1990 was introduced. However, a transferable tax allowance for married couples is also to be introduced. This marriage allowance can be paid to either partner depending on their relative tax positions. *The Times*, commenting on the Budget in a leader, praised this change and the abolition of multiple mortgage tax relief for unmarried individuals buying a joint house as moves to strengthen the nuclear family – 'a key institution for social stability'.

These views about the family and women's role run completely counter to the reality of a radically restructured labour market that is increasingly dependent on the low-paid waged labour of married women. But it is this very ideology of motherhood and rhetoric of the sanctity of the nuclear family that allows women's waged labour to be constructed as secondary, as peripheral, and so to be paid at levels far below the 'family wage' earned by male breadwinners. The assumptions that caring, nurturing, nursing and other kinds of servicing tasks are 'women's work' allows them to be undertaken 'for love' within the family and for inadequate financial rewards in the labour market.

Women and Politics under Thatcher

In this section I want to examine how the contradiction between the restructuring of waged labour based on women's increased participation, and social policies based on traditional gender divisions, has surfaced in political debates about equal rights since 1979. I also want to examine the implications for the strategies of the women's movement and feminist politics in the 1980s.

Despite the significance of the familial ideology in social welfare debates, there seems to have been neither an explicit policy to return women to their homes nor a commitment to extending equal rights to women during the three terms of Thatcher's Government. Indeed, Margaret Thatcher herself, in a rare speech about women's position, stated that 'the battle for women's rights has largely been won. The days when they were demanded and discussed in strident tones should be gone forever'. The Prime Minister seems to hold a view about women's dual roles that was common in the 1960's. Women can have their cake and eat it: by creating a happy domestic environment for their children when young and then by entering the labour market as their children leave home: '... women of our generation are often still comparatively young by the time our children are grown up and therefore we have the opportunity to develop our own talents ... For many that experience can enhance their lives and enlarge their interests' (Dame Margery Corbert-Ashby Memorial Lecture 1982, quoted in Wilson, 1987). That these opportunities are class-specific for women is glossed over. What Thatcher seems to have achieved is the containment of the ambiguous views of women reflected in her Government's policies. Simultaneously women have been placed on the agenda in both their new and their old roles. At a profound level she has succeeded in making women feel that they belong: either to the nation or to the family, or in the case of high flyers, to themselves and their careers.

Political Organisation

What have been the implications for organising around specifically women's issues in the 1980s? I have argued that gender is now at the forefront of the political agenda in a way that it has not been before. Despite the attack on the principle of collectivity which has been such a strong element in the ideology of the women's movement, the emphasis on individual liberty by right-wing Conservatives has opened up a space for women on the Right to organise around civil issues. A new generation of Tory women has begun to mobilise support for women's issues. These women have 'become self-consciously political about their gender. They are the confident voice of the dispossessed: the female Tory rebels who want argument, action and political definition. Yet differently from the feminists on the left, these women resist the categories of oppression and subjugation. Instead they exalt a female individualism and extend the right-wing libertarian values to include women' (Loach, 1987: 26). The Conservative National Women's Committee, for example, strongly criticised the proposed changes in the taxation system that would give wives at home a tax allowance and so act as a disincentive for women to enter the labour market.

Whether these types of campaigns can be subsumed under the label 'feminist', or at least the type of feminism that was constructed during the second wave of the women's movement from the 1960s, is debatable. Beatrix Campbell has argued that 'feminism may not describe the politics of Tory women, but Tory women more than most have a gendered politics and these days cannot exist entirely outside the frame of feminism' (Campbell, 1986: 298). The problem with Campbell's argument, however, is that it takes as self-evident the definition of feminism. But the main feature of contemporary feminism is its diversity and plurality. Women's politics and organisation have been characterised during the late 1970s and the 1980s by a variety of emphases, different interpretations of strategies and success, and by the different social bases of mobilisation. An extremely significant divide during these years, for example, has been on the basis of race. It is more accurate to argue that the politics of the 1980s has been a *gendered* politics rather than feminist politics, although this gendering, of course, is partly a consequence of earlier feminist organisation.

The several paradoxes that exist in Thatcherite ideology and policies – between individual rights and moral responsibility for family members, between the idea of fulfilment for women in waged work but the reality of increased exploitation for many, the reassertion of the obligations of male breadwinners in the face of radically restructured employment opportunities for many men – make it difficult for coherent strategies of opposition and resistance to be formulated.

The future of feminist politics on 'the Left' seems unclear at the moment. The recognition of experiential and theoretical diversity (Barrett, 1987; Phillips, 1987; Segal, 1987) makes unified political opposition more difficult to achieve. However, the centrality of gender issues in Thatcher's Britain – through the increased participation of women in waged labour and the attacks on their living standards because of cuts in state spending – means that feminist politics have an increased significance for socialism as well as for organisations outside the Labour movement. The central issues of gender politics and class politics are increasingly coincident. Changes in the nature of the labour process and the gender division of the labour force cannot be ignored by theoretical socialist analysis nor by socialist politics. Women's growing incorporation into the working class, in their own right, will (should!) alter the nature of socialist analysis and practices. In the last decade an unprecedented attack on the living standards and economic circumstances of many women and men has been launched and sustained by three terms of Conservative Government. Perhaps a new and strong socialist feminism will emerge as a consequence. The signs are there in the politics of some local authorities who have set up women's committees and introduced new programmes to involve women working in the community in a wide range of areas from child-care provision to transport. However, these very authorities have been the focus of a Conservative attack – through rate-capping and a public relations campaign to dub their policies 'loony'. At the national, rather than local, level signs are less hopeful. The Labour Party seems, despite its policy review initiated in 1988, unready to recognise the significance of the current restructuring of gender relations.

11
Transport Policy: Off the Rails?

John Whitelegg

Introduction

The organisation and delivery of transport services in Britain have undergone important changes in the last ten years. In evaluating these changes we must be very clear in what ways they represent radical departures from existing policies and in what ways they are merely extensions of trends, even if there are presentational differences. While there have been important changes in transport provision, the basic pattern remains unaltered. Successive right-wing Conservative governments have had little difficulty in working within the framework established or sustained by previous Labour administrations. Any shifts in transport policy are readily explicable by the post-war history of neglect of or indifference to all non-motorised modes and public transport. All post-war administrations have subscribed to the view that the needs of the car must be met, cities destroyed as living places, and planning defined so as to facilitate spatial changes which favour motorised travel against the pedestrian, cyclist and user of public transport.

Transport is a major item of public expenditure (£5.6 billion in 1986–7) and a major area of everyday experience for the population, but the frequency with which ministers change at the Department of Transport (DT), and its low esteem in the pecking order of Whitehall indicate the low status accorded to transport by government. This low status is inversely proportional to the importance of transport policies in the management of resources (particularly energy), environmental problems, road traffic accidents, public expenditure and the long-term future of cities as places where people would choose to live. In all these respects there have been no dramatic policy changes since 1973.

The benefits of transport are unevenly distributed between different groups in society. Car ownership is a symbol of success, prosperity and liberation; the image of the car as a status and sexual symbol persists (Bayley, 1986); and it confers benefits – notably those deriving from accessibility – denied to those without a car. There are important gender, ethnic and spatial inequalities in car ownership, and these inequalities may be growing in severity. The car is also responsible for social, economic and environmental damage, whether in the form of loss of life (some 5,000 deaths occur on the roads in Britain each year) or the imposition of stress, noise, congestion and pollution in urban areas (Hagerstrand, 1987; Holzapfel and Sachs, 1987; Roberts, 1987). All post-war governments in Britain have accepted these costs as a necessary price to pay for the pursuit of higher levels of motorisation, and this can largely be attributed to the strength of the road lobby and the importance of the motor vehicle industry and its related suppliers to the national economy.

Transport policy can produce a range of benefits by bringing people and facilities together through appropriate modes which maximise accessibility. This requires provision of walking and cycling facilities. For freight transport, advantages will accrue from low-cost movement by whatever means serves the purpose best, taking account of environmental issues and the availability of rail, water, roads and pipelines. In both cases, longer travelling distances, greater tonne-kilometre capacities and more vehicles are not synonymous with progress or improved efficiency. Indeed longer journeys to work and the growth in tonne-km of freight indicate maladaptation of location and the means of travel. Moving goods longer distances to reflect changes in the organisation of retailing, storage and distribution actually transfers expenditures from capital to the state (which responds to demands for road space) and to the consumer (in the form of increased travel costs and the environmental effects of increased traffic).

Transport policy has been the subject of considerable conflict: community opposition to road construction, railway closures, the anti-social activities of motorists, and the implementation of planning policies designed to serve the car and oppress the pedestrian, has flourished. Transport has also been an arena for conflict between central and local government where local authorities have pursued very different goals from those supported by central government.

Transport, therefore, has to be viewed from many different angles. As a major item of public expenditure it is subject to those forces which seek to limit or to expand such expenditures, depending on the ideological priorities of the government. Transport is also a focus of popular social protest, owing mainly to its creation of very clear losers and gainers in an urban system (and more generally). Transport also offers opportunities for a conversion from public to private provision and for the disengagement of local authorities from its provision. Hence it is important, in a wider consideration of the state or of public provision, to come to terms with transport.

In the next section I will identify elements of continuity and change in transport policy. In the third section I will review those areas which clearly do represent a departure from past approaches, and in the final section I assess the question of change versus continuity.

Continuity in Transport Policy?

The post-war period in Britain has seen strong elements of continuity in transport policy, regardless of which party has held office. The main elements of continuity are: the decline of railways; the rise of the heavy goods vehicle (HGV); the rise in car ownership; support for the company car; the allocation of transport investments and the nature of investment appraisal.

This situation arises for several reasons. The most important influence on transport policy is the growth in ownership and use of the private car. This is an expression of consumer preference and status and of broader societal goals related to freedom of choice, self-improvement and economic growth. These powerful forces are sustained by a dense network of political, corporate and consumer patronage. Policy changes which would threaten this system are simply not seen as feasible, particularly when large sections of the economy are in difficulties and the motor vehicle and road construction industries so obviously depend on policies which support road transport. In addition, transport policy is prone to action based on mythology. It is still generally believed that building roads is good for the economy. Similarly, roads are still built (in cities) to 'relieve' traffic congestion. Yet there is no evidence for the former, while new roads actually create *more* traffic. A final argument in support of the position of continuity rather than change is that a coherent transport policy has never really existed: rather, transport is an area of poorly co-ordinated pragmatism.

The decline of railways

The basic picture for rail in the UK can be seen in Table 11.1. The decline in rail, whether in physical or financial terms, has happened under both Labour and Conservative administrations in post-war Britain (see Bain, 1985, and Gourvish, 1986). One of the milestones of railway history, the Beeching Report of 1963, was produced under a Conservative administration but largely implemented by its Labour successor. The broad philosophy of this report has not subsequently been challenged, though there was some slackening off of closures in the late 1960s and the Conservative administration in 1970–4 reprieved some Welsh railway lines. More recently the 1970s and 1980s have seen relatively little rail closure activity, and a spate of station reopenings has brought improved services to parts of Scotland, West Yorkshire and the rural areas along the Settle–Carlisle railway line, although paradoxically the latter line has been the subject of the largest closure proposal for many years (Whitelegg, 1987). The main focus of rail's decline has been the successive cuts in the level of grant aid from central government (the Public

Table 11.1   The decline of Britain's railways, 1965–84

	Length of line (km)	Passengers carried (millions)	Passenger-km (millions)	Tonnes carried (millions)	Net tonne km (millions)
1965	24013	865	30116	232	25229
1970	18989	824	30400	209	24500
1975	18118	730	30255	175	20896
1980	17893	766	31700	155	17640
1981	17769	724	30700	155	17505
1982	17668	635	27200	142	15876
1983	17435	701	29500	145	17504
1984	17221	708	29700	78	13357

Source: ECMT (1987), *Statistical Trends in Transport 1965–1984*.

Services Obligation (PSO)). The loss of rail freight is a different issue as the freight sector must operate without a subsidy. A lack of investment in new lines or existing infrastructure produces a lowering of service quality and by comparison with European railways British Rail (BR) is severely disadvantaged in this respect (TEST, 1984a).

Some investment is taking place on Britain's railways with the electrification of the east coast main line and some modest improvements in Kent and the London area as part of the Channel Tunnel project. By European standards these are small schemes and in the case of the works associated with the Tunnel they are grossly inadequate to meet the needs of an enlarged freight share. There is no provision for an improved line to London which would avoid congestion arising from conflicts between commuter and freight traffic, and there is no provision for any cross-London route to serve the North of England. Any gains have been won against government opposition and after considerable delays, but they will not be enough to rescue urban and commuter rail services, eliminate the dereliction of a large part of the provincial sector, and combat the near-terminal illness of the freight sector.

BR's changing financial circumstances, measured by the size of the government grant, are shown in Table 11.2. The decline in support for rail since 1979 reflects a distinctive view of disengagement from the business of running railways. The rhetoric is stronger than the reality, however, and the actual degree of 'underfunding' of Britain's railways has not altered dramatically in comparison to our European neighbours since the mid-1970s. BR has extracted more funds from fares, has developed the inter-city business and gener-

Table 11.2   British Rail's receipt of government grant aid (£ million at 85–6 prices)

	84–5	85–6	86–7	87–8	88–9
Inter-city	208	125	90	82	–
Network SE	294	257	216	217	211
Provincial	530	520	482	476	477
Total grant	1032	902	788	775	688

Source: British Rail, *Corporate Plans*, 1986, 1987.

ated funds for new investment from its own borrowings. The decline in PSO is real and has led to a dramatic fall in service quality and reliability on BR, but it is not the root cause of BR's problems, nor a distinctively new facet of transport policy of the post-1979 era. Since nationalisation in 1948, BR has never received the support necessary to produce efficient urban rail, long distance passenger and freight systems. Moreover, such new investment as is taking place in BR is inadequate, too late, and has to be justified against far more stringent criteria than those which apply to road investment schemes. It is also generated from within the industry and this limits what is available as well as contributing to higher fares.

The Beeching philosophy resurfaced in the Serpell Report of 1982. This philosophy assumes that rail services can be cut back to bring expenditure into line with revenue, that there should be no wider assessment of rail investment, such as might be carried out with a cost-benefit analysis, and that there should be no comparability of assessment of road and rail investment. This contrasts with several European countries, where road and rail investments are assessed on more equal terms.

Serpell was a depressingly negative document: it is difficult to understand why Serpell proposed major cuts in the size of the network, since the Beeching 'axe' had not solved any financial problems. The gains that were made post-Beeching were made as a result of new investment (Gourvish, 1986). This point was ignored by Serpell.

The decline of BR affects employment and local economic prosperity. Since 1970, 70,324 jobs have been lost through contraction, closure and privatisation of services such as the sale of hotels. As many as 52,274 have been lost on the railway itself and in the rail workshops and 15,157 are due to go in the next five years. Five out of thirteen British Rail Engineering Ltd (BREL) workshops have closed since 1979 and a privatisation programme is now agreed with the possibility of more closures/rationalisations. In 1987 the BR *Corporate Plan* announced massive cost cutting with job losses in the freight sector. The forecast outcome in this sector is £53 million profit, of which £45 million will be achieved by reduced working expenses. This points to job losses at depots and marshalling yards in a sector already suffering from low market share and capable of a greater contribution to the movement of freight and elimination of environmental problems.

A remarkable factor in BR's decline under the Thatcher governments has been the complicity of the rail industry itself in its demise. Rather than make a vigorous case for rail expansion and support from public funds, BR has produced successive corporate plans which aim to reduce the PSO grant. Central government has accepted this planning base but has demanded the reduction of PSO in a much shorter timescale. BR has proposed the closure of lines which clearly have revenue potential and has instituted studies of converting rail to road as in the case of the Marylebone 'coachway'. BR's attitude is not the sole cause of its rapid decline but, in combination with an anti-rail government stance, it has produced a negative approach to marketing and development which impedes the development of any revenue-led rail initiatives and brings cost-cutting to the fore.

The attitudes of both BR and central government stand in stark contrast to the European experience. In many countries, particularly Germany and France, rail is seen as an essential part of urban renewal, environmental strategies and energy and land-use policies. Investment in urban rail systems obviates the need for expensive and inefficient road projects, and new high-speed railways, though not without problems, are seen as an important stimulus to the economy and regional development (Whitelegg, 1988a). In Britain negative attitudes and successive rounds of cuts have produced a railway which operates on or below the margins of what is acceptable both to the consumer and in terms of its contribution to economy and environment. Further cuts in the PSO will seriously threaten rural railways like the Settle–Carlisle line and the 'Cinderella' cross-country routes which serve places like Norwich and Lincoln. Britain's most important commuter railway will also find life very difficult with reduced funding for the continuation and extension of 'Operation Pride' which has made some inroads into the poor physical quality and service reliability of London commuter services.

The Rise of the Heavy Goods Vehicle (HGV)

The growth in numbers and weight of HGVs is one of the most important transport characteristics of the last twenty years. Some measures of the increasing importance of HGVs are given in Table 11.3. There has been a decline in tonnes carried but a rise in tonne-

Table 11.3   Trends in HGV numbers and use

	Tonnes (m)	Tonnes-km (1,000m)	Vehicle km (m)
1965	1590	68.8	36,300
1970	1610	85	38,600
1975	1439	89	37,720
1980	1349	93	41,330
1984	1375	103.8	43,300

Source: ECMT (1987), *Statistical Trends in Transport 1965–1984.*

km, reflecting an increase in the length of haul and substantial changes in the food, drink and tobacco industries which have rationalised production, storage and distribution with a small number of centres, thereby increasing journey length. This tendency produces an increase in vehicle-km just as the decline in heavy industries such as steel-making produces a fall in tonnes.

The problem of HGVs is multi-faceted and has not been tackled effectively by any post-war administration. The Department of Transport is currently embarking on a programme of expenditure worth £2 billion to upgrade pre-1922 bridges to a 40-tonne standard to cope with bigger lorries. This will pave the way for a further increase in weights and size which, at 38 tonnes, is below the EEC's preferred standard. HGVs cost public authorities at least £600m per annum in road damage repair alone (National Audit Office, 1987). Their true costs include the costs of noise and air pollution, damage to buildings and road traffic accidents. Currently there is no mechanism for calculating these costs and relating them to vehicle taxation. The increasing size of the HGV fleet represents a serious drain on public funds and is the result of sustained political lobbying in favour of road construction and a liberal regime for the HGV (Hamer, 1987). Roads are justified on the grounds that they will improve economic performance, and this link between lorries, roads and economic gain is accepted by government: 'by offering a combination of speed, convenience and flexibility, freight carriage by lorry plays a vital role in cutting costs and increasing efficiency for industry and commerce' (Department of Transport, 1987b).

Such statements cannot be found in support of rail investment and this view of the relative merits of road and rail is a long-standing one with its origins in post-war expansion programmes and fundamental changes in the location and organisation of manufacturing. The belief that road investment is good for the economy or generates local economic benefits as opposed to placeless corporate benefits has been challenged (Whitelegg, 1985b; Vanke, 1987) but is still strongly held; Labour and Conservative policies do not differ on this point, and the trade union movement, in particular the TGWU, is in agreement with representative organisations from the employers' side.

In a situation of all-party support for road construction and lack of interest in lorry restraint, the run-down of rail is more easily understood. This is unlikely to change, given the balance of interests and their respective weights in the area of lobbying. EEC transport policies will also add emphasis to the growing importance of HGVs as liberalisation of transport proceeds alongside plans for removing customs controls in Europe and implementing measures which ensure that Europe functions as one internal market (see Whitelegg, 1988b).

The Rise in Car Ownership

The growth of car ownership and use is one of the clearest components of change in transport over the last twenty years. Car ownership is seen as desirable in itself, as a necessary prerequisite of longer journeys to work, as a means of coping with inadequate public transport and as a response to changes in retailing, health service and education provision which all involve the substitution of longer journeys to bigger centres for shorter journeys to smaller centres. The car is deeply embedded in the structure of the economies of 'developed' societies and living with the car has become a process of adaptation. In exchange for the supposed economic benefits of the car-based society, children have surrendered their use of streets as play areas and for the majority of urban residents streets are noxious, dangerous places to be avoided, rather than the focus of social interaction and community which they once were. In this most fundamental area of transport policy there is no difference in approach on the part of any government. Table 11.4 illustrates the steady growth of car ownership and use in Britain. Between 1958 and 1982 the penetration of cars into British society has grown

Table 11.4   Car ownership and use in Britain

	Passenger-km (millions)	Cars per 1,000 persons	New car registrations per 1,000 persons
1965	191,000	168	21
1970	260,000	213	20
1975	294,000	252	22
1980	365,000	294	28
1984	410,000	293	31

Source: Department of Transport, *Transport Statistics*, 1987.

dramatically (Plowden, 1985). Car ownership is still highly variable between groups and between regions. A list of local authority areas ranked according to the percentage of households without a car shows a clear division between the top ten and the bottom ten (Whitelegg, 1985a), mirroring wider socio-economic divides within Britain.

Within small areas of cities, car ownership rates will be even more variable and they certainly convey a strong impression of the inadequacy of transport policies which deprive cities of good public transport and give them large traffic volumes. Townsend *et al.* (1988) in examining car ownership rates at ward level found percentages of households without cars as high as 70–80, particularly in Newcastle-upon-Tyne and Middlesbrough. Car ownership and use continues to be one of the most important inputs to transport policy. The unrestrained use of cars regardless of environmental and social

Table 11.5   The development of car ownership in Britain

No. of cars in household	1958 %	1982 %
None	77	39
One	22	45
Two or more	1	16

Source: Plowden (1985).

Table 11.6   Local authority areas in Britain at the extremes of car ownership rates

Highest percentage without a car (top ten)	Lowest percentage without a car (bottom ten)
South Shields	High Wycombe
Glasgow	Aldershot
Sunderland	Maidenhead
Coatbridge	Bishops Stortford
Peterlee	Woking and Weybridge
Mexborough	Horsham
Liverpool	Bracknell
West Bromwich	Hertford and Ware
Paisley	St Albans
Hartlepool	Guildford

Source: Whitelegg (1985a).

losses has been a principle of post-war transport planning and represents a remarkable degree of continuity in transport policies.

The Company Car

The company car is a clear example of governmental support for motorisation among the relatively affluent members of society. The 1978–9 National Travel Survey shows that 11.1 per cent of cars available for use in private households had been paid for entirely, and 1.5 per cent in part, by a company. In 1982 41 per cent of all new cars were registered in a company name. Because of registration of such cars in private names the actual percentage is much higher: the Inland Revenue estimate that 70 per cent of new cars are paid for by companies. The annual subsidy to company car users is £1.5 billion, mainly derived from the low effective tax rates on the benefit (TEST, 1984b). Moreover, two-thirds of the mileage of company cars is for private and leisure activities and includes commuting. The support of private motoring on this scale represents a considerable distortion of transport markets condoned by those who argue against public transport subsidy. The use of the company car is preferable to any public transport option even for longer journeys where there is an attractive inter-city rail alternative. This socially regressive system transfers resources to the more affluent while contributing to the loss of income to public transport and hence its decline. This has serious consequences for those groups without access to the private car (Whitelegg, 1984; TEST, 1984b).

Company cars have been available to highly paid employees and company chairmen since at least the early 1960s. In 1970, 50 per cent of company executives received the full use of a company car and in 1982, 78 per cent. Governments have generally supported this system, despite its implications for loss of revenue to the exchequer. In 1959 the Conservative government limited tax relief and depreciation allowances that companies could claim to a maximum of £2,000 or £11,700 at 1984 prices. In contrast a Labour government in 1977 reduced the deposit payable on long-term lease of cars from ten months to three. This gave a considerable boost to the company car. The current Conservative administration has adopted the view that company cars are not subsidised and, while the scale values which determine the cash equivalent value of cars for taxation purposes have been increased, there are no plans to reform a unique institution for large-scale public support of private motoring. This view does not differ from that taken by previous Labour administrations and was not significantly adjusted in the 1988 Budget which increased the amount of tax that would be paid by company car beneficiaries.

Transport Expenditure and Investment Appraisal

It is appropriate to link expenditure and appraisal because the former is the result of the latter and the methods of appraisal reveal much about the unspoken but pervasive assumptions which underlie transport policy. I argue that public expenditure on transport has shown a systematic bias towards road expenditure, particularly construction. Expenditure on rail and bus, both infrastructure and revenue support, has declined in recent years (Table 11.7), through deliberate decisions to cut budgets (as in the case of the PSO) and through appraisal systems with in-built discriminatory tendencies. Because of problems of comparability of monetary units over time, and changes in statistical categories, it is not possible to cover 1975 to 1985 in the same table. Table 11.7 shows a decline in road expenditures in the first few years of the current Conservative administration from a high point under Labour. Expenditure on rail

Table 11.7 Transport expenditures, 1975–84 (£ million: current prices)

	75–6	76–7	77–8	78–9	79–80	80–1	81–2	82–3	83–4
Roads inc. motorways (trunk)	728	607	431	446	467	422	460	460	460
Local Roads	540	514	319	307	342		375	456	503
BR passenger subsidies	496	455	445	409	449	454	474		
Local passenger subsidies	429	401	344	348	341	335	310		

Source: Department of Transport, *Transport Statistics*, 1981.

was relatively stable, though at the low level established by previous administrations. Local passenger subsidies, mainly to bus operators and in support of concessionary fares, fell noticeably.

In the 1980–6 period there were different trends, as expenditure on the national road system rose from £2.5 billion to £3.3 billion. Local road expenditure also increased from £426m to £531m. Support to BR also increased in the early years of the Conservative administration before the cuts described earlier. The level of PSO rose from £595m in 1980–1 to £851m in 1983–4 before BR were given more stringent targets to achieve. Official statistics fail to convey an impression of the size of the gap between road and rail investment. Railways receive a very small share of total investment in transport while investment in roads and road vehicles has risen from £10,874m in 1981 to £15,643m in 1984. (The equivalent figures for rail are £364m and £382m respectively.)

Spending on roads at an increasing rate is not new. Van Rest (1985) refers to the 1960s as a period when roads were relatively popular and increasing amounts were devoted to them. In May 1970 Fred Mulley, the Minister of Transport, launched the Primary Strategic National Network, promising £4,000m (at 1970 prices) for new construction. Road expenditures have risen and fallen in response to various circumstances, and a predilection for road expenditures has not been a source of party political dissent. Barbara Castle (1980) has described her disappointment with Labour Party transport policies. It was a Conservative government that effectively brought a stop to urban motorway construction and introduced government-supported fare subsidies. Starkie (1982) actually suggests that 1973 represents a watershed in transport policy. After this date the emphasis moved away from urban road construction and into the area of traffic restraint and managing the demand for urban road space. With hindsight it can be seen that this did not come to much in terms of the development of a distinctive British approach to urban design and coping with the car. By comparison with Germany, for example, there was very little change in the general direction of UK policies. Starkie's point remains, however, correct.

The decline in all forms of collective transport investment in comparison with the demands of motorisation has been facilitated by methods of appraisal (Leitch, 1978). Existing methods give road schemes more than a head start in the competition for funds in comparison with rail, cycling or pedestrian facilities which must meet more stringent conditions. The advantages of a very broadly based cost-benefit analysis are denied to all forms of public and personal transport. The economic return calculated by cost-benefit analysis will usually be higher than the straightforward financial return (House of Commons, 1987).

Cost-benefit analysis allows road schemes to build-in time savings which have a financial value. Thus speed is valued as a benefit regardless of its relationship with road traffic accidents, and slower modes will fare badly if assessed on a time basis. It is debatable whether or not reduced journey times are actually beneficial, though this principle is uncritically enshrined in the appraisal methodology for road projects. One consequence is a bias in favour of those who travel most by car (the majority of whom are men), while those for whom speed is irrelevant in comparison with safety, reliability and cost (the elderly, children, and those who care for them, the majority of whom are women), are denied new investment because the method of appraisal so effectively discriminates against them. This has been condoned by successive governments and has not been the subject of political debate.

Rail investment projects would clearly perform better if social, environmental and safety considerations were built into their assessment; conversely, road projects would fare less well. If a range of alternatives were assessed within the same framework, then for the first time road schemes could be compared with other transport solutions to some previously identified problem. This does not happen at the moment and road schemes are approved without any evaluation of alternatives (Lancaster City Council, 1987).

The current resurgence of road expenditure and the attack on rail are entirely consistent with the well-established procedures for assessing transport investments. The lack of sensible, small-scale transport improvements for pedestrian and cyclist groups is also a result of this distortion. Investment appraisal techniques are not just obscure technical procedures, they are a fundamental obstacle to a balanced transport policy which will serve the interests of the majority of the population. There has been no disagreement between the main political parties in the last twenty years on this point and any further deterioration in the transport environment is entirely consistent with this long-standing neglect of basic issues.

Elements of Change in Transport Policy since 1979

The topics dealt with in the previous section strongly suggest an element of continuity in transport policy and one which has been based on neglect and pragmatism rather than any thorough assessment of alternatives and priorities. Both Labour and Conservative governments have given transport a low priority, and their policies have been almost indistinguishable. This has not been the case at local level where a small number of Labour administrations – notably the GLC and South Yorkshire, but also Merseyside, West Yorkshire and Lothian – have pursued radical and egalitarian public transport policies. The contrast between national and local Labour policies heightens the similarity between Labour and Conservative policies at national level.

The continuity described in the previous section is far wider in its extent than the topics covered. A detailed study of walking, cycling, urban design, planning and road safety would add further weight to the continuity argument. No post-war administration has distinguished itself by a fundamental attack on these problems. The occasional ebb and flow of policy which might give rise to the idea that there are differences in transport policy are superficial in character and more presentational than substantial. It is in this general context that the changes of the last nine years should be assessed. One problem in such an assessment is perceptual. The

Thatcher administration has a high political profile with much rhetoric being produced in support of policies which are under discussion. This produces the impression that more is happening than is the case, and it is unlikely that the changes which have been initiated could be described as a significant watershed in transport policy. Two important areas of change – bus deregulation and road construction – are examined in detail. Rail finance will be returned to in the conclusion.

Bus Deregulation

Bus deregulation came into effect in October 1986 and ended fifty years of regulation in the bus industry. In particular it ended the monopoly of municipal and National Bus Company (NBC) operators which had been maintained by the Traffic Commissioners. Henceforth there were to be no restrictions on new entrants and on competition beyond the satisfaction of some safety and organisational requirements. Municipal and NBC operators were to be privatised and local authorities would no longer have a duty to co-ordinate public transport. The intention was that the market would ensure that demand was met and local authorities were to operate a tendering system to fill such gaps as might emerge after the new pattern of commercial services had been registered. None of this was to apply to London which is still regulated. The arguments for deregulation assume that public monopolies are inefficient and that the private sector is much more capable of delivering a service at a lower price to the consumer. Deregulation would make all this possible and lead to a rush of new entrants who would raise the standards of service, lower fares and increase efficiency. Most importantly this would reduce the demands for public funds to be used as subsidies to public transport (similar arguments have been used elsewhere, e.g. in the National Health Service (NHS); see Chapter 13). Counter-arguments would point to the nature of a public transport service which depends on a network, the facility to switch between modes, reliability and safety. It is very unlikely that a privatised system could achieve the degree of co-ordination required for a high quality service to match the attractions of the car. A failure in public transport supply would further accelerate its decline and make life very difficult indeed for those groups (mainly children, women and the elderly) and areas (mainly rural areas and large cities) most dependent on the bus.

Assessing the effects of deregulation is difficult, given its novelty, the many different circumstances in which bus deregulation is working, and the absence of a reliable independent monitoring system. In this latter respect Guiver and Turner (1987) describe the role of a national voluntary organisation, Buswatch.

Various analyses of the results of bus deregulation suggest that the claims of government ministers are exaggerated. Moyes (1988) and Knowles (1988) identify very little new competition. The effects are patchy with Merionydd, for example, having five new entrants into the bus business. ATCO (Association of Transport Coordinating Officers) (1987) found that ten per cent of routes had been subject to some kind of competition with an average of two to three new entrants per county or region. Farrington and Mackay (1987) found fierce competition in Glasgow and Edinburgh though the total increase in the supply of bus services was only 2.8 per cent (measured in miles). Knowles (1988) found fare increases in conurbations, particularly Manchester, whilst ATCO (1987) found fare changes insignificant. There are no reports of fare reduction, though for some groups of regular travellers there have been some gains in the form of weekly tickets and other marketing initiatives. Guiver and Turner (1987) find a decline in reliability post-deregulation. Other studies do not consider this aspect of consumer impact. ATCO (1987) found that the previous level of service had been secured by councils though there were serious losses of evening and weekend services. Knowles (1988) finds severe off-peak cuts in conurbations. Farrington and Mackay (1987) comment on the same effect and note an increase in peak services as well as a decline in off-peak services.

Moyes (1988) is alone in recording the very serious effects of bus deregulation on the conditions of service of employees. He found redundancies and losses of earnings of up to £23 per week for employees as companies cut costs to produce lower tendered prices.

Bus deregulation does represent an attempt to change the boundary between the public and private sectors. Privatisation, however, has taken a different form from that seen in the NHS, in air transport or in telecommunications. Municipal services are still run by their local authorities, albeit under a different fiscal regime and with a transport committee transformed into a 'board of directors'.

NBC subsidiaries have been sold to employees in a series of 'management buy-outs' and both sets of changes have not produced the dramatic effects predicted by the Government, but neither have they been the disaster predicted by opponents of bus deregulation. The bus industry was underfunded and not performing well before deregulation, and this situation remains largely unchanged. Deregulation has been little more than an ideological exercise in re-sorting the components of a complex industry; it remains to be seen whether these changes have improved or reduced its long-term chances of survival.

Road Construction

Recent government statements describe road expenditures very positively:

> The M25 is complete. It has been one of the most ambitious and significant engineering projects undertaken in this country . . . at a cost of nearly £1000 million. In total 108 motorway and trunk road schemes in England have been completed, an investment of nearly £1.5 billion (since 1973). (Department of Transport, 1987b.)

Expenditure on roads and road maintenance in 1985–6 was £2,978 millions, almost a third higher than in 1980. The commitment to the roads programme is as great as in the late 1960s and early 1970s; what is novel is the commitment to urban road construction (even urban motorways, though the term 'motorway' is carefully avoided), and the commitment to private sector involvement. Both trends are combined in London where the Government is supporting a proposed new four-lane bridge across the Thames for south-bound traffic from Thurrock to Dartford. This will be privately financed and, like the Channel Tunnel, will be facilitated by a 'hybrid bill' which enables long and complicated public enquiries to be by-passed. The Government describes as 'exciting' the prospect of private sector involvement in road construction. The Government is also encouraging the private sector to get involved in running 'unprofitable' railways like the Settle–Carlisle line. Other projects under consideration for similar treatment include the Mersey and Severn barrages, the second Severn bridge, the Avon Metro and a Heathrow Terminal 5.

Privatisation of transport infrastructure provision will have a very damaging effect on transport as a whole because it can only proceed case by case in those circumstances where financial forecasts justify the involvement of the private sector. The private sector will not be interested in the damaging effects of increased traffic flows in the vicinity of major new links. The traffic-generation effects of major new links are well known and are thus a very desirable market item. Links built in isolation from other policies and from the consequences of their construction will destroy many urban communities and lead to an increase in the number of car owners and users, whose needs can only be 'satisfied' (though only in the most illusory sense) by more new construction. What is excellent news for financial consortia and civil engineering firms is very bad news indeed for those communities living in the vicinity of the East London river crossing or near any new urban road scheme. Transport and land use planning as currently understood cannot function alongside a privately funded transport infrastructure which depends on precisely those forces which planning must contain and regulate in the interests of everyone.

The main effects of this resurgence in road investment are to be found in London, though National Parks in deeply rural Britain have also been the subject of large road schemes, e.g. Okehampton in Devon and Gargrave in North Yorkshire. The abolition of the GLC has made it easier for central government to take a direct interest in the transport problems of the capital and this has shifted the policy thrust from public transport solutions to road construction. The DT (Department of Transport) have proposed substantial expenditure on London's roads of up to £1.5 billion, stating clearly that: 'The existing programme gives high priority to completing the comprehensive improvement of the North Circular Road and the A40 Western Avenue, and to improving access to East London' (DT, 1987). The government is also considering the result of the London Assessment Studies which examined transport issues in four corridors of London (East, West, South and the South Circular). Even though these studies were to report on a wide range of possible solutions including public transport, the Government's determination to implement East London 'improvements' in the teeth of fierce opposition and hard evidence of environmental, economic and community severance damage, supports the view that the assessment studies are a preparatory phase for large-scale road construction. Given the possibility of private sector involvement and of hybrid bills to smooth the passage of unpopular measures, the likelihood of new road construction in London is greater than at any time since the motorway box plans of the 1960s.

Conclusion

There are elements of change and continuity in transport policies over the last twenty years. Bus deregulation, with its strong ideological basis, is a major change, but the measure has not yet produced much change that can be perceived by the consumer. It may still be too early for a full assessment, and bus deregulation does pave the way for more radical changes in road provision and in the rail industry. It ended fifty years of consensus on the way the bus industry should be organised. Deregulation has not produced many tangible effects because of the sluggish response of the private sector, and partly because of the efforts of local authorities to keep the fabric of public transport intact. Bus deregulation will also undermine the importance of local government in transport matters. If the powers of local government are further limited (see Chapter 5) then radical and damaging changes in public transport become much more likely.

The dramatic decline in rail services since 1979 has far more continuity than any other policy dimension. Rail has been neglected by all governments and the industry itself. The case of the Settle–Carlisle closure proposal (Whitelegg, 1987) shows the extent to which BR is prepared to go in cutting its own throat. Similarly in the case of the Channel Tunnel BR's commitment to landward-side improvements has been modest, so that it is highly unlikely the Tunnel will provide the boost to rail freight and regional development that was hoped for (Whitelegg and James, 1987). Britain's rail industry has been neglected for so long that rail management cannot see its own business in the strong positive light which West Germany's railways have cultivated. Rail's decline is now locked into a culture of operator and government neglect, and a pessimism which will be very hard to dislodge.

Road investment has the right ingredients to win support from an avowedly 'free market' administration. It is an area which responds to simplistic arguments about economic growth and the need for good roads. The same argument is never used for rail freight and the detailed case for a link between economic benefits and road construction has not been proved. A very well-organised road lobby in Britain, coupled with a lot of pseudo-scientific evidence for road construction as an environmental and road safety benefit, has ensured a healthy road programme. Strong governmental links with large engineering firms, dating back at least twenty-five years, also ensure a degree of harmony between government and industry (see Hamer, 1987).

Transport, in so far as its characteristics impinge on most people, has not altered dramatically in the last ten years. There has been a deterioration in bus services as a result of deregulation and in large cities transport policies have shifted from public transport revenue support to other policies. The abolition of the GLC and metropolitan councils has had a dramatic effect on transport policy formulation and innovation. In London and in some other cities a process of policy evolution which has introduced some of the benefits of transport planning in continental cities has been brought to an end and Britain is once again characterised by the discredited production of road plans as a solution to transport problems. This can be seen in London but also in smaller cities such as Lancaster where the local authority is planning to push a four-lane highway through the centre of a small and compact urban area.

The Lancaster experience shows the extent to which things have changed very little in over twenty years of transport planning in Britain. In comparison with the real advances made in other European countries (see Whitelegg, 1988b) Britain remains locked into a narrow view of transport policy as catering for increased levels of motorisation and denying the necessity of catering for the pedestrian, cyclist and large numbers who depend on public transport.

The transport policies of the Thatcher era are not radical departures from previous administrations, either Labour or Conservative. They contain the seeds for really radical change, for example to break up the railways into private companies and a return to turnpike-road systems, but this is only possible because sustained neglect of broad transport objectives has starved this sector of both funds and popular support. A private retreat into the steel-reinforced womb of the automobile and a public retreat from high standards of accessibility and environmental quality is the unavoidable consequence of historical neglect and a clear political philosophy based on the imperatives of market forces.

12
The Political Geography of Housing in Contemporary Britain

Chris Hamnett

Introduction

Since the election of the first Thatcher government in 1979, there have been major changes in government housing policy. These changes, particularly the introduction of tenants' 'right to buy', the massive cuts in council house building, and the reorientation of housing subsidies away from council housing and towards owner occupation, have led to major changes in both the tenure structure and geography of British housing. Over a million council houses have been sold off, and the tenure composition of new building has shifted markedly in favour of the private sector. Council house building is now at the lowest peacetime level for fifty years. As a result, the erratic but continuous growth of council housing in Britain since 1919 has been thrown into sharp reverse. The absolute number of council houses and their proportion of the total stock has fallen sharply since 1979 while the dominance of owner occupation has been further reinforced.

But the incidence of sales and cuts has not been geographically even across the country as a whole. The impact of the cuts has been most strongly felt in the large industrial cities and inner city areas where the concentration of council housing and housing need is greatest. Conversely, sales have been concentrated in the more desirable parts of the housing stock, particularly in the small towns and villages and suburbs of Southern England. There have been relatively few sales in the inner cities (Dunn, Forrest and Murie, 1987; Kleinman and Whitehead, 1987). Consequently, the geographical differences in the distribution of council housing and owner occupation have become more marked. When these changes are considered alongside those in the social composition of the two tenures, the uneven geographical impact of house price inflation, the redistribution of financial assistance for housing, and the growth of council waiting lists, homelessness and in the use of bed-and-breakfast accommodation, it can be argued that the political economy of Thatcherism has reinforced the existing inequalities in the British housing market. The division between the haves and have-nots is wider than ever.

The Politics and Ideology of Housing Provision in Britain

These changes are of considerable importance for the structure and geography of housing in Britain, and they highlight the extent to which housing provision in contemporary Britain is affected by changes in government housing and economic policy. But while the changes wrought by Thatcherite policies are particularly visible today, state housing and economic policies have played an important part in shaping both the structure and the geography of housing provision since the Labouring Classes Dwelling Houses Act of 1866 enabled local authorities to borrow money to buy land and erect dwellings for the working classes. Private renting and owner occupation have been greatly affected by government housing and fiscal policies, and the growth of housing associations since the mid 1960s is almost entirely a product of government policies, and the ideological assumptions which underpinned them (Back and Hamnett, 1985).

But, as a result of the great growth of council housing from 1919, when direct state-subsidised provision was first introduced, to 1979 Britain has been unique amongst western capitalist countries in the scale of its directly state-owned and subsidised housing sector. In other Western European nations, social housing is not directly state-owned or controlled, and in Canada and the USA social housing comprises a negligible part of the total housing stock: less than 2 per cent in the USA. As a result, the size and role of the public housing sector, the scale of provision and the form and level of subsidy have been the subject of constant political conflict in Britain. Whereas Labour have traditionally strongly supported the public sector as a form of general housing provision, Conservative support has been much more reluctant, and they have generally seen large-scale council provision as an interim measure to rectify short-term shortages, to head off potential social discontent or to win electoral support (Merrett, 1979). When such short-term problems have been resolved, the Conservatives have looked to the private sector to provide housing for general needs, leaving council housing to provide for special needs such as slum clearance and redevelopment. This has led to a geography of council housing differentiated by type and quality.

Despite these differences, there was a broad political consensus during the 1950s and 1960s that council housing had a major role to play in British housing. Under Macmillan in the mid-1950s, new council building reached its highest ever level. This consensus did not last. When re-elected in 1970, the Conservatives reduced new council building and introduced the 1972 Housing Finance Act which raised council rents and reduced Exchequer subsidies to council housing while leaving tax relief to owner occupiers untouched. This Act was repealed in 1974 by the Labour Government, but the dispute over the costs of council house subsidies was intensified during the mid-1970s by the rapid rise in inflation and building costs and the front-loading of interest payments, and by Labour's decision to hold down council house rents below the level of inflation as part of its anti-inflation strategy. As a result, Conservative party opposition to council housing hardened rapidly during the mid-1970s. The rightward drift in Conservative thought culminated in their commitment to 'rolling back the frontiers of the state' and to a reassertion of the role of the market as a means of increasing freedom of choice. In housing, this meant the expansion of owner occupation and the revival of private renting, and a halt to the rise of the council sector and council housing expenditure. The sale of council housing was an ideal policy which killed these two birds with one stone.

Harloe and Paris (1984) have interpreted sales of council housing and the cuts in council housing spending in terms of growing fiscal austerity and the pressure to reduce state spending and the Public Sector Borrowing Requirement. They point to the fact that Labour also carried out substantial cuts in council housing in 1976 in the wake of the IMF (International Monetary Fund) crisis. This is true, but I would argue that the scale and nature of the cuts implemented under the Conservative Government is quantitatively and qualitatively different and reflect a very different set of social and political priorities from the reduction of state spending *per se*. Whereas Labour cut housing expenditure by approximately 18 per cent, the Conservative Government cut housing expenditure by 64 per cent in real terms between 1979–80 and 1988–9. Between 1979–80 and 1983–4 housing accounted for some 75 per cent of all public expenditure cuts (Forrest and Murie, 1987a). At the same time mortgage interest tax relief has grown to £5 billion in 1986–7 – double the £2.4 billion spending on public housing. What has occurred is arguably not a reduction in state housing expenditure, but a *reorientation* which has favoured owner occupation at the expense of council housing. To the extent that this is correct, fiscal austerity has not been the principal motive force behind Conservative housing policy.

The Objectives of Conservative Housing Policy

Council house sales and the expansion of owner occupation represent a cornerstone of the Conservatives' 'housing' policy and Malpass (1986) suggested that it is better seen as a 'tenure' policy rather than a housing policy. Margaret Thatcher clearly sees the growth of owner occupation as central to the creation of a mass property-owning democracy which will foster greater self-reliance, give more people a 'stake in the system' and wean the electorate away from the siren song of socialism. The Conservatives have been willing to pay a high financial price in terms of lower revenue from sales and a higher burden of mortgage interest tax relief to achieve this goal. They have even been prepared to 'massage' estimates of the potential financial benefits from council house sales (see Kilroy, 1982). Michael Heseltine, the then Secretary of State for the Environment, stated in 1980 that 'as a matter of policy they (the Government) wanted to encourage owner occupation and give very substantial fiscal incentives to do that' (quoted in Whitehead, 1983). This policy of subsidised owner occupation has been a principal factor underlying the decline of the private rented sector (Hamnett and Randolph, 1988), but the Conservatives have taken the view that the abolition of rent control and the creation of a free market will lead to the revival of the private rented sector. This is highly unlikely and, in general, ideology rather than economics has been the key determinant of Conservative housing policies since 1979 (Hamnett, 1987).

While it may seem inconsistent for a government committed to market forces to offer discounts on council housing and tax relief on mortgage interest, Farmer and Barrell (1981) argue that 'the apparent inconsistency arises from an attempt to elide two quite distinct policy objectives: that of developing a vigorous free-market economy with as little government interference as possible, and that of guaranteeing the fundamental conditions for the existence of such an economy' (p. 329). This is precisely what the Government have attempted to achieve by promoting the growth of owner occupation and reducing the size of the council sector.

As the annual rate of sales has fallen from its 1982 peak of 200,000, so the Government has increased the size of the discount and reduced the length of residence qualification in an effort to stimulate demand. The maximum discount for flats is now 70 per cent and some Conservatives have suggested that if council housing cannot be sold it should be given away. The alternative, as some Conservative-controlled local authorities have realised, is to sell whole estates to private landlords and developers. The power to do this, and to evict tenants from their homes if necessary, was included in the 1986 Housing and Planning Act. The Housing Act 1988 extends this by proposing that council tenants should be able to choose their landlords, and recent Conservative Ministers of Housing – John Patten and William Waldegrave – have both suggested that large-scale state landlordism is redundant. As William Waldegrave put it: 'It is an oddity confined largely to Britain among European countries that the State goes on landlording on this scale' (*Independent*, 29 August 1987).

The Government have also substantially reduced the autonomy of local councils to determine their own housing policy in several key respects. First, the Housing Act 1980 gave tenants a right to buy irrespective of local housing conditions, and councils who attempted to resist this were threatened with the imposition of government Housing Commissioners (Forrest and Murie, 1985). Second, the DoE (Department of the Environment) severely curtailed local government financial autonomy in several ways (see also Chapter 5). First, the DoE announced a series of large rent increases for council housing. Although these were non-mandatory (local rent policies being the prerogative of local government), they were *assumed to have been implemented* for the sake of calculating the level of central government subsidy for each local authority. Whether or not local authorities made the increases, their level of central government subsidy was reduced as though they had. In addition, council spending was severely restricted, and councils who exceeded these limits were subjected to the progressive loss of central government rate support grant.

As a result, some Labour-controlled councils who refused to raise rents or cut expenditure and services lost most or all of their rate support grant. This led these councils sharply to increase local rates to make good the revenue deficit. This then resulted in the rate-capping of some overspending councils and, more recently, in the development of creative accountancy schemes whereby councils have sought to raise cash by selling assets to banks and leasing them back. This has now been stopped, along with most new council building. Local government has been effectively brought to heel and forced to implement central government policy on housing. But to appreciate the impact of some of these changes in housing policy on the geography of housing they must be located in the context of the tenurial and geographical transformation of British housing since 1919.

The Changing Tenure Structure and Geography of British Housing

The tenurial structure and the geography of British housing have seen a profound transformation since 1919. The geography of Britain's housing was not laid down uniformly at a single point in time. Like the geological map, it is the result of phases of deposition, uplift, denudation and metamorphism which have been differentially superimposed upon one another. In the 'pre-Cambrian' period, up to the First World War, the geography of housing in Britain varied according to its size, rent and living conditions. It also varied sharply by class. Whereas the middle and upper classes lived in spacious, well-equipped houses, the majority of the working class often shared badly overcrowded and poorly equipped houses. But in one crucial respect, that of tenure, the housing market was largely homogeneous. In 1919, 90 per cent of households in Britain rented from private landlords. Council housing was negligible – 25,000 dwellings at most, and only 10 per cent of households owned their own home. Although there were regional variations, private renting was the dominant housing tenure across most of the country. Britain may have been two nations in many respects, but it was one nation in terms of housing tenure.

The dominance of private renting was eroded by a combination of factors. The building of new privately rented houses had begun to decline from 1910 onwards as profitability declined. This decline was accelerated, but not created, by the introduction of rent control in 1915. Then in 1919 Lloyd George introduced state-subsidised council housing. Despite political vicissitudes, council housing grew to 1.1 million dwellings in England and Wales by 1939 – some 10 per cent of the total stock (Jennings, 1971). Owner occupation grew even more rapidly. Between 1919 and 1939 some 3 million new private dwellings, most built for suburban owner occupation, were constructed in England and Wales (Marshall, 1968), increasing the proportion of home owners to over 25 per cent. As a result of these changes, the dominantly privately rented inner cities were encircled by rings of suburban owner occupation interspersed with the occasional council estate.

The relative importance of the two tenures varied regionally as did the rate of new house building. Just as unemployment in the 1930s was highest in the older industrial regions and lowest in the Midlands and the South East, so too the private housing boom of that decade had an uneven impact. In England and Wales the number of houses rose by just over half between the wars. But the increase was 76 per cent in the South East, 47 per cent in the North and only 28 per cent in Wales. In Middlesex, Surrey and Hertfordshire the housing stock more than doubled. The tenure mix was also very variable. In the South East no less than 82 per cent of all new housing was privately built, and the South East also accounted for 45 per cent of all new private building between the wars. In the Midlands and the North, council housing accounted for a higher proportion of new building than in the South East – 33 to 40 per cent (Marshall, 1968).

In the post-war period the main features of this new geography of housing were intensified on a much larger geographical scale. Between 1945 and 1975, 3.9 million new owner-occupied dwellings were added to the housing stock of England and Wales, the majority built on the urban periphery or in commuter villages – reinforcing the suburban ring of owner occupation. Over the same period, 3.9 million council dwellings were built, and it should be stressed that of the standing council stock in 1975, 80 per cent had been built post-war. But while some were built on the urban periphery or in new towns, a large proportion of council building during the late 1950s and 1960s took the form of high-rise blocks of flats which were actively promoted by central government and subsidised by the DoE (Dunleavy, 1981). These were strongly concentrated in the inner cities, and the distinction between suburban houses and inner city blocks of flats has played a key role in the geography of sales since 1979. In addition some 4 million private rented dwellings have been sold for owner occupation since 1919.

As a result of these changes, the proportion of owner-occupied households rose to 59 per cent by 1979, households renting from a council grew to 31 per cent, while private renting was reduced to 10 per cent of households: a complete reversal of the situation in 1919. The resultant improvement in housing quality and facility provision, if not in environmental terms, for the majority of the population has been immense. The absolute numbers and proportions of households living in houses deemed unfit for human habitation, sharing dwellings and basic facilities such as kitchens, bathrooms and toilets and living in overcrowded conditions, have all declined sharply since the early 1950s. Donnison and Ungerson (1981) claim that the development of council housing since the war has broken the link between poverty and poor housing. This claim is debatable but the scale of the transformation is not.

The Social and Geographical Consequences of Thatcherite Policies

Murie (1982) argued that the changes in government policy:

> imply a new era for council housing in which a concentration on special needs is accompanied by a reduction in the size of the council stock, a minimal rate of new building, a decline in the quality of new and existing council dwellings and a reduction in subsidy for council housing. It involves a rejection of the ideas of optimal public service provision and a reassertion of the role of the market backed by a minimal poor law service.

Murie's predictions have subsequently been proved correct. The level of new council building has fallen to 30,000 per year, most of which is special needs housing of one kind or another. And, as a result of council house sales, the overall size of the council stock has fallen from a peak of 6.5 million dwellings (31 per cent of the stock) in 1979 to 5.8 million dwellings (26 per cent of the stock) at the end of 1987. Waiting lists and homelessness have increased, and because sales have been concentrated in the better parts of the stock, in suburban houses rather than inner city flats (Forrest and Murie, 1986a), and because money for repairs has been very restricted, the condition of the council stock has declined. The Association of Metropolitan Authorities estimated in 1985 that some £20 billion was required to bring the council sector up to standard (Cantle, 1986). The Government have made it clear that money will not be forthcoming on anything but a very limited scale and, as a result, conditions will continue to decline.

This may represent more of an opportunity than a problem for the Government because the rate of individual council house sales has now dropped sharply from the levels of 1981 and 1982 as those who were able to buy have done so. Because local councils lack the financial resources to repair defective blocks, they are now faced with the choice of either seeing an increasing proportion of their stock falling into disrepair and lying empty or selling off parts of it to private developers in order to raise cash to repair the remainder (Forrest and Murie, 1986b). This increases the rate of sales which the Government welcomes on both tenurial and political grounds. In some Conservative-controlled London boroughs such as Westminster and Wandsworth, the councils have taken the lead in selling blocks to developers (*The Guardian*, 4 September 1987; *Roof*, July 1986). In Wandsworth this is an acknowledged part of the council's strategy to restructure the borough socially and politically, as highly paid owners replace low-paid tenants and Conservative voters replace Labour voters. The chairman of the property sales committee was quoted in *The Guardian* (19 June 1987) as saying: 'I don't think any of us have ever tried to hide the fact that we have sought not just to run Wandsworth more efficiently but to change Wandsworth into a Conservative borough ... a borough that will stay Conservative regardless of national swings'. It was widely suggested in the press that similar social changes may have helped Labour lose the marginal seats of Battersea and Hammersmith in the 1987 general election. This process of social restructuring through changes in the price and tenure of the housing stock has also taken place on a large scale in Docklands: Goodwin (forthcoming) terms it 'the replacement of a surplus population'.

The social restructuring of the housing market by tenure has been intensified by Thatcherism, but it has actually been going on since the early 1960s. Prior to the rapid expansion of owner occupation from the late 1950s onwards, council housing was seen as a highly desirable alternative to private renting. But because rents were relatively high and supply was limited, it tended to be dominated by skilled manual workers. The less-skilled and lower-paid were concentrated in the large private rented sector. As the private rented sector contracted and the council and owner-occupied sectors grew in the 1960s and 1970s, the highly-skilled and better-paid were channelled into owner occupation and the less-skilled and the poor went into council renting. Simultaneously, some skilled manual workers left the council sector for owner occupation. As a result, the social composition of the two tenures diverged markedly whether in terms of socio-economic composition, income, or concentration of supplementary benefit recipients (Hamnett, 1984; Bentham, 1986; Forrest and Murie, 1987b). All measures show a rising degree of socio-tenurial polarisation and a trend towards what has been variously termed the social residualisation or the pauperisation of council housing (Malpass, 1983; Forrest and Murie, 1987b). Although these trends pre-date Thatcherism, they have been intensified and reinforced by council house sales to better-off tenants, the rises in council rents and the decline of the stock. They have also led to increased geographical polarisation, as the poor and less-skilled are concentrated in the less attractive remaining inner city and peripheral housing estates, and suburban owner occupation expands (Hamnett, 1987).

The Government's solution to the problem of decaying council estates is transfer to the private sector for renovation, and the Housing Act, 1988 provided for both a tenant choice of landlord and the establishment of Housing Action Trusts which will take over estates from local councils for renovation and partial sale. The declared rationale for allowing tenants to choose their own landlord is that this will increase tenant choice and break up large bureaucratic and inefficient local authority landlords. The underlying reason is to break up the council sector and transfer large parts of it to private or quasi-social ownership. During 1988 several Conservative-controlled councils were negotiating with housing associations for the sale and transfer of their entire housing stock; this is likely to grow.

What is certain is that by reducing the number of units available for low-income households, sales will exacerbate the growing problem of homelessness. The Greve Report (1986) calculated that the number of households accepted as homeless by local authorities under the 1977 Homeless Persons Act has increased 700 per cent in London from 1970 to 27,000 in 1985. This excludes the large number of ineligible homeless single persons sleeping rough. Because of the cuts in new council building and the low level of new lettings, two-thirds of the households accepted as homeless are first placed in temporary accommodation and approximately half of these are placed in private bed-and-breakfast accommodation – the new slums of the 1980s. An increasing number of hoteliers and landlords have seen the profit potential of this market and expanded provision accordingly.

The number of households in bed-and-breakfast accommodation in London at any one time has risen from 1,000 in 1981 to 4,000 in 1985, and the length of stay varies from a few days to a year or more. This accommodation is very expensive, and as the cost of such accommodation is generally higher than allowed for in social security payments, London boroughs have been making top-up payments estimated by Walker (1987) to average £92 per week per household in 1984–5 – a total of £15 million per year. Walker shows that the estimated annual cost of building new council housing for homeless households in London is much less than the cost of paying for bed and breakfast, half as much for family-type housing, but councils are prevented from building by the financial limits placed on them by central government.

Inequalities in the Owner-Occupied Housing Market

The growth of owner occupation – from 11.8 million dwellings in 1979 to 14.1 million in mid-1987 – represents a triumph of Thatcherism. After the decline in new private building in 1980 to a low of 99,000 dwellings, a level not seen since the collapse of the owner-occupied market in 1974, the level of building has continued to increase steadily and in 1987 it reached 190,000. But the level of new building has been extremely geographically uneven. In 1985 the South East accounted for 38 per cent of new private building, compared to under 30 per cent between 1974 and 1980 (Figure 12.1). While the share of the South West and East Anglia has increased

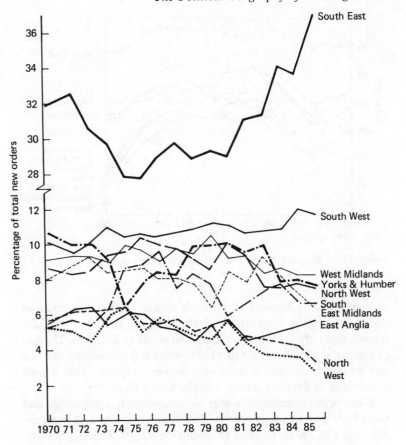

Figure 12.1   The regional distribution of new private house building, 1970–85

slightly since 1980, the share of most other regions has dropped sharply.

This geographical unevenness is also reflected in the large gap which has opened up from 1983 onwards in regional house prices and rates of house-price inflation. This gap is a long-standing one. But whereas its size tended to fluctuate cyclically in the 1970s – at its peak in periods of rapid house-price inflation and at a minimum in periods of lower inflation – it has widened considerably during the mid/late 1980s (Figure 12.2). In 1971–3 and 1979–80 the price of the

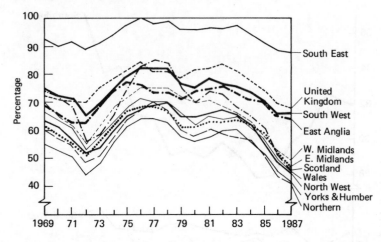

Figure 12.2   Regional house prices as a percentage of London's, 1969–87

average house in London was double that of the average house in the North and in Yorkshire and Humberside. In 1976–7 the difference was only 1.5 times but in 1987 it stood at 2.7 times. The size of the gap is all the more remarkable when it is considered that the mix of properties varies markedly between regions, with a high proportion of flats in London and the South East.

When prices of terraced houses are compared, it is noticeable that these vary by a factor of four – £20,000 in Yorkshire and Humberside and £79,300 in London (Nationwide Anglia Building Society, 1987; Nationwide Building Society, 1987; Hamnett, 1988).

Four related problems arise from this geographical unevenness in the owner-occupied market. First, Thorns (1982) has argued that there is a dual owner-occupied market in Britain which parallels the differences in regional employment, incomes and prosperity, and reinforces the social and geographical division of Britain into 'two nations'. Recent work has confirmed the close statistical relationship between owner-occupied house prices and general labour market and economic conditions in different labour market areas of Britain (Champion, Green & Owen, 1988).

The second problem is that of labour mobility. While unemployment remains high in the North, there is evidence of labour shortages in the South East (Incomes Data Services, 1988). But, because house prices are high, private rented accommodation is scarce and expensive (Hamnett and Randolph, 1988), and council rented property is in short supply, it is very difficult to move South in search of work. This clearly demonstrates the failure of the private housing market to move towards equilibrium, as many neo-classical economists suggest. Their response, and that of the Conservative government, is to argue that the imperfections in the market are the result of excessive controls (Minford *et al.*, 1987). The solution put forward in the 1987 Housing Bill is the removal of rent control to allow rents to rise to economic levels and supply to come back into the market. But while the returns and rents on private rented housing are determined by prices in the subsidised owner-occupied market this is unlikely to work. Once again, free-market ideology has triumphed over economics.

The third problem is that of housing affordability in London and the South East. The house price:income ratio has always been higher in London and the South East than elsewhere, but the gap has widened very markedly since the early 1980s (Nationwide Building Society, 1987). Figure 12.3 shows that the ratio of house prices to household incomes of borrowers from the Nationwide Building Society in the South East had risen from around 3.0 in the early 1980s to 4.0 in 1987. In the northern regions the ratio has remained constant at around 2–2.5. Given that the price paid by the average first-time buyer in London in 1987 was £47,000 this means that

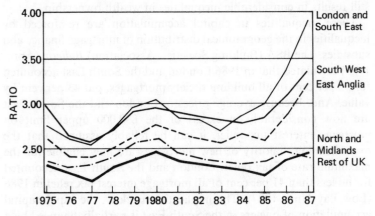

Figure 12.3   Ratio of house prices to incomes: Nationwide borrowers, 1975–87

many potential first-time buyers will have either been squeezed out of the market entirely or forced to club together to purchase a house or flat collectively. Until the 1988 budget abolished the tax loophole, single people were allowed to claim separate tax relief on the same house.

Fourthly, rapid house price inflation in the South East has generated large potential capital gains which have increased inequalities in wealth ownership between owners and non-owners and between owners in the North and South. In 1970 the average house price in Britain was £5,000. In late 1987 it had reached £50,000 – an increase of 900 per cent. At current prices, a buyer in 1970 would now have a capital gain of £45,000 and a buyer in 1981 would have a gain of £25,000. None of these gains would have accrued to tenants. The regional differences in capital accumulation are even more marked. A buyer in London in 1970 would have paid £6,800 on average. In 1987 the average price of property bought in London was £80,000 – a capital gain of £73,000. Given that an increasing proportion of dwellings now bought in London are flats, this considerably understates the capital gains made by a house buyer in 1970. In the North and in Yorkshire and Humberside the average capital appreciation in the same period has been about £26,000 – a third or a quarter of that in London. As a result, existing owners in London now have large capital assets which can be realised and disposed of in several ways. While this capital accumulation arguably represents enforced savings through high mortgage payments, it still results in considerable inequalities in wealth ownership.

These inequalities in capital accumulation are reinforced by inequalities in the geographical distribution of mortgage finance and subsidies. The BSA (Building Societies' Association) *Bulletin* (April, 1987) calculated that in 1986 London and the South East accounted for 33 per cent of all building society mortgages, but 43 per cent by value. And, because average prices in London and the South East are now considerably in excess of the £30,000 upper limit on mortgage interest tax relief, it can be reliably assumed that the overwhelming majority of new mortgages are now eligible for the maximum rate of tax relief. London and the South East accounted for no less than 41 per cent of all mortgage interest tax relief in 1986 (Low Pay Unit, 1987). The implication is clear: the rapid capital accumulation of owners in the South East is partially financed by a redistribution from tax payers in the less affluent parts of Britain.

This amounts to a hidden regional policy towards owner occupiers in the South East.

Conclusions

It has been argued that Thatcherite housing policy represents a radical break with the policies pursued by previous governments. The traditional, if sometimes reluctant, acceptance of a role for both owner occupation and the council sector has been replaced by a private sector housing policy which stresses owner occupation, the revitalisation of the private landlord, and a greater role for housing associations and other forms of quasi-social housing to replace council rented housing. The public rationale for this policy is to increase choice in the housing market. This is very desirable in principle, but the way the Government has gone about this is imposing major constraints on the operation of local councils, by dismantling the council sector at a rapid rate and by increasing the subsidies to owner occupation. This is not the maximisation of choice, but the reshaping of the structure of constraints and opportunities in such a way as to propel people into the private sector. The reality is likely to be a reduction of choice, as households are forced either into owner occupation or, for those unable to afford it, into renting from private landlords. This is a return to Victorian values with a vengeance. If the landlords are housing associations or building society ventures such as the new Nationwide 'Quality Street', and the rents are subsidised in some way, there is a possibility that the new arrangements may work. But, as with the restructuring of the economy in the early 1980s and the associated rise in unemployment, the transitional social effects of the Government's attempt to restructure housing provision in Britain are proving severe for millions of people.

13
Commercialisation and Centralisation: Towards a New Geography of Health Care

John Mohan

Introduction

It is easy to exaggerate both the extent of consensus surrounding the NHS (National Health Service) and the unity of the political forces which brought it about; after all, the Conservative opposition voted against the Bill introducing the NHS on its third reading, an almost unprecedented indication of a party's total opposition to the principle of a Bill. In similar vein, it is also possible to underestimate the extent to which there has, since 1979 and especially since 1983, been a radical departure in health policy. The Government has persistently proclaimed its support for the NHS, and some commentators, for example Klein (1984), have been persuaded that the 'reality of politics', notably public support for the NHS and the influence of powerful vested interests, have prevented fundamental change. On this view, change has been marginal: administrative reforms, limited increases in funding, and small concessions to private health care represent piecemeal change which contrasts sharply with the strident rhetoric of at least some Conservative spokespersons (Klein, 1984). Here I extend the critique of Klein's position developed by Davies (1987), for whom Britain is presently entering an age of 'welfare pluralism'. If anything, Britain is entering an age of 'welfare commercialism' in which, while superficially little has changed, the ground has systematically been prepared for fundamental change in the concept of a comprehensive health service, the way this service is funded and managed, and the roles of private and public, formal and informal sources of care in such a service.

It is worthwhile recalling that there were sound technical and political reasons why all political parties agreed on the necessity of a comprehensive health care service during the Second World War. Technically, the pre-war part-state, part-private health care 'system' offered a patchwork of *ad hoc* developments, was uneven in quality, and was unevenly distributed geographically (Abel-Smith, 1964). Full state funding was regarded as the only way to provide comprehensive health care, since demonstrably neither private charity (the voluntary hospitals) nor municipal effort (the local authority hospitals) had done so.

Commentators differ on the relative importance of political parties, the medical profession and individual politicians in creating the NHS, but there is general agreement on the progressive, reformist character of the service. However, that reform is limited. The NHS has always been curative, hierarchical and oriented towards acute hospital care (Doyal, 1979). There was never any serious challenge to the economic power of those private sector activities dependent on health care, such as the pharmaceutical companies, nor has there been a commitment to the elimination of class inequalities in health status. For many critics these points demonstrate the class character of the NHS (e.g. Navarro, 1978).

Nevertheless the basic principle of the NHS – access to health care shall be guaranteed for all in need of it, irrespective of ability to pay – remains substantially unchallenged. However, I argue that if the NHS itself remains substantially intact, it is being run on ever-more commercial lines; that, while a commitment to the elimination of spatial inequality in the distribution of NHS revenue resources is being pursued, since 1983 this has been a zero-sum game in which redistribution is taking place at the expense of certain geographical areas; and that a novel departure has been the open encouragement of private provision of health care. These three departures point towards a system in which market criteria play a growing role in determining access to health care.

Commercialisation and Centralisation: the Funding and Management of Health Care

All governments have increased NHS resources in real terms (even if the extent of growth has been questioned (e.g. House of Commons,

1988)). Recent policies betray an overriding concern with the limitations of public funds and an emphasis on the need for non-Exchequer sources of revenue. Furthermore, the novelty of recent reorganisations of NHS management lies in their commercial inspiration and character. These developments may prefigure a market-based reform of the whole service.

Rising NHS costs have plagued all governments. Wartime estimates were hopelessly optimistic, and NHS expenditure appeared regularly on the Cabinet agenda between 1948 and 1951, ultimately leading to the famous split within the Labour Government regarding the imposition of prescription charges at a time of rising defence expenditure. Subsequently an inquiry into the cost of the NHS refuted charges of extravagance, criticised the limited spending on health care, and recommended an expanded programme of capital investment to improve efficiency (Guillebaud Committee, 1956). By 1957 the Conservative Cabinet was concerned about whether the country could continue to afford comprehensive health care, to the point where the introduction of charges for some services (e.g. hospital boarding charges) was debated (see Webster, 1988). Despite this in 1962 the MacMillan Government announced the largest-ever capital development programme in the NHS (Ministry of Health, 1962), and from the 1950s to the late 1970s the NHS seemed to have entered a period of stability.

During this period, expenditure on the NHS grew steadily, although spending on health care as a proportion of Britain's GNP was consistently low in comparison to other nations. The Royal Commission on the NHS in 1979 saw no case for a departure from the system of tax-based finance, however. At first this seemed to be accepted by the 1979–83 Conservative Government. Their election pledges to honour public sector wage settlements agreed under the outgoing Government meant that there were actually substantial increases in NHS expenditure in their first years of office. However, private health care was encouraged in several ways and health authorities were exhorted to take account of voluntary and domestic sources of care in developing services, suggesting a move towards a 'mixed economy' of health care in which District Health Authorities (DHAs) play 'a coordinative, almost entrepreneurial role' (Davies, 1987: 306).

There were also attempts to examine alternative sources of funds for the NHS. Right-wing policy institutes argued for expanding charges for services and increasing competition within the service (e.g. Adam Smith Institute, 1981). In 1982 the Central Policy Review Staff suggested reducing public expenditure on health care by introducing charges for visits to GPs and hospital stays, and – in the longer term – by replacing the NHS with an insurance-based system. A well-publicised leak of this document extracted the Prime Minister's pledge that 'the NHS is safe with us', although some Conservative MPs felt that the 1983 election 'should, and could, have been won without that pledge' (Bow Group, 1983).

The validity of that pledge remained open to doubt. Following the 1983 general election events showed clearly that the Government was prepared, with the cushion of an increased parliamentary majority, both to curtail the rate of growth of NHS expenditure and to dictate the way health authorities spent their resources. Within six months of the election, the following happened: a 1 per cent across-the-board reduction in the budgets of health authorities; revised long-term revenue growth assumptions, involving real reductions in the allocations for the Thames RHAs (see below); staff reductions; and the introduction of competitive tendering for ancillary services.

Further indications that public funds are to be limited have been the steady increases in prescription charges and the 1987 Health and Medicines Bill, which empowers health authorities to engage in income-generating activities to supplement their NHS allocations. Charitable finance has also been encouraged: witness the appeal launched by the world-famous Great Ormond Street Children's Hospital for funds to cover that proportion of the cost of redevelopment which will not be met by the Government – an indication, perhaps, that where possible, funding will be off-loaded on to voluntary and private effort. Whether the NHS is 'underfunded' is not the issue here: the crucial point is the systematic attempt to place more of the burden of providing health care on the private sector.

One strand of Conservative policy has thus been to stress the limits on state funds and therefore to encourage alternatives. Another, possibly more insidious, has been radically to alter the nature of management of health care. Here Government policies have been shaped by a perception that the public sector is inherently inefficient. The administrative reforms of 1982 removed one tier of NHS administration (DHSS, 1979) but did not introduce any new management methods. The Griffiths Report (DHSS, 1983) did: it recommended the installation of general managers, each with clearly defined responsibility for a particular unit and who were required to foster financial control and to monitor and review performance.

The emphasis on efficiency is central to Government strategy and is underpinned by a belief that extra volumes of services can be generated through higher levels of performance. To this end DHAs had 0.5 per cent of their budgets ('efficiency savings') deducted at source in the financial years 1982–3 and 1983–4. Centrally determined efficiency savings are no longer insisted upon, but all authorities must now agree 'cost improvement' programmes. These are now crucial to the financial viability of DHAs – indeed they are perhaps the only way they can develop new services, not least because of the systematic (until 1988) underfunding of NHS pay awards. The emphasis in all these developments is on *self help*: health authorities must generate resources internally through greater efficiency. These policies can be bracketed with the new systems of 'performance indicators' as 'quasi-market discipline(s) for those parts of the public sector that could not be privatised or subjected to the sanitising effect of the trusty market' (Pollitt, 1986: 319).

This implicit commercialisation has been accompanied by a centralisation of decision-making. This has been explicit in some cases, for example ministerial interference in privatisation of ancillary services (Ascher, 1987), in hospital closure decisions (London Health Emergency, 1987), or in the imposition of reduced staffing levels (Mohan and Woods, 1985). Elsewhere it has been implicit: for example, health authorities have been directed to attain targets for particular operations (hip replacements or coronary artery bypass grafts), while central control is facilitated through formal annual reviews of regional, district, unit and even individual performance, the effect of which is usually to specify quantitative targets on particular programmes (e.g. to make savings of a specified size through competitive tendering, or to rationalise or develop services in a particular way). If performance was a neutral concept, this would be unobjectionable, but absent from the whole range of performance measures to date have been measures of outcome or of consumer satisfaction, leading critics to observe that performance measurement is narrowly conceived to conform to centrally determined notions of efficiency (Pollitt, 1986). It is not that there is no scope for improvements in service delivery, nor is performance assessment undesirable. Rather, there is a limit to what health authorities can do within their finite budgets, and – more fundamentally – greater dependence on private sources of funds and on private-sector management methods seems to herald a move towards some sort of market-based reform of the NHS.

Spatial Resource Allocation and Territorial Politics in the NHS

Despite the egalitarian aims of the NHS, initially there was no sustained attempt to remove spatial inequalities in the distribution of NHS resources. There was a 'steady stream of criticism' of the uneven pattern of hospital provision from various Regional Hospital Boards, but resource allocations had been dictated largely by the 'inherited pattern' and inequalities had 'become entrenched' by the late 1950s (Webster, 1988: 292–8), due to the incremental budgeting system adopted in the absence of any objective measure of 'need' for health care, and in a context of limited resource growth. Although the 1962 Hospital Plan was primarily aimed at modernising the acute hospital system, it also sought to redistribute resources through differential capital investment, though its implementation was curtailed by public expenditure cuts and political disagreements on hospital closures.

The 1964–70 Labour Government attempted to adjust regional revenue allocations to begin to remove inequalities, but only in 1976 was any serious attempt made to allocate resources in a manner responsive to need. The Resource Allocation Working Party (RAWP) related existing resource allocations to the estimated needs of health authorities for services (DHSS, 1976). Broadly, the Thames RHAs were deemed to be overfunded while much of the north and west of the country was underfunded. Between 1976 and 1983 redistribution took place by differential growth: all RHAs received growth in their budgets but some received more than others so that, over time, interregional differences would be ironed out, while easing the pace of change in the 'overfunded' RHAs – principally the Thames RHAs, covering London and South East England.

This picture changed dramatically in 1983: within two months of the 1983 general election, the Government had cut the budget for the Hospital and Community Health Services (HCHS) by 1 per cent and announced new long-term growth assumptions, under which the Thames RHAs were to lose, in real terms, between 0.3 and 0.5 per cent of their budgets each year to the mid-1990s. Hence growth in the underfunded regions was occurring only at the expense of actual reductions in the budgets of the overprovided regions. Even in 1984 this was causing serious difficulties, and the Social Services Committee concluded that, given the limited growth in the NHS's revenue budget, 'it may be unwise to expect the RAWP process to go much further' (House of Commons, 1984). Partly in recognition of this, and partly to offset the adverse publicity caused by hospital closures and service reductions in the Thames RHAs, these regions have more recently been allocated marginal percentage increases in their revenue allocations. They have also been granted what have euphemistically been termed 'transitional allocations' of additional money to bail them out towards the end of the financial years 1986–7 and 1987–8. Consequently redistribution is now a zero-sum game, with some RHAs gaining only at the expense of others. Klein (1984) argues that this is a necessary consequence of the politics of retrenchment and recession, and implicitly congratulates the Government on achieving at least some growth in NHS resources and so giving the service priority. In so doing he ignores the crucial point that other branches of public expenditure – notably defence and law and order – were accorded much higher priority: differential cuts were only necessary because the Government chose not to give the NHS the scope to manage its services without substantial net transfers from the Thames RHAs.

Such resource transfers may be manageable at the RHA scale, but disparities between present and target levels of revenue between DHAs are much greater, budgets are smaller, and much of the revenue budget is spent in acute general hospitals, especially in inner urban areas, whence substantial net transfers of resources are taking place. Some DHAs are losing up to 2 per cent of their revenue budgets in real terms each year. This is putting severe pressure on DHAs, whose adverse financial circumstances necessitate a rapid run-down in acute hospital capacity. Regional and sub-regional specialty services receive some financial protection in resource allocation formulae, and specialist services are vociferously defended by hospital medical staff. Hence the search for economies has focused on local acute services. Considering only non-psychiatric acute services, 8,730 beds (6.3 per cent of the total) were lost in England between 1983 and 1986; 159 out of 191 DHAs experienced reductions in bed numbers. In some places these reductions in hospital capacity have made it almost impossible to admit patients for elective surgery and some DHAs have refused to treat patients referred from outside their designated catchment area for local acute services (Beech *et al.*, 1987). These developments raise the question of whether the NHS is providing comprehensive health care.

One response by DHAs has been to increase patient throughput and intensify the use of hospital beds. This is seen by central government as a symbol of greater efficiency, but paradoxically this may impose additional financial pressure on DHAs. Increased throughput is cash-demanding: as patients are discharged quickly, they spend proportionately less time in hospital recovering and proportionately more of their time receiving treatment – which is the expensive part of hospital costs (House of Commons, 1988). Perversely, therefore, central government demands for efficiency have further exacerbated the financial problems of DHAs from which resources are being transferred. Among the (as yet) unquantified effects of this are the repeat admission of patients who have been discharged prematurely, and the additional costs borne by Social Services departments and by families of those discharged quickly from hospital (see Radical Statistics Health Group, 1987).

Although RAWP's basic aim is to release resources from the 'overprovided' areas to benefit the less well-off parts of England, all is not well, even in RAWP-gaining regions. Surveys have shown that, in the 1986–7 financial year, only 26 out of 148 DHAs would be able to develop their services as planned, owing to the combined effects of underfunded pay awards, the impact of demographic change, and the costs of implementing policies such as community care (National Association of Health Authorities (NAHA), 1986). A worse situation was anticipated for 1987–8, with several DHAs claiming that they were no longer able to make savings without implementing direct cuts in services to patients (NAHA, 1987). In short, the pace of redistribution away from over-target RHAs is forcing health authorities to implement direct cuts in patient services in order to contain expenditure. This situation is unlikely to change, given the present pace of redistribution. Crucially, therefore, over-target districts must still bear the painful costs of rationalisation: there may be minor adjustments to RAWP but these will only slightly reduce the pace of resource redistribution.

Given the scale and pace of change, a key issue is why opposition to Government policies has made almost no impact. Most opposition has taken the form of *ad hoc* anti-cuts campaigns protesting at the closure of individual hospitals, but in some cases opposing the whole thrust of central government policies on the NHS. In some areas, notably London, these campaigns have been backed by local government agencies, and have mobilised vociferous opposition and produced numerous critical documents (Association of London Authorities, 1986; London Health Emergency, 1987). There have been similar campaigns elsewhere (e.g. Newcastle Health Concern, 1986). In terms of the territorial politics of the contemporary political scene, bed reductions and hospital closures mainly affect inner-city areas not known for allegiance to the government. It is debatable whether such electoral considerations have influenced government decisions on the pace of redistribution in the NHS, but they certainly minimise the political costs of change.

Within Parliament, the Labour and other opposition parties have regularly attacked the Government's record on the NHS, but much debate has consisted of territorial pleading, with MPs detailing the latest cuts to affect their constituency and vying with one another to obtain a hearing for their case. Although some backbench Conservative MPs have been involved, their opposition has not yet forced the Government radically to reconsider NHS expenditure and Ministers have retaliated to stories of cuts with tales of service developments in RAWP-gaining areas and of additional hospital activity and increased numbers of staff employed (for a good example of this see Hansard, 26 November 1987, cols. 397–480).

Rather more influential was the willingness of the medical profession to publicise evidence about the local impact of funding difficulties on the NHS. Doctors in several places campaigned publicly against Government policy, and the support given by the Presidents of the Royal Colleges of Medicine added credibility to these claims. Such protests and the mounting media coverage of the NHS 'crisis' seem to have forced the Government to allocate extra resources. Ironically, however, these protests have allowed the Government to claim that these difficulties are symptomatic of the impossibility of ever meeting all the demands for health care, thus permitting radical options to be placed, once again, on the agenda, as in the recent review of the NHS.

In summary, differential cuts, rather than differential growth, are now the order of the day in the NHS; even in RAWP-gaining localities, DHAs are experiencing difficulty in developing services.

Klein (1983) claims that the problems of geographical inequality would resolve themselves, given sufficiently rapid economic growth, yet despite several years' growth, the process of redistribution is still extremely slow and is imposing severe strain in certain areas. As well as these developments, with their spatially concentrated effects, the rapid growth of private health care is adding a new layer to the geography of health services.

Commercialisation and Privatisation: a Two-Tier System?

Although a small private sector continued to exist after the setting up of the NHS in 1948, it covered no more than 1 million people until the early 1970s, and its hospitals were typically run by charitable or non-profit organisations. The key date in its recent growth is 1976: Labour's attempt to abolish paybeds from NHS hospitals created a climate in which private sector developers could invest with confidence in new hospitals, secure in the knowledge that private beds within the NHS were on the way out. The Conservatives simply picked up on this trend and began systematically to encourage growth in private health care, and in non-state finance and provision of services, for three reasons.

First, the Government has regularly stressed the limitations on public funds, blamed the high PSBR for Britain's poor economic performance, and consequently claimed that higher public spending must follow from rather than take precedence over improved national economic performance. For these reasons non-state provision has been welcomed.

Secondly, in terms of the politics of support for Thatcherism, it has been argued that successive governments have pursued a 'two nations' strategy in which they practice a systematic politics of inequality (Jessop *et al.*, 1984; see also Chapter 1). This view sees the 'productive' members of society being rewarded through the market for their contribution to production (e.g. through company-paid private health care schemes), while placing greater responsibility for service provision in private hands creates new material interests in private care (owners of nursing homes, proprietors of private ancillary services, etc.). This expands a constituency with a vested interest in the private sector while eroding the numbers dependent entirely on the NHS.

Thirdly, in terms of the ideology of the 'New Right', emphases on freedom of choice, competition, and individual responsibility are linked to Conservatism's traditional stress on the family and the 'community' as social support networks, and to the New Right's anti-statism and belief in the virtues of the market-place. Hence the expansion of private care creates competition for the NHS while community care draws on untapped, informal sources of support. Implicit in this is a new notion of the state's role in health care in which there are definite limits on what the state can do and there is scope to mobilise other agencies. Several initiatives have flowed from these principles, including support for private acute hospital care, finance of private nursing homes, and 'Care in the Community'.

Taking private acute sector growth first, this is at least partly due to the intended and unintended consequences of Government decisions. Growth has indeed been rapid: over 200 acute hospitals now exist, providing between them over 10,000 beds (Association of Independent Hospitals, 1987). The private acute sector's contribution to hospital activity is no longer marginal: in South West Thames RHA over 20 per cent of all operations in certain specialties are carried out privately (Williams *et al.*, 1984). The character of private hospital care has also changed, with greater commercialisation and, in particular, the entry of multinational hospital chains, to which market leadership has passed (Rayner, 1987).

A more direct form of encouragement of private sector growth has been the expansion of payments to proprietors of private nursing homes for the elderly; these payments now total some £1000 million pounds annually. This direct subsidy to the private sector has produced extremely rapid growth in private nursing homes: there are now over 50,000 beds in such institutions, compared to less than 25,000 in 1982 (DHSS, 1987). In some DHAs, the number of places available in private nursing homes now exceeds the total number of NHS beds.

This has led to speculation about the existence of a *de facto* two-tier health care system. While the total number of beds in private hospitals and nursing homes is some 12 per cent of the NHS total, in some areas – central London and the South Coast – either acute hospital beds or nursing home capacity are larger in the private sector. There are also counties – notably in the Outer Metropolitan Area – where private medical insurance coverage exceeds 15 per cent. Hence there are substantial sections of the population who do not require the NHS save in emergencies. This is a growing political constituency with a material interest in private service provision; the same is true of private proprietors of nursing homes and of commercial ancillary services. The very *irreversibility* of this form of privatisation is its most notable feature: it has established the commercial sector as a permanent presence in the British health arena.

One form of privatisation has thus been the increased role envisaged for *formal* providers of private health care. The Government has also sought to develop *informal* sources of care through the 'Care in the Community' initiative. This is laudable in principle as it involves the de-institutionalisation of long-stay patients and their care in small, less formal settings. However, it has been implemented at a time when health authority and local authority budgets have been so tightly constrained that they have collectively been unable to develop community care services in tandem with the discharge of patients from long-stay hospitals (House of Commons, 1985). The net effect has been to shift the burden of providing accommodation on to the private sector (usually bed-and-breakfast or privately rented accommodation), to transfer the burden of finance on to the non-cash-limited funds of the Social Security budget, a move branded as 'perverse' by the Public Accounts Committee (1988), and to shift the burden of care into the 'private' sphere of the family and community. This not only leads to care being available in unplanned locations and unplanned quantities, it also raises the question of whether all 'communities' are able to provide support for those discharged from long-stay institutions (Audit Commission, 1986).

Conclusions

What is perhaps surprising about the first ten years of the Thatcher governments is the limited and selective change introduced in health care policy. To regard this as evidence of their commitment to and indeed prioritisation of the health service would, however, be a mistake, given (as indicated above) the initiatives which have altered the very character of health care delivery. On funding, the screws have gradually been tightened, especially since 1983, and this has led to the reductions in services which have provoked so much debate on the 'crisis' in the NHS. Yet, paradoxically, the extent of public on the 'crisis' in the NHS. Yet, paradoxically, the extent of public concern at and media coverage about the crisis in the NHS has not only been a political problem for the Government, it has offered the best opportunity yet to effect far-reaching change. Government thinking is moving on two related paths. Firstly they have criticised inefficiencies in the service, highlighting regional and local variations in costs and treatment rates and arguing that this betokens inefficiency; from this will follow examination of options for internal reforms of the way hospitals are funded. Secondly, they have claimed that the problem with the overall funding of health care in Britain lies in the nation's relatively low level of spending on *private health care* compared to other states, and this suggests examination of the possibilities for introducing more private finance into the health care system.

One possible response to inefficiencies in the NHS would be some variant of an 'internal market' scheme, under which health authorities would seek out low-cost providers of hospital care (whether public or private) while having to keep their own costs low in order to attract custom. This would involve a higher level of mobility of patients and the competitive logic underpinning it could bankrupt older hospitals whose outdated capital plant would hinder their ability to compete. Many NHS hospitals would be disadvantaged, and one effect would be to boost the private sector since it has spare capacity and (generally) modern plant and could therefore offer operations at low costs.

Secondly, further steps will be taken to expand non-Exchequer sources of funds for the NHS. The 1987 Health and Medicines Bill has empowered health authorities to raise funds from commercial and charitable sources, and estimates suggest that some £70 million (only 0.3 per cent of annual spending on the NHS) could be so raised. The encouragement of charitable support is also well known but, again, is unlikely to make more than a marginal impact. What these developments will both do, however, is to increase the importance of local effort and finance in the provision of health care, and it seems likely that there will be great variations in the ability of hospitals and health authorities to raise funds in these ways. More far-reaching possibilities seem to be on the agenda. An insurance-based system can be ruled out because of the evidence from the USA that it fails to provide comprehensive coverage, and because of the massive transitional costs of moving to this model. But right-wing commentators are increasingly calling for incentives to individuals to take out private medical insurance and the possibility of people contracting-out of the NHS has been raised. It might be possible to be sanguine about these developments if there was convincing evidence that they were being contemplated for their technical superiority and not as crude political expedients. Moreover, because they are market-based, they will inevitably lead to segmentation and inequality in both social and spatial terms. By provoking the present 'crisis' of funding in the NHS and by creating or strengthening a constituency with a substantial material interest in the private sector, the Government has systematically prepared the ground for much more radical reform. The 1989 White Paper on the NHS proposes much greater competition between health authorities and hospitals, and between the NHS and the private sector. It also reduces local accountability since health authorities will no longer include nominees from local authorities. For many of the Government's critics these developments foreshadow the break-up of the NHS and its replacement, in the 1990s, by a largely private health care system.

Note

I should like to acknowledge the financial support of an Economic and Social Research Council (ESRC) Postdoctoral Research Fellowship, grant no. A23320036, and also the helpful comments of David Smith on an earlier draft of this chapter.

14
Policing the Recession

Nicholas R. Fyfe

Introduction: Police, Politics and Geography

> The practice of policing provides citizens with one of their most
> immediate and tangible experiences of the state.
> (Bradley, Walker and Wilkie, 1986: 203)

The theoretical and substantive importance of this claim has been
surprisingly neglected by political geographers. Despite significant
developments in theorising about the state (see for example Clark
and Dear, 1984) and a widening of the empirical focus of political
geographical studies, the police remain conspicuously absent from
these accounts. By contrast, theoretical developments in political
sociology have re-established the importance of the state's powers of
coercion, a power which is the distinctive resource of the police (see
Giddens, 1985, and Nicholson, 1984), while the images and experiences of contemporary policing on the streets, on picket lines
and at demonstrations have made the police conspicuously present
in everyday life. This neglect of policing in political geography
would appear to be for both political and geographical reasons.

First, there is the popular belief that the police are above politics,
that they are 'the servants of all the people, not the politicians'
(Leslie Curtis, Chairman of the Police Federation, quoted in *The
Standard* 25 May 1983). The notion of political neutrality underpinning this view centres on the police's role in the impartial enforcement of the law and the maintenance of order. However, the realities
of limited resources, information and time mean that the law must
be enforced selectively: 'political decisions must be made about
which laws to enforce, when, where and against whom' (S. Smith,
1986a: 102). These decisions are taken within a constitutional

structure insulating the police from direct control by elected authorities. This structure, comprising central government, local government and the police, is described in the second section. The restructuring of relations between these three parties during the recession, described in the third section, demonstrates that policing in Britain is, however, unequivocally political.

Secondly, the notion that policing has a geography sits uncomfortably alongside an image of the police as an organisation which embraces 'a national identity, and turn[s] a unified face towards civil society' (Brogden, 1982: 1). The British policing tradition is, however, founded on localism: there are forty-three separate forces in England and Wales (see Fig. 14.1), eight in Scotland and one in Northern Ireland. This tradition is now being threatened by increasing central government intervention in local policing, transforming the political geography of policing in Britain. This transformation is sketched out in the third section, beginning with the aftermath of the riots in 1981 and then examining the policing of the miners' dispute in 1984–5. In the final section I develop the notion of a geography of policing by considering the contrasting territorial strategies for policing the streets and the growing concern to develop place-specific policies in consultation with the local community. The success of such strategies, however, appears to be compromised by the restructuring of central–local relations identified in the third section. This tension between localism and centralism is rooted in the constitutional context of British policing with which I will begin.

Centralism versus Localism: Policing in its Constitutional Context

The statute of Winchester in 1285 might seem a perverse starting point for discussing policing in the 1980s, but its affirmation of the principle of local collective responsibility for peace-keeping has informed all subsequent police legislation (see Jefferson and Grimshaw, 1984, and Critchley, 1978). Modern professional policing in Britain began in 1829 with the formation of the Metropolitan Police; subsequent legislation established local constabularies in the counties and boroughs of England and Wales. That legislation sustains the commitment to localism, in part to counter nineteenth-century fears inspired by the French Revolution of a state-directed police force. Nevertheless, it also reveals the tightening grip of central

Figure 14.1   Police forces in England and Wales, 1987

government on these local police forces, a phenomenon for which historians offer a variety of interpretations. In the 'orthodox' or 'cop-sided' police histories (for example, Critchley, 1978) this restructuring of central–local relations represents a check on partisan, local interests interfering in impartial law enforcement; in contrast, radical historians (for example, Bunyan, 1976) view the same changes as the centre usurping local democratic control of a key local function (for summaries of these police histories see Reiner, 1985a).

Under the present constitutional arrangements, set out in the Police Act of 1964, this tension between centralism and localism continues. Responsibility for policing in Britain is set within a tripartite structure consisting of central government (via the Home Secretary), local government (via police authorities) and the police (via chief constables). Central government's constitutional relationship with the forty-three local constabularies in England and Wales (see Figure 14.1) is defined in section 28 of the Act, which requires the Home Secretary to 'exercise his powers ... in such manner and to such an extent as appears to him to be best calculated to promote the efficiency of the police.' The powers at his disposal include amalgamating forces, ratifying senior appointments, making regulations on administration and conditions of service, and calling for reports from chief constables. The main lever of central government influence, however, is not legal compulsion but, as in other areas, financial sanction (see Chapter 5) for central government provides 50 per cent of the cost of local policing. This grant can be withheld if the Home Secretary is not satisfied with the efficiency of the force. Indeed, given that 'efficiency' is nowhere defined in the Act it is potentially a highly political construct to 'be defined more or less explicitly in accordance with the influence which the Secretary of State wishes to exert on policing policy' (Weatheritt, 1986: 102).

Against this broad set of central powers, the local components of the tripartite structure are the chief constables and the police authorities. The chief constables have responsibility for the 'direction and control' of the local forces (section 5, Police Act, 1964). These terms are not defined in the Act but in practice chief constables have 'operational autonomy'; they have sole responsibility for enforcing the law in particular cases and in decisions over the allocation and deployment of their resources. While their role in specific instances of law enforcement remains unquestioned, the extent of their autonomy in decision-making over the use of police resources is now being tested as both central government and police authorities attempt to exercise greater influence.

The police authorities (now known as joint boards in the metropolitan areas) are the main form of local representation in policing. They are made up of elected councillors and appointed magistrates in the ratio 2:1, except in Scotland where all members are councillors, and the Metropolitan Police District (which includes Greater London) where the Home Secretary is the police authority. Under the 1964 Police Act each authority has a duty to maintain an 'adequate and efficient' force, and again these terms are undefined. The authority contributes 50 per cent towards the expense of maintaining the local force and must provide buildings and equipment, approve budgets and the force size, appoint senior officers and deal with complaints against them, and may call for reports from the chief constable. All these functions, however, are subject to the Home Secretary's approval. Given the vague and ambiguous character of the Act, the extent to which the police authority can in fact influence the decisions of the chief constable depends largely on the particular working relationship between them (Weatheritt, 1986: 101). In the words of the former Chair of the Merseyside Police Authority: 'the resolution of the built in contradiction between the political obligation to ensure the service is efficient and the professional responsibility for its actual operation has been left to the mercy of circumstance and individual personality' (Simey, 1982: 53).

The distribution of power within this tripartite structure is clearly uneven. The greatest influence lies with the Home Secretary and the chief constables, the latter exercising considerable corporate influence through the Association of Chief Police Officers (ACPO). By contrast, the police authorities have many responsibilities but little authority. With the exception of London, however, where the absence of any locally elected representation in policing has been the focus of campaigns for reform ever since the Metropolitan Police were established, the politicisation of the asymmetries in the 1964 Police Act has been a product of a combination of changes, beginning in the 1960s, in the organisation and style of policing both at a national and local level. Nationally, successive Home Secretaries have used their powers to promote the efficiency of the police by amalgamating forces, reducing the number of constabularies from 158 in 1962 to 43 today. Policing has thus increasingly become 'a tightly integrated, national network of highly professionalised, autonomous police bureaucracies' (Baldwin and Kinsey, 1982: 104). Locally important changes in police strategy have further distanced police from public. The police response to the inexorable rise in crime (a 68 per cent increase in the last ten years) has increasingly been dominated by a 'fire brigade' style of policing, centred on rapid response and lowering the status of the beat bobby. These national and local level changes, and their unintended consequences in terms of deteriorating police–community relations, have clearly occurred unevenly (see S. Smith, 1986b: 134–9). The contours of this 'policing crisis', indexed by poor crime clear-up rates and public disorder, predictably reveal inner-city areas as the places where the gap between the police and sections of the community, particularly ethnic minorities, is at its widest. It was in these areas that concern about the lack of local democratic influence on policing became most acute and where demands for making the police more *accountable* to local representatives were first voiced. When these areas erupted with street violence in 1981, however, it wasn't only local politicians who began to scrutinise their relationship with the police: central government also began to reassess its influence over the local constabularies, initiating a restructuring in the tripartite relationship to which I now turn.

From Scarman to Scargill: Restructuring Central–Local Relations

... the British people watched with horror and incredulity ... scenes of violence and disorder in their capital city, the like of which had not previously been seen in this century in Britain.

(Scarman, 1981, para. 1.2)

The 1981 riots mark a watershed in British policing, prompting important changes in thinking, attitude and policy among the police and central and local government. Here I consider the restructuring of central–local relations initiated by the riots and then further developed by the policing of the miners' dispute.

Scarman and the New Tripartism

In the summer of 1981 outbreaks of civil disorder occurred in many cities across Britain but the most violent clashes were on the streets of Brixton in London, Toxteth in Liverpool, and Moss Side in Manchester. It would be foolish to ignore the spatial coincidence of these riots with areas of high unemployment (Hamnett, 1983), but we should recognise that the competing analyses of the riots tell us more about the ideological points of view of the authors than the reality of the rioting. Whether police abuse of their powers (the 'liberal' thesis) or an alien culture lacking social discipline (the 'conservative' thesis) is accorded causal status (see Lea and Young, 1982) such explanations suffer from an 'empirical emptiness', failing to specify what actually took place (Keith, 1987).

Lord Scarman's explanation and interpretation of events in Brixton had most influence on central government's national response to the riots. He stressed the economic plight of the inner-city communities and in particular the ethnic minorities whose experiences of discrimination in social and political as well as economic life provided a set of *conditions* 'which create a predisposition towards violent protest' (Scarman, 1981, para. 2.38). The disorders themselves 'were essentially an outburst of anger and resentment by young black people against the police' (*ibid.*, para. 3.110). This had occurred in a context where the police had lost the confidence and support of large sections of the local community (*ibid.*, para. 4.1) brought about in part by policing methods, such as use of special squads and the perceived indiscriminate use of 'stop and search' powers. Scarman recognised, however, that a 'basic principle of policing a free society is the need to ensure that the police operate not only within the law but with the support of the community' (*ibid.*, para. 4.60). To ensure that support he noted that under present constitutional arrangements the police were accountable to police authorities, arrangements he believed were satisfactory. The problem, he argued, was the link between consultation and accountability which was 'tenuous to vanishing point in the Metropolitan Police District; [and] more effective, but insufficiently developed, in the police areas outside London' (*ibid.*, para. 5.58). He therefore recommended establishing statutory community–police liaison committees.

This recommendation was incorporated into the Police and Criminal Evidence Act 1984, signalling the beginning of a more interventionist stance by the Government within the tripartite structure. This was made easier because police forces across the country were looking to them to offer short and long-term guidance on how to deal with the consequences of the riots (Weatheritt, 1986: 104). The main mechanism for this increased intervention was however, provided not by legislative change but by increased use of Home Office circulars, produced to inform local constabularies and police authorities of new regulations or administrative changes. Since 1981 the scope of these circulars has increased, prompting speculation that the police are now subject to 'government by circular' (Loveday, 1987: 206). One of the clearest examples of this new climate of central interventionism is Home Office circular 114/83 on *Manpower, Effectiveness and Efficiency in the Police Service*, spelling out to the police that the themes which inform government policy in other activities are to be introduced into policing. The police will be expected to give 'value for money' by setting and evaluating priorities and making effective and efficient use of resources. Indeed, central government's view of the Scarman proposals on consultation is informed by this thinking. The police liaison committees are to encourage 'self help' by informing communities of their responsibilities in activities such as crime prevention, and should enhance 'consumerism' by seeking to adopt policing policies to the identified needs of the local community (see R. Morgan, 1985). This is the key to police effectiveness (for the police depend on the public to solve crimes) and thus to police efficiency. Paradoxically perhaps, this much is common ground to those on the Left and Right of the political spectrum. Disagreement, however, centres on the fact that the Conservative Government believes this can be achieved *within* the tripartite structure: the Left argue there has to be effective local, democratic control of police policy. The refusal of both Scarman and the Government to accept this has fuelled the politicisation of policing at local government level.

In London, where policing has rarely been off the political agenda, Scarman's rejection of proposals for an elected police authority was greeted angrily by the Police Committee of the Greater London Council (GLC). Arguing that Scarman's recommendations 'fell far short of providing a satisfactory system for ensuring the accountability of the police to the community they serve' (Greater London Council, 1982, para. 115), they began a campaign to publicise how the Metropolitan Police are out of democratic control, a campaign taken up locally by Labour borough councils forming their own police committees, and by the GLC funding local police-monitoring groups. Clearly, however, the current constitutional position precludes local government in London from having any more than a marginal influence in policing issues.

Outside London, Scarman hoped that giving police authorities a responsibility for establishing consultative arrangements would lead them to 'act more vigorously and with greater confidence' (Scarman, 1981, para. 5.68). In Liverpool, however, scene of some of the fiercest rioting and where CS gas was used to disperse crowds, the riots themselves encouraged those in local government to re-examine the role of their police authority. The Chair of Merseyside Police Authority commented that the riots meant that 'The question of responsibility suddenly took on an inescapable urgency. Given the riots, could the Authority be said to have fulfilled its duty to ensure the provision of an adequate and efficient force?' (Simey, 1982: 54). The Authority came to the 'painful conclusion' that it had 'failed to fulfil its responsibilities as a vital cog in the machinery for governing police as a public service' (*ibid.*). In trying to correct this, the Labour-controlled Merseyside Police Authority attempted to make more effective use of the tripartite structure, seeking greater influence both with the local chief constable and the Home Secretary. The Authority was, ironically, assisted by central government's commitment to 'value for money' from the police because Home Office Circular 114/1983 recognises that greater efficiency can only be achieved by specifically involving the police authority (Loveday, 1985: 130). This attempt by local government to play a more active role in the tripartite structure has, however, been frustrated for two major reasons. First, the chief constable retains his autonomy over police policy; second, central government can, and has, used its power to overrule local police authority decisions. The policing of the miners' dispute provides clear examples of both these aspects.

The Miners' Dispute 1984–5

> Whilst trying to maintain public order on the coalfields, the police service has unwittingly allowed itself to be portrayed as Margaret Thatcher's puppet . . .
>
>   (Letter from police officer to *The Guardian*, 6 January 1985.)

In interpreting the miners' dispute the explanatory focus has moved from the economic criteria on which pits are run to questions of trade union power (see Chapters 7 and 8). Nevertheless, some of the most enduring images of the dispute are of the clashes between police and pickets, bringing the politicisation of law and order to the centre of attention (see Fine and Millar, 1985). These often violent confrontations reversed a trend of declining picket-line violence which has occurred since the late nineteenth century (Geary, 1985). The increased riot-control training police officers have received since the 1981 riots has left them ill-equipped to deal with the more restricted conflict of the picket line, where they now tend to escalate any violence by the use of public order tactics (*ibid.*, p. 143). The policing of the dispute must, however, also be set in a broader context because from behind the scenes of police officers opposing miners on picket lines emerged a fundamental restructuring of the relations between central government, local police authorities and chief constables.

The organisational police response to the mass picketing was the activation of the National Reporting Centre (NRC) at Scotland Yard. Formed after the 1972 miners' dispute, when the police presence was insufficient to prevent pickets closing the Saltley coke depot, the NRC has only been activated very occasionally since, the main time being during the 1981 riots when 30,000 officers were deployed to aid eight forces (Kettle, 1985: 25). It is controlled by the President of the Association of Chief Police Officers who administers the mutual aid system whereby police officers, grouped in Police Support Units, are sent to forces requesting aid; it is not, ACPO insist, an operational centre. The numbers deployed in the coalfields varied from below 4,000 to over 8,000 officers according to levels of picketing, often staying up to a week in the areas where they were sent. These activities had serious consequences for the police author- ities in the areas both sending and receiving aid.

Activation of the NRC undermined the role of the local police authorities. Aiding authorities never knew from day to day how many officers were available to them, thus cutting across their statutory duty to provide adequate and efficient policing. Margaret Simey described the experience of the Merseyside Police Authority thus:

> What happens is that the NRC ring up our Chief Constable and say 'We want 500 men on standby' and he says 'O.K.' When we passed a formal resolution asking him to cease sending support units to the strike, he laughed out loud at us and said he wasn't going to take any notice.
> (*The Guardian*, 11 August 1984)

The central concern of the police authorities receiving this aid was how to pay for it: in Nottinghamshire, for example, aided by thirty- seven forces, the dispute was costing £2.5 million per week, compared with a normal annual budget of £42 million (Spencer, 1985: 37). Eventually, seven months into the dispute, police authorities were told that they would have to find a maximum of a 0.75 pence rate beyond which any further costs would be met by the Exchequer. In effect, therefore, central government was giving the police a blank cheque. Thus despite the Government's commitment to reduce policing costs, when it suited the Government's political purpose money was not an issue. This immobilised the most effective mechanism a police authority has for influencing policing: budgetary control. Where an authority attempted to exercise such control, the Government intervened. The South Yorkshire Police Authority, for example, rejected a request by their Chief Constable to pay the cost of billeting officers sent in from other forces and so the Attorney General was called in to apply for a judicial review to quash the Authority's decision.

This alliance of central government and chief constables has brought about what has been evocatively described as 'The Eclipse of the Police Authority' (Spencer, 1985). This, combined with the sight of large numbers of police officers travelling across Britain, has raised 'in the fearful British mind the bogey of a national police force' (Scarman, 1985: 11). The role of the NRC and ACPO and their close contact with the Home Office are used as evidence to argue that Britain now has a *de facto* national police force (Reiner, 1985b) or, as more radical commentators claim, a *de jure* National Riot Force (Coulter *et al.*, 1984: 56–7). Others, however, are more cautious, arguing for example that the NRC is the necessary product of a police system which retains a commitment to decentralisation, but which on occasions requires inter-force co-ordination: 'A dozen men, with no independent budget or premises, who coordinate intelligence and requests for manpower, are hardly the nucleus of a national police force' (Lustgarten, 1986: 24–5). Indeed, it is important not to underestimate the commitment of chief constables to their local autonomy. The former Assistant Chief Constable of Derbyshire stressed that operational command of officers sent as aid into his area remained entirely in the hands of the Derbyshire police (Leonard, 1985: 101). Clearly, though, any post-Scarman attempts at achieving a more balanced tripartism were undermined by the policing of the dispute. Local democratic influence in policing is not the only casualty of this restructuring: the traditional image of the local bobby has been threatened by that of 'The Long-Distance Policemen' (Lustgarten, 1985). The post-Scarman commitment to new forms of community policing has occurred in parallel with the provision of more riot training and equipment. It is these aspects of policing the recession which I now consider.

The Changing Beat: Policing the Streets in the 1980s

> The line of riot shields opened up and roughly twenty mounted police galloped out, some to the left and some to the right, scattering demonstrators in all directions. Many protestors fell under the hooves as the police forced the crowd back down the road.
>
> (*Daily Telegraph*, 26 January 1987)

> I adhere strongly to the concept of the police officer on the beat, working closely to the community, as the main point of public contact and the most important crime prevention agent.
>
> (Sir Kenneth Newman, *The Way Ahead, 1986–1988. A Guide to the Strategic Report of the Commissioner of Police of the Metropolis to the Home Secretary*)

These contrasting and conflicting images of the British police have clearly emerged during the policing of the recession. The officer on the beat, policing by consent – the twin hallmarks of the British policing tradition – is now also the officer who possesses riot overalls, a shield and a long truncheon and who also polices by coercion. Nevertheless, policing of riots, picket lines and demonstrations still only constitutes a small fraction of police work. In Merseyside, for example, the percentage of officers' time spent on policing the coal dispute was 4.5 per cent, all made up from overtime (Kinsey, Lea and Young, 1986: 52), while in the Metropolitan Police only 2 per cent of officers' time is given over to policing special events such as demonstrations (Policy Studies Institute (PSI), 1983, vol 3, p. 40). Day-to-day policing involves mainly low-profile activities, incorporating everything from responding to emergency calls to directing traffic. The preferred self-image of many officers is that of the crime-fighter, and this is the most important function in the view of the public (Kinsey, Lea and Young, 1986: 13–4; see also Jones, Maclean and Young, 1986). As the crime figures quoted earlier indicate, however, police effectiveness in the fight against crime appears to be rapidly declining. This is in part due to the increased reporting of crimes such as burglary and theft of vehicles which are notoriously difficult to 'clear up'; the irony is, however, that the decline can also be traced to the breakdown in 'policing by consent' caused by police strategies employed to deal with rapidly rising crime. I consider this first before examining current attempts to reconstruct 'policing by consent'.

Consensual or community policing attempts to encourage the preventive and non-conflictual aspects of policing, such as crime prevention panels and community liaison (Weatheritt, 1987). It is argued that a supportive public will readily pass on information helpful in crime detection, making the targeting of offenders that much easier (Kinsey, Lea and Young, 1986: 43). This style of policing contrasts starkly with the 'military-style' policing which some commentators claim has increasingly come to characterise the inner city (Kinsey, Lea and Young, 1986). The transition from consensus to military-style policing is prompted initially by the police employing 'swamp' tactics to combat a perceived rise in actual crime (see Fig. 14.2). This can initiate a vicious circle, because as sources of information dry up and sections of the community respond to the indiscriminate use of 'stop and search' by viewing any attempts at arrests as a symbolic attack on the community (so

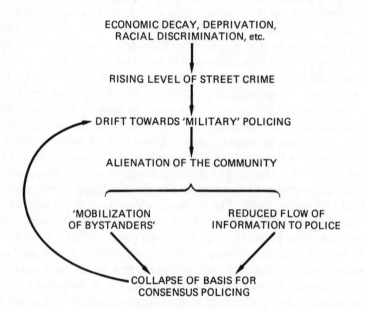

Figure 14.2   The vicious circle of the collapse of consensus policing
Source: Kinsey, Lea and Young, 1986.

'mobilising bystanders'), the police bring in specialist units and make greater use of surveillance technology. The policing of Britain is increasingly becoming polarised between these two strategies:

> Consensus policing serves quite well in low crime, affluent areas of the country where there is substantial support for the police and least need for them. The move towards military-style, hard policing is seen most clearly in the inner city areas, where it augments the growing alienation and exacerbates the community's problems of crime control.
>
> (Kinsey, Lea and Young, 1986: 51)

Military-style policing is also seen as characteristic of Northern Ireland, but it would be misleading to view Northern Ireland as a 'social laboratory' in which policing methods are tried out before being imported to the mainland. Nevertheless, importation in terms of the form and organisation of policing may have occurred by default, given that in some cases personnel responsible for policing in the province have also had responsibility for policing on the mainland. Sir Kenneth Newman, for example, was Chief Constable of the Royal Ulster Constabulary before becoming Commissioner of the Metropolitan Police (Hillyard, 1987: 304).

In Brixton, military-style policing was characterised by the use of the Special Patrol Group in saturation policing operations such as 'Swamp '81' (and which Scarman identified as one of the proximal causes of the riots), the now-repealed 'sus' law (being a suspected person loitering with intent to commit an arrestable offence) and the use of 'stop and search'. These methods focused on young blacks who, as the victims of societal and institutional racism, are disproportionately represented in the unemployed, inner-city street population, the target of police 'order' maintenance work (Reiner, 1985c: 176). This, combined with allegations of the under-policing of racial attacks, has led to the catastrophic breakdown in relations between the police and black community.

This breakdown is symptomatic of a more widespread withdrawal of support for the police among sections of the community, as the police, through the use of the methods described above, appear to be becoming 'a corps d'elite set apart from the rest of the community' (Scarman, 1981, para. 5.3). These related crises of legitimacy and effectiveness have prompted a whole repertoire of local policing initiatives which are being developed to 'breathe life' back into the proposition that there can be 'policing by consent' (R. Morgan,

1987: 32). Many are community-based, such as neighbourhood watch; others have required changes in police organisation, such as neighbourhood policing, giving officers a 'geographic responsibility' for an area in which they are to take the initiative in developing links with local community organisations. Critics argue that these initiatives are 'an attempt at the surveillance and control of communities by the police' (Gordon, 1984: 56; see also Wolmar, 1984). They point also to the parallel development of 'hard' policing methods through the investment in riot equipment and public-order training and to new pieces of legislation such as the Police and Criminal Evidence Act 1984 and the Public Order Act 1986, which have increased police powers (see Benyon, 1986; Christian, 1983). I want to focus briefly on one of these initiatives, community–police consultation, which usefully brings together some of the themes of this chapter: central government intervention, the politicisation of policing in local government and the operational autonomy of the police.

Community–police consultation now has statutory backing under section 106 of the Police and Criminal Evidence Act 1984. This simply states that arrangements are to be made for obtaining peoples' views on policing and their co-operation in the prevention of crime. Home Office circulars about consultation do refer to flexibility in the form local consultation can take but it is assumed throughout that committees will be formed, which has resulted in a broadly similar interpretation of section 106 across the country (R. Morgan, 1985). In London, where the Commissioner has responsibility for implementing consultation (in contrast to the rest of the country where it is each police authority's responsibility), the guidance betrays the Government's concern about the politicisation of policing in the capital by restricting local council representation to five members, while placing no limit on community representation (see Fyfe, 1987). Labour and Conservative councils alike view this as an attempt to undermine the authority of democratically elected representatives. More specifically, some Labour councils oppose the initiative because it would undermine the campaign for full accountability 'by giving a false impression of control when in reality the police remain accountable to no one' (Greater London Council, 1983: 14). In the area of operational police policy the impact of consultation seems to be strictly limited. The groups have been able to develop joint action between the police, the local community and the local authority to deal with specific problems, such as crime on council estates. However, the main determinants of local policing – decisions about priorities, tactics and manpower allocation – are generally fixed centrally within police headquarters or the Home Office. Indeed, in London the policing of the News International dispute at Wapping revealed the powerlessness of both consultative groups and local police officers in the face of policy decisions taken centrally. The concern, of both consultative groups and police, that the drain on local police resources caused by sending an average of three hundred officers a day to Wapping was having an adverse effect on local policing, made little difference to the policing of the dispute. The lack of power and influence of consultative groups on local police policy has led many of those most critical of the police, in particular the ethnic minority communities and some Labour politicians, to boycott consultation.

The rioting on Broadwater Farm in October 1985 confirmed for many on the Left that the post-Scarman initiatives will never be truly effective unless set in the context of elected local authority control of police policy, while for the Government it signalled the need for yet another round of investment in riot shields and armoured vehicles.

Conclusion: The Future Politics of Policing

These contrasting responses to the 1985 riots neatly illustrate the highly politicised debate which now surrounds British policing. Recent developments in the form and organisation of policing have been made possible by a 'law and order' Government committed to using the police to deal with the conflicts resulting from its social and economic policies. The response from many on the Left has been to demand local democratic control of policing but with little analysis of how this would work and what it would achieve; anything less is viewed as mere window-dressing. In such a conflict-ridden political environment the notion of policing by consent seems increasingly hollow. Securing such consent by *locally* sensitive policing and crime-control strategies (see S. Smith, 1986b: 191) is now recognised by many in the police and local government as an effective way to proceed. But it is the increasing influence of central government and national organisations like ACPO and the strictly limited influence of local government and communities which are now, as in many other policy areas, the distinctive features of the contemporary political geography of policing in Britain.

Indeed, the restructuring in central–local relations described in this chapter appears to be gathering momentum. The Local Government Act 1985 has replaced police authorities in metropolitan areas by joint boards and has given the Home Secretary the powers to determine the budget, the rate precept and the staffing levels of these metropolitan forces. Further, the expanding use of Home Office circulars is now encroaching on territory previously thought to be the sole responsibility of chief constables, such as the issue of firearms and police response to racial attacks. One commentator concludes that as a consequence: 'it is no longer realistic to describe policing in England and Wales as being a local function. Structural change has led, in effect, to the *de facto* nationalisation of the police in metropolitan areas' (Loveday, 1987: 210).

15
Environmental Politics and Policy in the 1980s

Philip Lowe and Andrew Flynn

Introduction and Background

The active political forces shaping environmental policy in Britain since the late 1970s include: Conservative policy, the European Community, and the environmental movement.

The pace and direction of change have been constrained by the established administrative and legislative context, and so despite the radical and iconoclastic rhetoric of some politicians and lobbyists, change has been piecemeal and incremental. On the other hand, major new challenges for environmental policy have arisen from the extensive restructuring of the British economy that has occurred since the mid-1970s. Before considering the main political forces and their impact on policy, therefore, it is important to consider these two factors which, more than any others, have determined the terrain of environmental politics: the administrative and legislative context; and the consequences of economic restructuring.

Administrative and Legislative Context

A diverse structure of agencies, procedures and statutes concerned with the environment has evolved in an *ad hoc* and pragmatic manner since the mid-Victorian period. By the early twentieth century this included a range of measures to safeguard public health, contain industrial pollution, preserve historic monuments and protect wild birds. By mid-century there had been added a detailed land-use planning system and protective measures for important landscapes and habitats. Legislation in the 1950s and 1960s rationalised and extended controls over air and water pollution and bird protection, promoted rural and urban conservation, and addressed the growing problems of noise and toxic wastes.

Under pressure from the environmental lobby, the late 1960s and early 1970s saw an accelerated pace of reform. Existing environmental agencies were strengthened, and comprehensive pollution controls were introduced. The planning system was overhauled and provision made for public participation. The Department of the Environment (DoE) was set up in 1970 and a number of advisory bodies were established to bring environmental opinion to bear on central policy making. In retrospect, this period represents a peak of reforming activity.

The fourfold increase in oil prices of 1973–4 and its impact on the economy had major consequences for environmental politics. The faltering growth rates, inflation, recession and mass unemployment experienced since then have polarised British society and undermined the political consensus on which the key post-war policies for social and economic management had been built. Environmental policy did not remain unscathed. Before reviewing subsequent and contemporary developments it is important to note the principal characteristics of environmental policy as of the mid-1970s. The following four major features are noteworthy.

First, government structures and law relating to environmental protection have been (and largely remain) an accretion of common law, statutes, agencies, procedures and policies. There is no overall environmental policy other than the sum of these individual elements, most of which have been pragmatic and incremental responses to specific problems and the evolution of relevant scientific knowledge: a 'tactical rather than strategic approach' (G. Richardson *et al.*, 1982: 33) has dominated the history of pollution control in Britain. Richardson and Watts (1985: 8) suggest that this arises from 'a very reactive approach to problem solving', characteristic of British policy-making generally. Environmental problems, however, are intrinsically cross-sectoral, and this, in part, also accounts for the fragmented nature of an environmental policy that has emerged piecemeal. Even the formation of the DoE left many key environmental concerns in the realm of other Ministries (Kimber *et al.*, 1974). Not surprisingly, there are glaring procedural inconsistencies, such as the differing rules governing public access to information (DoE, 1986).

Secondly, environmental regulation has been highly devolved and decentralised. In most cases responsibility for taking direct action has fallen to local government or an administrative agency. Central government usually retains responsibility for promoting general policies, exercises financial control and often has reserve powers. Where the problems are especially complex (e.g. hazardous waste), sensitive (e.g. radioactive waste), or are extra-territorial (marine pollution), central government has retained control, but even then enforcement responsibilities are often delegated to semi-autonomous agencies.

Third, environmental control, like many other aspects of state regulation in Britain, is pervaded by administrative rather than judicial procedures. The approach pursued is informal, accommodative and technocratic rather than formal, confrontational and legalistic (Vogel, 1986). Legislation tends to be broad and discretionary; regulatory agencies are usually given wide scope to determine and enforce environmental objectives. In contrast with many other industrialised countries, there has been an avoidance of legislatively prescribed standards and quality objectives.

Fourth, the approach traditionally adopted in dealing with private concerns seeks to foster co-operation and strives to achieve the objectives of environmental policy through negotiation and persuasion. This has often meant encouragement of voluntary measures (as in the removal of detergent effluent from inland rivers), self-regulation (e.g. the Pesticides Safety Precaution Scheme, as it existed until 1985), or codes of practice (such as the National Farmers' Union (NFU)'s strawburning code). Regulatory authorities are sensitive to the economic and practical constraints that private concerns face, and this often leads to a certain protectiveness on the part of the regulators towards industrial interests, not least in the secrecy with which they preserve information collected from firms in the course of pollution-monitoring (Frankel, 1974).

The Environmental Consequences of Economic Restructuring

Since the mid-1970s the established panoply of environmental protection has encountered new issues thrown up by the restructuring of the national economy. Associated with the economic recession was a decline in house building, curtailment of the New Towns programme, government postponement of major capital projects such as the third London airport and the Channel Tunnel, a slow-down of public works such as reservoir and power station construction and road-building – all of which delayed major threats to the environment. Industrial decline diminished some environmental pressures; large-scale closure of plant, especially in traditional heavy industries, eliminated long-standing sources of air and water pollution. One of the few established industries to grow steadily throughout the recession was agriculture, reflecting its highly protected status; not surprisingly, therefore, farm pollution and the impact of agricultural intensification on wildlife and the landscape have emerged as major issues in the 1980s (Lowe *et al.*, 1986).

Another general consequence of the recession was a slowdown in public and private investment in pollution control and environmental improvements. The low level of industrial investment meant slower replacement of inefficient or obsolete equipment, which is often a prime source of pollution. Pressure mounted from industrialists for relief from environmental controls, and authorities were reluctant to press clean-up measures on firms hit by the recession, especially where local employment seemed at stake (Blowers, 1984). Public expenditure cuts meant that much-needed capital investment in waste treatment facilities was either shelved or indefinitely postponed; hence ten years after it was passed, much of the Control of Pollution Act, 1974 could still not be implemented (Levitt, 1980; Pearce, 1986).

One welcome consequence of the oil shocks of 1973 and 1979 was the impetus and urgency they gave to resource conservation. The consequent drive to save energy, with government backing, also had positive implications for the efficient use of other resources, either because energy saving or recovery facilitated other forms of recycling, or because increasingly cost-conscious manufacturers were induced to look for other ways to reduce their raw material costs. These efforts, in turn, alleviated problems of pollution and waste disposal. Thus, through a combination of industrial decline and slow recovery, and greater efficiency in the use of fossil fuels, total sulphur dioxide and nitrous oxide emissions in the United Kingdom fell progressively from the late 1970s to the mid-1980s (OECD, 1985a). The improvement, however, has not been sufficient to placate Scandinavian countries suffering from acid rain, and other countries committed to a 30 per cent reduction on 1980 levels of SO_2 pollution by 1993 (Park, 1987).

The economic recovery since 1982 is revealing the extent to which improvements in air and water quality during the late 1970s and early 1980s were fortuitous consequences of industrial decline and previous infrastructural improvements rather than tangible results of the steady application of control measures. The reversal in the mid-1980s of the downward trend of sulphur emissions and of the progressive improvement over many years of river quality suggests that the scope for living off past investments in pollution abatement has been exhausted, and that continued progress in curbing pollution will demand major new investment in control measures and treatment facilities.

Moreover, Britain's industrial structure and its regional distribution have changed markedly (see Chapter 6). Though some changes have been environmentally benign, particularly the decline in traditional industrial pollution, others pose significant and novel threats.

First, the growing technology-based industries (such as microelectronics and biotechnology) are creating new pollution problems. Toxic materials are used in their production, and cases of soil and groundwater contamination have been reported (OECD, 1985b: 223; Olivierin *et al.*, 1985). The accidental or deliberate release of genetically modified organisms into the environment poses novel and unknown risks (Fowle, 1987). Technological advance and the diversification of the materials used in production are also leading to a great expansion in the number of chemicals in industrial use (Crone, 1986), but the knowledge and procedures to regulate their transport, use and disposal are woefully inadequate.

A second feature is an increasingly polarised social geography of amenity, reflecting the sharply contrasting economic fortunes of different localities (Champion *et al.*, 1987). Examples of the divergent environmental pressures include:

1. Traditional industrial towns and cities, where the decline of heavy industry has left a legacy of extensive dereliction and land contamination;
2. Inner cities, where counter-urbanisation and reduced public and private investment have resulted in urban decay and declining infrastructure;
3. Smaller settlements and the countryside, experiencing diffuse development pressures as well as threats to landscape and wildlife from agricultural intensification and afforestation.

These divergent pressures, mediated through local political and state structures, yield great variations in environmental politics, for example:

1. In most industrial cities, a strongly pro-development outlook, articulated by local businessmen, trade unionists and politicians, tends to predominate, and is often linked to a concern not to make environmental controls too stringent for established or incoming firms;
2. In inner cities and blighted industrial areas, environmental improvement is heavily dependent on government-sponsored urban renewal and job creation schemes;
3. Throughout much of the South East and the lowland countryside, anti-development preservationism predominates, expressed mainly by middle-class residents and oriented towards the protection of amenity;
4. In the remoter rural areas, especially in Scotland and Wales, conflict is often found between agrarian, forestry and mineral interests, on the one hand, and, on the other, national pressure groups and statutory agencies promoting recreation and conservation.

Conservative Policy

The implementation and elaboration of environmental policies since the mid-1970s have encountered not only an adverse economic climate but also the political resurgence of business interests, alarmed by the 'limits to growth' debate, and the emergence of 'New Right' politicians unsympathetic to business regulation and *dirigiste* policies of any kind. These counter-pressures have had a considerable impact on thinking within the Conservative Party and the Thatcher Government. The Government's approach to environmental policy, nevertheless, combines several strands of Conservative philosophy and has also been influenced by Margaret Thatcher's distinctive style of government.

Many commentators have noted the importance to the policies of the Thatcher governments of neo-liberal ideas, especially in economic management, where the Government has emphasised the superiority of the market over state intervention. Traditional Tory paternalism still remains influential in other, less central areas. In addition, the Government's radical economic liberalism coexists with a reactionary impulse, an 'authoritarian populism' (Jessop *et al.*, 1984). So Thatcherism rests on a dualism: the promotion of a free economy and a strong state. Conservative environmental policy has reflected both this dualism and a strong undercurrent of Tory paternalism (see Chapter 1). Which element is to the fore has depended on ministerial inclinations and the balance of sentiments within Cabinet and Parliament. Also crucial has been the centrality of the issue to Government policy and party politics, and the sensitivity of the party leadership, backbenchers and peers to various influences including development, financial, industrial, farming and land-owning lobbies as well as certain constituency pressures, not least the Conservative-voting residents of the leafy suburbs and shires.

Thus there has been little sympathy with any regulatory controls if they are perceived to obstruct growth or development. Perhaps the initial instincts of the Thatcher Government towards environmental controls were best captured in leaked Cabinet papers which recorded the intention of her first administration to 'reduce over-sensitivity to environmental considerations' (*Sunday Times*, 18 November 1979). However, it and subsequent administrations have avoided an overtly anti-environmental stance, seeking instead to put pressure on regulatory agencies to minimise the burdens placed on business – pressures reinforced by cuts in budgets and staff and changes in the composition of their governing councils and advisory boards in favour of business interests (Brotherton and Lowe, 1984; Pearce, 1986).

Neo-liberal ideas have been most strenuously brought to bear on land-use planning, and here deregulation has been explicitly pursued as a political priority, though not to the same extent everywhere (Thornley, 1981). In the major conurbations and industrial cities not only has deregulation been pushed furthest, but the imperative needs to promote urban renewal in the wake of inner-city rioting and to defeat municipal socialism have also unleashed the more authoritarian side of Thatcherism (see also Chapter 5). In contrast, in the countryside, the heartland of Conservatism, paternalistic ideas still set the tone of environmental policy. Finally, the interface between the urban and the rural – the green belt and the surrounding commuter belt – has become something of a battleground between rival versions of Conservatism and their attitudes towards market forces.

The reform of the planning system has involved both deregulation and the promotion of private development. The reduction of the scope of the planning system has included the repeal of the Community Land Act, which undermined the positive role of local authorities in the development process, and the elimination of strategic planning through the scrapping of the Regional Economic Planning Councils, the abolition of the metropolitan counties and the GLC, and the attenuation of the planning powers of County Councils. Revisions to the Use Classes Order and the General Development Order have also involved some relaxation of development control powers. In addition, ministerial statements and Government circulars have repeatedly exhorted local authorities to adopt a liberal attitude towards development.

There have, in parallel, been efforts actively to promote private development. Initially these involved the introduction of Enterprise Zones (EZs), followed by Simplified Planning Zones. In these developers enjoy considerable freedom of action supplemented, in EZs, by substantial rate and tax exemptions. Local democracy has also been bypassed through the setting up of Urban Development Corporations and British Urban Development (BUD), a new company which will supplant the traditional local authority role of land assembly and basic site redevelopment. These changes embody the authoritarian side of Thatcherism and have resulted in 'less public participation, less control by the local authority and greater power exerted by central government' (Thornley, 1986: 21).

In contrast to its efforts to weaken and contain the planning powers of urban councils, the Conservative government has initiated significant extensions of environmental policy in rural conservation and heritage preservation. These are archetypal concerns of Tory paternalism. Both the countryside and the historic heritage are seen as repositories of traditional values at once glorifying the nation's past, expressing its eternal character and emphasising social continuity (Paterson, 1984). In both cases, government legislation has involved some extension of state agency, but there has also been an emphasis on private and voluntary initiative, stimulated by grant and tax concessions, rather than on statutory controls (Hewison 1987; Lowe *et al.*, 1986). By comparison, in Scotland, safeguards for National Scenic Areas, introduced in 1980, have involved a reinforcement of development control procedures, as well as greater centralisation, by giving the Countryside Commission for Scotland

and the Scottish Development Department supervisory functions over local planning decisions that might affect these areas (SDD Circular 20/80).

Subsequent ministerial attempts to relax planning controls in the countryside – to satisfy the house-building industry, diversify the rural economy and wean farmers off agricultural supports – have provoked staunch resistance from back-bench, mainly shire MPs and rural preservation interests, most notably the Council for the Protection of Rural England (CPRE). In the autumn of 1983 this combination mounted a successful campaign against two draft circulars on *Green Belts* and *Land for Housing* which would have relaxed green-belt controls (Elson, 1986). Another draft circular, also from the DoE, provoked a similar backlash in the spring of 1987. The circular sought to overturn the post-war assumption that agriculture should have first claim on rural land, by removing, in most cases, the requirement that planning authorities should consult the Ministry of Agriculture where planning applications would involve loss of farmland to building. Lobbying pressures ensured that the final version was amended to stress 'the continuing need to protect the countryside for its own sake', if no longer for its agricultural value (Circular 16/87). These struggles between Ministers and backbenchers continued into 1988, as the Government looked for greater release of land for housing in the southern counties and, in an unusual display of organised dissent, over ninety Tory MPs formed a group called Sane Planning, to resist additional major development pressures on the countryside.

Overall, during the Thatcher years, there has been a significant erosion of the comprehensive land-use planning system of the post-war period. In its stead one can discern the essential ingredients of a *de facto* zoning approach in planning. On the one hand, areas of high environmental value, including National Parks, Areas of Outstanding Natural Beauty, Sites of Special Scientific Interest, Conservation Areas and National Scenic Areas, have not only been largely exempted from the relaxation of planning powers but have also been given additional safeguards. On the other hand, in Enterprise Zones, Simplified Planning Zones and areas covered by Urban Development Corporations, planning constraints have been streamlined and weakened, to allow market criteria to prevail. Elsewhere, the previous system remains, though now less public-sector led and more private-sector driven, and less oriented towards community needs and more towards market demands. It has been suggested that 'We no longer have a planning system but three planning systems' (Thornley, 1988: 18). As yet, though, the government has not explicitly embraced a formal zoning approach, although it has been urged to do so (e.g. Adam Smith Institute (1984)).

A final influence of Thatcherism on environmental politics has been the Prime Minister's distinctive style of government, with its projected image of conviction politics and firm direction. The Thatcherite vision of Conservatism places a premium on the resolute enunciation of political principles in determining policy, and downplays the need for wide consultation or the role of detached expertise. In practice this has meant somewhat diminished consultation opportunities for environmental interests and reduced levels of formal political access.

The early years of the Thatcher Government saw the sweeping away of several advisory bodies set up during the previous decade to incorporate environmental interests into policy-making, including the Clean Air Council, the Noise Advisory Council, the Commission on Energy and the Environment and the Water Space Amenity Commission. The Government has, moreover, shown a marked aversion to establishing new advisory bodies or committees of inquiry. The one major advisory body to remain – the Royal Commission on Environmental Pollution – was, perhaps, too influential to axe, being oriented more towards the scientific establishment than the environmental lobby, and it has assumed enhanced significance as an authoritative source of independent judgement and policy analysis.

Efforts to expedite key development projects have also been criticised for bypassing local democratic procedures and curtailing the scope for public scrutiny. The use by the Government of Special Development Orders, for example, allowed exemptions from planning control for the Hay's Wharf development on the Thames and for the exploratory investigation of potential sites for the disposal of low-level nuclear waste (Blowers, 1987). Likewise, private bill procedures have been pursued, successfully, to authorise the construction of the Channel Tunnel and, unsuccessfully, for a bypass to cut through part of the New Forest; and though affected interests can make representations to the relevant parliamentary committee, the scope for scrutiny by objectors is much less than in a wide-ranging public inquiry.

It is notable that, in the environmental field, Thatcherite reformism and deregulatory zeal have focused on the land-use planning system. Of all the types of environmental regulation, this is the one most accountable to local democratic procedures and offering the greatest scope for public participation. Most other forms of environmental regulation are much more corporatist in their operation and thus more attuned to the consequences of regulation for businesses and firms. There is no evidence that, say, manufacturers or farmers were as discontented with the regulations they faced as were developers with the planning system. During the late 1970s, the construction industry actively campaigned against difficulties and delays in obtaining planning permission and the costs incurred as a result (House of Commons Expenditure Committee, 1977). Given the close association of major construction interests with the Conservative Party, it was perhaps inevitable that those concerns would be to the fore when the Tories took office. Finally, the administration of the planning system by local authorities has meant that it has inevitably been embroiled in the Government's sustained challenge to the autonomy of local government (see Chapter 5).

The European Community

Increasingly, states must co-operate in tackling common environmental problems that do not respect national boundaries. Pollutants are carried across borders, and the global commons – the atmosphere, the seas and international rivers and lakes – are universally abused. Securing solutions to these transnational and international concerns is extremely difficult, involving sustained collaboration between states with divergent interests and different political and administrative structures. Although many multilateral conventions have been signed on the protection of the environment, progress in implementing most of them has been very slow. The efforts of EEC countries to co-ordinate their environmental policies present an interesting exception. The European Community differs from all other international organisations in having powers and institutions of its own which are binding on member states. The Community's Environmental Action Programme was initiated in 1974. A primary motivation behind the Environmental Programme was to ensure that different national standards and regulatory procedures did not become an obstacle to free trade and business competition. In all, the Community has adopted over a hundred legal instruments covering water quality, air pollution, hazardous chemicals, noise, wastes, protection of wildlife and the safety of nuclear installations.

The Single European Act 1987 has formalised and made explicit the Community's involvement in this field. Article 25, which defines the general objectives and scope of the Community's environmental policy, states that the Community shall take action relating to the environment where the objectives 'can be attained better at the Community level than at the level of the individual Member States'.

Decision-making within the Council of Ministers is such that the pace of reform is usually dictated by those states in the rearguard on the matter. Thus, depending on the issue, there are lead states that are pushing for change and see the Community as something of a brake on their own progress, and lag states which react to and constrain Community initiatives. In the environmental field, the lead states have included Denmark, the Netherlands and West Germany.

The British Government's record has been rather mixed, especially in relation to efforts to tighten up and standardise pollution controls. Unlike some member states, however, the British are interested less in having correct or admirable laws than in legislation that is workable. The British Government, therefore, tends to scrutinise proposed community legislation most closely and insists on modifications to ensure that it is capable of being implemented. In the main, the consequence has been that most Community directives have had no more than incremental effects on the development of domestic environmental policy. Thus, although substantial parts of the two most important pieces of British environmental legislation of the past fifteen years – the 1974 Control of Pollution Act and the 1981 Wildlife and Countryside Act – were crucially shaped by Community directives, most directives could be implemented under existing law.

The more significant effect of Commission initiatives has been to probe the traditional basis of British procedures by obliging the government fully to explain and justify these. One consequence has been to make explicit principles that were previously implicit or merely rhetorical. Not only does this establish a more definite framework in which the achievements of regulation can be assessed and challenged, but it has also opened up a wide-ranging debate about established practices and alternative strategies of environmental protection (Haigh, 1984).

Another inevitable influence of the European Community has been a trend towards greater centralisation of policy-making which has reinforced the Gaullist tendencies of the Thatcher Government (Macrory, 1986). It is, after all, the central government that is responsible for negotiating with the Community and for ensuring implementation of agreed measures and policies. This has involved it taking a much more active and prominent role in setting policy objectives and standards and obliged it to take a more strategic approach to environmental policy. Still, much of the administration of environmental policy remains decentralised, if subject to greater central monitoring. In water management, though, regulation is to become highly centralised. In 1986 the Government was obliged to abandon its initial proposals for privatising regional water authorities *in toto*, under strong criticisms from the environmental lobby. Legal opinion sought by the CPRE had deemed that placing water pollution control in the hands of private companies would be illegal under European Community law. Revised privatisation proposals issued in 1987 will retain the regulatory duties of the water authorities in the public sector through the establishment of a National Rivers Authority with powers over pollution control and responsibility for land drainage, fisheries, conservation and recreation. A trend related to centralisation is one from voluntary and informal regulation to statutory regulation. One of the motives, for example, behind the replacement of the voluntary Pesticides Safety Precautions Scheme with statutory controls under the Food and Environment Protection Act 1985 was to make British procedures more acceptable and consistent internationally.

Finally, the European underpinnings of environmental policy-making have established a broader context of accountability for British policy and actions (Brackley, 1987). Through the institutions of the Community, international pressures have been more effectively brought to bear where Britain has seemed out of line. On some issues, including the sea dumping of nuclear wastes, radioactive discharges into the Irish Sea and acid rain, Britain has found herself isolated, and the Government has felt obliged to make concessions to international opinion. In addition, in acceding to Community Directives the Government accepts commitments that it cannot lightly abdicate. In a number of instances, including sewage contamination of bathing water and nitrate contamination of drinking water, the consequence has been to force the pace of remedial action and significantly enlarge its scope despite government complacency.

In general terms, one might conclude that the integration of British environmental policy-making into a European framework has challenged a twofold insularity: an administrative insularity which in the past has exhibited a certain self-satisfaction over a system of environmental regulations that has evolved in an *ad hoc*, pragmatic and piecemeal manner; and a geographical insularity which, through exploiting the capacities of the prevailing winds, fast-flowing rivers and surrounding seas, has pursued a 'dilute and disperse' approach to solve, or at least dispel, major pollution problems.

The Environmental Movement

Britain has perhaps the most highly organised environmental lobby of any European country (Lowe, 1988). It achieved a peak of influence in the late 1960s and early 1970s. Subsequently it faced a much more unfavourable political climate as the deepening recession generated a hostile and pervasive mentality of 'growth at any price'. Periodically commentators and politicians have been ready to pronounce it a spent force politically but invariably they have been confounded. Of the social causes that came to prominence during the 1960s, including feminism, consumerism, and minority rights, environmentalism has best weathered the economic tribulations of the 1970s and 1980s and the right-ward shift in national politics. Indeed the contemporary environmental lobby would appear to enjoy greater legitimacy and influence than some traditional sources of social power, such as the trade union movement.

Its resilience is due to certain fundamental strengths. First, environmental groups command mass support. They include some of the biggest voluntary organisations in Britain, with a combined membership of between three and a half and four million. Membership is predominantly middle class, but evidence from opinion surveys suggests that passive environmental concern is even more widespread and socially much more broadly based. Moreover it is evident that popular support for environmental protection and conservation remained buoyant through the recession and subsequently. It also appears that only a small minority of the public is willing to sacrifice some degree of environmental improvement for economic growth when offered a choice in a trade-off question:

indeed, a sizeable majority gives priority to protecting the environment, even if this means restricting economic growth or raising taxes or increasing prices (MORI, 1987; Young, 1985; European Commission, 1983, 1986).

Because of the strength of its popular support, environmental opinion is an important factor in government decision-making although environmental groups are less of an influence than major economic interests. Not being of central importance to the effective performance of government or the economy they do not have the close, symbiotic relationship with senior civil servants in the central departments which corporate interest groups enjoy. They are not automatically included, therefore, in the most formative stages of policy-making, though they are usually consulted but often at a later stage.

Failure to be closely involved with policy formulation in the crucial initial stages often means that national environmental groups are later faced with an uphill campaign against a course of action to which Ministers, officials and major interests have become committed. Good media and parliamentary relations can compensate to a certain extent by enabling groups to raise issues for government attention and by ensuring considerable opprobrium for any official initiatives with blatant and damaging environmental implications. Many MPs and peers are sympathetic to conservation issues, and most groups have good contacts with the mass media and can count on a ready and usually favourable treatment for their views. Environmental topics are public-interest issues of a non-partisan nature which makes them an attractive and important outlet for campaigning and investigative journalism. As a result, a combination of public censure and parliamentary pressure can prove an effective weapon, enabling environmental groups to take the offensive against recalcitrant government departments and win important concessions (Lowe and Morrison, 1984).

Environmental groups in Britain pursue reformist strategies, and incidents of militancy have been few in number and mainly in keeping with the British dissentient tradition of civil disobedience of a non-violent and often symbolic kind (Lowe and Goyder, 1983). On the whole, the environmental movement has not adopted a radical stance. Oppositional elements seeking structural rather than policy change have not emerged as a significant political force. Most other advanced industrialised countries, in contrast, have witnessed the emergence of radical green movements during the past decade (Rüdig and Lowe, 1989). Having faced a similarly harsh climate for environmental concerns during this period, it is of interest to speculate why Britain has not followed suit.

First, in comparative terms, British environmental groups enjoy relatively easy access to government and the political system. However, unlike some other countries, such as the United States, Sweden, Denmark and Switzerland, where the environmental lobby is also highly integrated into established political processes, access for groups in Britain is entirely by discretion and custom. Maintaining good links with the executive, therefore, is of particular importance for pressure groups because of the absence of such alternative institutional mechanisms for pursuing dissent as are provided elsewhere by federal constitutions, popular referenda, the separation of the legislature from the executive, or judicial review of executive actions. Consultative status is gained and maintained by adhering to an unwritten code of moderate and responsible behaviour. It may be forfeited if a group is too outspoken in its criticisms or fails to show the necessary tact and discretion. Overall, the general receptivity of the British political system to group activity, pervasive cultural pressures and fear of disrupting established relationships reinforce a tradition of moderation and pragmatism and discourage militant and unorthodox approaches.

The predominant ethos of activism within the British environmental movement inclines in a quite different and apolitical direction, towards practical action, inspired by an ethos of voluntarism and a liberal ideology implicitly sceptical of state action. Most environmental groups see themselves as *voluntary* organisations; indeed, they fulfil a range of executive tasks of their own, including education and research, the provision of information and technical advice, practical conservation work, and the ownership and management of land and property. With the growth of such responsibilities, their role as pressure groups has diminished, though not necessarily their influence. Finally, most groups are charities and therefore, in principle, are debarred from overt political activities. Consequently, their lobbying is discreet and restrained, and their efforts to inform opinion are presented as public education and not propaganda.

The Political Management of Environmental Issues in the 1980s

Partly because of the above constraints and traditions, the style of environmental politics has not changed greatly during the past ten years, though individual groups have adjusted their tactics. Three features of the continued political management of environmental issues are worth noting.

First, lobbying groups have had to confront the peremptory style of the Thatcher Government. Recognising that the limited influence they have enjoyed through established channels is insufficient to achieve major reforms, groups have tended to adopt a more populist style of campaigning. The newer groups, particularly Greenpeace and Friends of the Earth (FOE), have led the way in this direction, but many older groups have also assumed a much higher public profile and adopted more adversarial, media-orientated tactics, while taking care not to disrupt their established relationships with government or to alienate the sympathy of their more conservative members.

The trend towards more open and indirect lobbying has been reinforced by changing patterns of political access. The somewhat diminished consultation opportunities for environmental interests and reduced levels of formalised access to central government have been offset by the extension of other arenas of influence, particularly within Parliament and the European Community. The new system of parliamentary select committees introduced in 1979 has increased opportunities for groups to promote their views and influence parliamentary opinion (Drewry, 1985). The Environment Committee certainly has been an important forum in which environmental groups have been able to raise issues, develop their criticism of policy and offer an appraisal of the evidence of official agencies and departmental witnesses. Some of the other specialist committees have also been welcomed by environmental groups as a means of challenging the orthodoxy of policy commitments in fields such as agriculture, energy and transport where the groups' influence and access are limited.

Two House of Lords Select Committees have also carried out important inquiries on environmental topics. The Science and Technology Committee's investigation of the disposal of hazardous wastes, for example, led to the establishment of the Hazardous Waste Inspectorate. The other Lords Select Committee (first appointed in 1974) reviews European Community legislative and policy proposals. Consideration of draft environmental directives has become a significant part of its proceedings which thus provide environmental groups with an opportunity to shape both UK and European policy.

More generally, the European Community has provided environmental groups with new arenas in which to pursue their concerns and exercise influence. Twenty-one British groups along with eighty from the rest of the Community (together representing some 20 million European citizens) are members of the European Environmental Bureau (EEB) which provides them with access to the European Commission and the Council of Ministers. The British member groups of the EEB – through their particular experience of domestic lobbying – have adapted more easily than many of their counterparts to the successive rounds of consultation and detailed redrafting of directives and regulations which characterise Community decision-making. They have used their involvement not only to influence European policy but also as a means of shaping the context in which domestic policies will be determined (Lowe and Goyder, 1983, ch. 10).

A second notable feature of environmental management is the expanding voluntary and practical activities of environmental groups. These now include not only traditional conservation tasks but also others such as local clean-up campaigns, waste recycling and building restoration (Pettigrew, 1984). Public authorities and social activists have encouraged 'urban greening' projects as part of broader renewal strategies (Davidson, 1988), environmental groups have fostered voluntary action to bolster their support, and the Conservative Government has promoted these activities as part of its philosophy of reducing dependence upon the state. Job creation schemes, notably those sponsored by the MSC (Manpower Services Commission, now the Training Commission) have helped expand the practical role of environmental groups, and there has been direct government financial support for environmental groups and voluntary activity, even to the extent of creating new organisations, such as UK 2000 and the Groundwork Trusts. There are, of course, drawbacks: the influx of new staff, especially under MSC schemes, alienated many volunteers (Willis, 1987), with a consequent drop in voluntary activity (Rankin, 1987). Furthermore, government funding can compromise the independence or distort the objectives of environmental groups. Groups are obliged to seek funds for activities that government is inclined to support, for example practical conservation rather than campaigning, lobbying or background inquiry. Cases of overt political interference are few, but there is certainly evidence that groups dependent on official funding are wary of offending the government, and this concern can reinforce a generally conservative tone in a group's political outlook and lobbying activities (Lowe and Goyder, 1983: 46).

The third notable feature about environmental political management in the 1980s is that, despite its image of conviction politics and resolute action, the Conservative Government, like its predecessors, has responded pragmatically and flexibly, even opportunistically, when environmental issues have threatened to become too contentious. Its political management of environmental conflict has also been facilitated by the way in which key issues with major protest potential, especially nuclear power, have evolved.

As in the 1970s, the public inquiry system has continued to play a crucial role in containing and channelling environmental opposition. This highly elastic mechanism has been particularly effective at defusing protest compared with the equivalent institutional procedures for processing environmental demands established in other advanced industrialised countries. These, though, have been put under more severe strain by the emergence of demands for fundamental change associated with the radicalisation of the environmental movement. The conflict over nuclear energy has proved singularly intractable, and in most cases this has been the catalyst for a radical shift in environmental politics.

After the oil shock of 1973 most advanced industrialised countries went for crash programmes of nuclear energy development. The political priority attached to the construction of nuclear power plants and the vehement opposition they provoked strained to breaking-point the integrative capacity of procedures for public consultation. The anti-nuclear movement became a rallying cause for oppositional elements, including radical environmentalists, New Left activists and disaffected local populations threatened by the construction of nuclear plants. The coalescing of these elements around electoral strategies has led to the formation and growth of green parties (Rüdig and Lowe, 1989).

The issue of nuclear energy has been of much less significance in Britain. Throughout the 1970s a number of factors, including lower projected energy demands, the country's large reserves of oil and coal, and technical problems with the Advanced Gas-Cooled Reactor, delayed the nuclear programme. In addition a siting policy, which in the 1950s and 1960s favoured remote coastal locations and subsequently has pursued a clustering strategy of putting new plant adjacent to existing stations, has served to minimise local opposition.

Events in the late 1970s did, however, lead to the emergence of an anti-nuclear movement. This occurred in the aftermath of the 1977 Windscale Inquiry, the conduct of which seemed to epitomise a strong and characteristic commitment to rational argument and due procedure. It was a great shock therefore when the inspector's report gave unequivocal backing to British Nuclear Fuels Ltd, and dismissed the major counter-arguments, almost to the point of ignoring them. Calls were made for direct action. More than 200 local groups emerged in a wave of anti-nuclear activity and an umbrella organisation, the Anti-Nuclear Campaign (ANC), was set up comprising all the major anti-nuclear groups, with the notable exception of FOE which had been the leading objector at the Windscale Inquiry. With the incoming Conservative administration of 1979 proposing to build ten reactors by the early 1990s and to switch to the controversial Pressurised Water Reactor (PWR) design, the scene seemed set for a nationwide campaign of co-ordinated protest, but for a number of reasons this did not materialise.

First, the Government followed a low-profile strategy. At the same time, plans for the first PWR reactor – to be built at Sizewell – were delayed, robbing the ANC of an immediate target. When local protest movements started to emerge in reaction to a proposed programme of test drilling to explore the potential for deep disposal of high-level nuclear waste, the Government quickly abandoned the programme. Site occupations to block the construction of a nuclear power station in Torness in Scotland and to obstruct site tests for the construction of another at Luxulyan in Cornwall were largely peaceable and the response of the police was very cautious with no attempt to clear the sites by force. In any case, the ANC did not give particular attention to these local conflicts. Instead, it concentrated on building up an alliance of trade unions against the Sizewell PWR, including unions concerned only about reactor choice rather than nuclear power as such. Thus the safety concerns of environmentalists continued to be deflected by the debate over the relative merits of the British Advanced Gas-Cooled Reactor and the US-designed PWR. The final blow to the anti-nuclear energy movement was the revival of the Campaign for Nuclear Disarmament (CND), which led to a large exodus of activists into the peace movement. The ANC extended its opposition to include nuclear weapons, but CND was lukewarm in reciprocating.

By the time the Sizewell Inquiry opened in 1983 the stage was largely left, as far as environmental opposition was concerned, to the moderate and established groups, including FOE, the Town and Country Planning Association and the CPRE. The inquiry – the longest in British history – lasted for a staggering 340 days and stretched over a two-year period. Inevitably, it absorbed much of the energy and resources of participating groups. Three more PWRs are planned, similar to Sizewell B. In a classic dilemma for the strong state and neo-liberal aspects of Thatcherism, however, their construction and the possibility of a second generation of more advanced PWRs will depend on the commitment to nuclear power embodied for strategic reasons in the privatisation of the electricity industry and its commercial acceptability.

Policy over radioactive waste disposal has been even more vacillating. In 1984 the sea dumping of low-level nuclear wastes was abandoned after international opposition, Greenpeace protests and a ban imposed by the National Union of Seamen. The following year the proposed nuclear repository at Billingham was dropped after strong local protest. Opposition intensified around three other sites short-listed for shallow disposal, and in 1986 plans to use them for intermediate-level waste were shelved in favour of low-level waste only. This did not placate local opinion and, just before the 1987 general election, proposals for shallow burial were withdrawn altogether. In this field at least the Government's record has been characterised by 'political indecision' which has led to 'policy flux and ambiguity' (Kemp, O'Riordan and Purdue, 1986: 13, 22). Nevertheless, anti-nuclear protest has been defused, at least for the time being.

More generally, the Conservatives have shown themselves alert to the potential electoral import of popular concern for the environment. In mid-1984, with her administration having attracted much adverse publicity over issues such as acid rain and nuclear wastes, Margaret Thatcher was widely reported to be revising her opinion of the political significance of environmental concern, particularly in the light of the electoral successes of green parties in Western Europe. 'Tories seek to win environmentalist vote' ran the headline in the *Financial Times* (16 July 1984). Previously, other parties, most notably the Liberals, had been much more to the fore in presenting their environmental credentials. With the heightened party competition in the wake of the formation of the Social Democratic Party, there followed an unprecedented wave of policy documents and position statements on the environment from all the political parties (Owens, 1986). It is in this way that environmental issues have become politicised in Britain – through competition between the established parties as well as the campaigning of environmental groups – and not through the electoral achievements of a radical green party. It is not that Britain is without such a party. Indeed, established in 1973, the British Green Party is the oldest in Western Europe; yet electorally it is the weakest (Rüdig and Lowe, 1989). The highest average share of the vote it has achieved was 1.5 per cent in the 1979 general election when it fielded 53 candidates. In 1983, with 109 candidates, its average fell to 1.0 per cent; and in 1987, with 133 candidates, the average recovered to 1.4 per cent. A number of factors can be adduced to explain its poor showing, not least the British electoral system, but the key factor is probably the lack of a radical ecological movement.

Conclusions

Environmental politics in Britain in the 1980s encapsulates certain paradoxes. On the one hand, despite its radical rhetoric and the alarmism of some of its critics, the Conservative Government's environmental policy presents a much greater degree of continuity with previous Governments than of change. Many long-established procedures and institutions have proved their durability, not least in accommodating affected interests. Significantly, although relief from environmental controls has been sought by hard-pressed firms, there has been no general support from industrial interests for widespread deregulation of environmental policy. The exception is the land use planning system, some of whose controls and procedures have been challenged by the construction industry, and here deregulation has been explicitly pursued as a political priority. Even so, the approach to reform, though tenacious, has been remarkably tentative, pursued through a succession of exhortatory circulars, ministerial statements, decisions on appeal, mostly minor legislative changes and limited experiments in relaxing and streamlining planning controls.

In part, the Government's more radical instincts have been held in check by back-bench and constituency pressures. Environmental opinion has also been another important influence, buoyed up by the considerable popular support enjoyed by the environmental lobby and the receptiveness to environmental issues shown by the mass media. The Government has shown itself especially pragmatic in seeking to defuse politically sensitive environmental opposition. Policy initiatives have also been shaped and modified by the various statutory sources of independent advice and scientific judgement, including the Nature Conservancy Council, the Countryside Commission and the Royal Commission on Environmental Pollution. An additional and novel constraint has emerged through the limitations on national sovereignty arising from Britain's membership of the European Community. A number of factors have combined to imprint on European environmental policy a temper of progressive reformism somewhat at odds with the outlook of the Thatcher Government. These factors include the regulatory and integrating inclinations of the European Commission, the corporatist interests of transnational business, the strength of the environmental and consumer movements across Western Europe, the pro-environmental stance of some of the leading member states, and the imperative need for community safeguards over sensitive aspects of public welfare to foster popular confidence in the process of economic integration.

Another paradox is that significant departures in domestic environmental policy outside planning have arisen less from the direct application of Thatcherite principles than from the working through, under the above constraints, of other major political or policy commitments. A prime example is utility privatisation. Proposals for the water industry have yielded a commitment to a National Rivers Authority and improved environmental safeguards. Likewise the privatisation of the electricity industry may eventually involve a significant demotion of Britain's nuclear commitments and will provide an opportunity for more explicit and possibly more stringent reduction of power station emissions. Similarly, when charges were introduced for the agricultural advice given to farmers in 1986, the Minister of Agriculture, under pressure from the environmental lobby, made an exception of conservation advice, with the consequence that this previously peripheral role of the Ministry's advisory staff has become much more central. In each of these cases, Thatcherite institutional radicalism, associated with the imperative of 'rolling back the state', has opened up established procedures to critical scrutiny and created opportunities for quite separate reforms. In this respect, the development of environmental policy has benefited from having a high public profile while not being a central feature of the Government's political programme.

One consequence has been significant moves away from the *ad hoc*, piecemeal and reactive approach of traditional environmental policy, towards a more strategic, integrated and anticipatory stance (Macrory, 1986). Important developments include the creation of a unified pollution inspectorate in 1987, a reform first proposed by the Royal Commission on Environmental Pollution in 1976 and formally rejected by the Government in 1982; and the statutory duty placed on Agriculture Ministers in 1986 to balance the conservation of the countryside with the support of agriculture, this again being a change for which environmental groups had long been lobbying but which, until then, the Government had equally firmly resisted.

Developments in European Community law are likewise obliging the Government to adopt a preventive approach, at least towards certain potential environmental problems. The so-called 'Seveso' Directive (no. 82/501) for example, adopted under pressure from the European Parliament following the explosion in Italy in 1976, places a general duty on manufacturers to prevent major accidents and requires those using any of about 180 dangerous substances to produce safety reports and emergency plans and to inform the public. Perhaps the most important environmental initiative by the European Community, which came into effect in 1988, is the requirement for the formal assessment of the environmental effects of major development projects (Directive no. 85/337).

These pressures, combined, have stimulated a major reappraisal of policy and, in what may prove to be an important milestone, the DoE in 1988 issued an environmental charter which enunciated for the first time certain basic principles of environmental policy. These included, for example, informing the public about the state of the environment and taking public feelings into account in developing policy; and recognising the international dimension to many environmental problems and taking international remedies accordingly.

In general the approach to be adopted should be preventive and precautionary, acknowledging the uncertainty about environmental impacts and hazards. It should also pursue an integrated (or cross-media) strategy towards environmental protection, recognising the futility of considering each medium (air, water, land) in isolation when devising or applying pollution controls, and seeking instead the so-called 'best practical environmental option'. Undoubtedly, this is a very significant statement of principles which if vigorously pursued could profoundly alter the philosophy and practice of environmental protection in Britain. The prospect of this would appear to have been significantly enhanced following speeches by Margaret Thatcher in the autumn of 1988 which were widely interpreted as marking a major new political commitment to environmental protection.

Bibliography

Abel-Smith, B. (1964) *The Hospitals 1800–1948*, London: Heinemann.
Adam Smith Institute (1981) *Health and the Public Sector*, London: Adam Smith Institute.
Adam Smith Institute (1984) *The Omega Report: Local Government Policy*, London: Adam Smith Institute.
Agnew, J. (1984) 'Place and political behaviour: the geography of Scottish Nationalism', *Political Geography Quarterly*, 3, pp. 191–206.
Agnew, J. and Mercer, J. (1988) 'Small worlds and local heroes', *Scottish Geographical Magazine*, 104, pp. 138–47.
Aldington, Lord (1986) 'Britain's manufacturing industry', *Royal Bank of Scotland Review*, 151, pp. 3–13.
Alford, B. (1975) *Depression and Recovery? British Economic Growth, 1918–1939*, London: Macmillan.
Allen, G. (1976) *The British Disease: a Short Essay on the Nature and Causes of the Nation's Lagging Wealth*, London: Institute of Economic Affairs.
Anderson, B. (1983) *Imagined Communities: Reflections on the Origins and Spread of Nationalism*, London: Verso.
Anderson, J. (1986) 'Nationalism and geography' in Anderson, J. (ed), *The Rise of the Modern State*, Brighton: Wheatsheaf, pp. 115–142.
Anderson, J. (1988) 'Nationalist ideology and territory' in Johnston, R. J., Knight, D., and Kofman, E. (eds), *Nationalism, Self-Determination and Political Geography*, Beckenham: Croom Helm, pp. 18–39.
Anderson, P. (1987) 'The figures of descent', *New Left Review*, 161, pp. 20–77.
Archer, J. and Taylor, P. (1981) *Section and Party*, Chichester: John Wiley.
Ascher, K. (1987) *The Politics of Privatisation: Contracting-Out Public Services*, London: Macmillan.
Association of Independent Hospitals (1987) *Survey of Independent Hospitals in the Acute Sector*, London: Association of Independent Hospitals.
Association of London Authorities (1986) *London's Health Service in Crisis*, London: Association of London Authorities.
ATCO (Association of Transport Coordinating Officers) (1987) *The Transport Act 1985: monitoring report*, Kingston upon Thames: ATCO.
Atkinson, R. (1986) *A New Approach to Regional Policy*, London: Bow Publications.
Audit Commission (1986) *Making a Reality of Community Care*, London: HMSO.
Back, G. and Hamnett, C. (1985) 'State housing policy formation and the changing role of housing associations in Britain', *Policy and Politics*, 13, pp. 393–411.
Bain, S. (1985) *Railroaded: the Battle for Woodhead Pass*, London: Faber and Faber.
Baldwin, R. and Kinsey, R. (1982) *Police Power and Politics*, London: Quartet Books.

Barker, E. (1983) *The British Between the Superpowers 1945–50*, London: Macmillan.
Barker, M. (1981) *The New Racism: Conservatives and the Ideology of the Tribe*, London: Junction Books.
Barratt Brown, M. (1988) 'Away with all the great arches: Anderson's history of British capitalism', *New Left Review*, 167, pp. 22–51.
Barrett, M. (1987) 'The concept of difference', *Feminist Review*, 26, pp. 29–42.
Barry, N. (1987) *The New Right*, Beckenham: Croom Helm.
Bartlett, C. (1984) *The Global Conflict 1880–1970*, London and New York: Longman.
Bayley, S. (1986) *Sex, Drink and Fast Cars*, London: Faber and Faber.
Beech, R., Challah, S. and Ingram, R. (1987) 'Impact of cuts in acute beds on services for patients', *British Medical Journal*, 294 (6573), pp. 685–8.
Beer, S. (1985) *Modern British Politics*, London: Faber.
Bentham, G. (1986) 'Socio-tenurial polarisation in the United Kingdom, 1953–83: the income evidence', *Urban Studies*, 21, pp. 157–62.
Benyon, J. (ed.) (1986) *The Police: Powers, Procedures and Proprieties*, Oxford: Pergamon.
Berrington, H. (1983) 'The British general election of 1983', *Electoral Studies*, 2, pp. 263–8.
Berrington, H. (1984) 'Decade of dealignment', *Political Studies*, 32, pp. 117–20.
Beynon, H. (ed) (1985) *Digging Deeper: Issues in the Miners' Strike*, London: Verso.
Beynon, H., Hudson, R. and Sadler, D. (1985) *Mis-Managing Horden*, Durham: Work and Employment Research Unit, University of Durham.
Beynon, H., Hudson, R. and Sadler, D. (1986) 'Nationalized industry policies and the destruction of communities: some evidence from north east England', *Capital and Class*, 29, pp. 27–57.
Beynon, H. and McMylor, P. (1985) 'Decisive power: the new Tory state against the miners' in Beynon, H. (ed), pp. 29–46.
Blackaby, F. (ed.) (1981) *Deindustrialisation*, London: Heinemann.
Blake, R. (1985) *The Conservative Party from Peel to Thatcher*, London: Fontana.
Blank, S. (1977) 'Britain: the politics of foreign economic policy, the domestic economy, and the problem of pluralist stagnation', *International Organization*, 31, pp. 673–722.
Bleaney, M. (1985) *The Rise and Fall of Keynesian Economics*, London: Macmillan.
Blowers, A. (1984) *Something in the Air: Corporate Power and the Environment*, London: Harper and Row.
Blowers, A. (1987) 'Transition or transformation? Environmental policy under Thatcher', *Public Administration*, 65, pp. 277–94.
Bogdanor, V. (1983) *Multi-Party Politics and the Constitution*, Cambridge: University Press.
Bosanquet, N. (1983) *After the New Right*, London: Heinemann Educational Books.
Bow Group (1983) *Beveridge and the Bow Group Generation*, London: Bow Group.
Brackley, P. (1987) *Acid Deposition and Vehicle Emission: European Environmental Pressures on Britain*, Aldershot: Gower.
Bradley, D., Walker, N. and Wilkie, R. (1986) *Managing the Police: Law, Organisation and Democracy*, Brighton: Wheatsheaf.
Brett, E. (1985) *The World Economy since the War*, London: Macmillan.
Bridges, L. and Bunyan, T. (1983) 'Britain's new urban policing strategy – the Police and Criminal Evidence Act in context', *Journal of Law and Society*, 10, pp. 85–107.
Bristow, M. (1976) 'Britain's response to the Ugandan Asian crisis: government myths and political realities', *New Community*, 5, pp. 265–79.
Brogden, M. (1982) *The Police: Autonomy and Consent*, London: Academic Press.
Brotherton, I. and Lowe, P. (1981) 'Agency or instrument: the role of Statutory Instruments in conservation', *Land Use Policy*, 1, pp. 147–53.

Brown, A. (1962) *The Tory Years, 1951–1962*, London: Lawrence and Wishart.

Brown, C. (1984) *Black and White Britain*, London: Heinemann.

Buchanan, J. (ed.) (1978) *The Economics of Politics*, London: Institute of Economic Affairs.

Bulpitt, J. (1985) 'The discipline of the new democracy: Mrs Thatcher's domestic statecraft', *Political Studies*, 34, pp. 19–39.

Bulpitt, J. (1986) 'Continuity, autonomy and peripheralisation: the anatomy of the centre's race statecraft in England' in Layton-Henry, Z. and Rich, P. (eds) *Race, Government and Politics in Britain*, Basingstoke: Macmillan, pp. 17–44.

Bunyan, T. (1976) *The History and Practice of the Political Police in Britain*, London: Julian Friedmann.

Butler, D. and Kavanagh, D. (1975) *The British General Election of October 1974*, London: Macmillan.

Butler, D. and Kavanagh, D. (1984) *The British General Election of 1983*, London: Macmillan.

Butler, D. and Stokes, D. (1969) *Political Change in Britain: The Evolution of Electoral Choice* (1st edn), Harmondsworth: Penguin.

Butler, D. and Stokes, D. (1974) *Political Change in Britain: The Evolution of Electoral Choice* (2nd edn), London: Macmillan.

Callinicos, A. (1988) 'Exception or symptom? The British crisis and the world system', *New Left Review*, 169, pp. 97–106.

Campbell, B. (1986) *The Iron Ladies: Why Do Women Vote Tory?*, London: Virago.

Cantle, T. (1986) 'The deterioration of public sector housing' in Malpass, P. (ed.), pp. 52–85.

Castle, B. (1980) *The Castle Diaries, 1974–1976*, London: Weidenfeld and Nicolson.

Cell, J. W. (1982) *The Highest Stage of White Supremacy*, Cambridge: University Press.

Central Statistical Office (1987) *Social Trends*, London: HMSO.

Central Statistical Office (1988) *Social Trends*, London: HMSO.

Champion, A., Coombes, M., Ellin, D., Green. A. and Owen, D. (1987) *Changing Places: Britain's Demographic, Economic and Social Complexion*, London: Edward Arnold.

Champion, A., Green, A. and Owen, D. (1988) 'House prices and local labour market performance: an analysis of building society data for 1986', *Area*, 20, pp. 253–63.

Childs, D. (1986) *Britain since 1945* (2nd edn), London: Methuen.

Christian, L. (1983) *Policing by Coercion*, London: Greater London Council.

Clark, G. and Dear, M. (1984) *State Apparatus: the Structures and Language of Legitimacy*, Hemel Hempstead: Allen and Unwin.

Coates, D. and Hillard, J. (eds) (1986) *The Economic Decline of Modern Britain: the Debate between Left and Right*, Brighton: Wheatsheaf.

Coates, D. and Hillard, J. (eds) (1987) *The Economic Revival of Modern Britain: the Debate between Left and Right*, Aldershot: Edward Elgar.

Cobban, A. (1944) *National Self-Determination*, London: Oxford University Press.

Cockburn, C. (1985) *Machinery of Dominance*, London: Pluto.

Commission for Racial Equality (CRE) (1984) *Race and Council Housing in Hackney*, London: CRE.

Conservative Party (1979) *1979 Election Manifesto*, London: Conservative Central Office.

Cooke, P. (1983) *Theories of Planning and Spatial Development*, London: Hutchinson.

Cooke, P. (1984) 'Recent theories of political regionalism: a critique and alternative', *International Journal of Urban and Regional Research*, 8, pp. 549–72.

Cosgrave, P. (1985) *Thatcher: the First Term*, London: Bodley Head.

Coulter, J., Miller, S. and Walker, M. (1984) *A State of Siege: Politics and Policing of the Coalfields Miners' Strike 1984*, London: Canary Press.

Cowell, D., Jones, T. and Young, J. (1982) *Policing the Riots*, London: Junction Books.

Cowling, K. (1986) 'The internationalisation of production and deindustrialisation' in Amin, A. and Goddard, J. (eds) *Technological Change, Industrial Restructuring and Regional Development*, Hemel Hempstead: Allen and Unwin, pp. 23–40.

Crewe, I. (1986) 'On the death and resurrection of class voting: some comments on *How Britain Votes*', *Political Studies*, 34, pp. 620–38.

Crewe, I. and Denver, D. (eds) (1985) *Electoral Change in Western Democracies*, Beckenham: Croom Helm.

Crewe, I. and Fox, A. (1984) *British Parliamentary Constituencies: A Statistical Compendium*, London: Faber and Faber.

Critchley, T. (1978) *A History of the Police in England and Wales*, London: Constable.

Croft, S. (1986) 'Women, caring and the recasting of need: a feminist reappraisal', *Critical Social Policy*, 16, pp. 23–39.

Crone, H. (1986) *Chemicals and Society: A Guide to the New Chemical Age*, Cambridge: University Press.

Cross, M., (1983) 'Racialised poverty and reservation ideology: Blacks and the urban labour market', paper presented to the 4th Urban Change and Conflict Conference, Clacton-on-Sea.

Cross, M. (1985) 'Black workers, recession and economic restructuring in the West Midlands', paper presented to the conference on 'Racial Minorities, Economic Restructuring and Urban Decline', Warwick.

Cross, M. (1986) 'Migration and exclusion: Caribbean echoes and British realities' in Brock, C. (ed) *The Caribbean in Europe*, London: Frank Cass, pp. 85–110.

Curtice, J. and Steed, M. (1982) 'Electoral choice and the production of government', *British Journal of Political Science*, 12, pp. 249–98.

Curtice, J. and Steed, M. (1984) 'The results analysed' in Butler, D. and Kavanagh, D. (eds), pp. 333–73.

Curtice, J. and Steed, M. (1986) 'Proportionality and exaggeration in the British electoral system', *Electoral Studies*, 5, pp. 209–28.

Curtice, J. and Steed, M. (1988) 'Appendix 2: analysis' in Butler, D. and Kavanagh, D. (eds) *The British General Election of 1987*, London: Macmillan, pp. 316–62.

Cutler, T., Williams, K. and Williams, J. (1986) *Keynes, Beveridge and Beyond*, London: Routledge and Kegan Paul.

David, M. (1986) 'Morality and maternity: towards a better union than the moral rights family policy', *Critical Social Policy*, 16, pp. 40–56.

Davidson, J. (1988) *How Green is Your City?*, London: Bedford Square Press.

Davies, C. (1987) 'Things to come: the NHS in the next decade', *Sociology of Health and Illness*, 9, pp. 302–17.

Dean, D. (1988) 'Coping with colonial immigration, the Cold War and colonial policy: the Labour Government and black communities in Great Britain, 1945–51' *Immigrants and Minorities*, 7, 305–34.

Denver, D. (1987) 'The British general election of 1987: some preliminary reflections', *Parliamentary Affairs*, 40, pp. 451–7.

de Jonquieres, G. (1987) 'Privatisation: irreversible, warts and all', *Financial Times*, 25 March.

Department of Employment (1988) *Employment Gazette*, April.

Department of the Environment (1986) *Public Access to Environmental Information*, Pollution Paper no. 23, London: HMSO.

Department of the Environment (1988) *Protecting Your Environment – A Guide*, London: DoE.

Department of Trade and Industry (1988) *DTI: the Department for Enterprise*, Cmd. 278, London: HMSO.

Department of Transport (1981) *Transport Statistics, 1970–1980*, London: HMSO.

Department of Transport (1987a) *Transport Statistics, 1976–1986*, London: HMSO.

Department of Transport (1987b) *Policy for Roads in England*, London: HMSO.

DHSS (1976) *Sharing Resources for Health in England: the Report of the Resource Allocation Working Party*, London: DHSS.

DHSS (1979) *Patients First: the Reorganisation of the NHS*, London: DHSS.

DHSS (1983) *NHS Management Inquiry Report (the Griffiths Report)*, London: DHSS.

DHSS (1987) *Independent Sector Hospitals, Nursing Homes and Clinics in England*. London: DHSS.

Dickens, P., Duncan, S., Goodwin, M. and Gray, F. (1985) *Housing, States and Localities*, London: Methuen.

Dixon, D. (1983) 'Thatcher's people: the British Nationality Act 1981', *Journal of Law and Society*, 19, pp. 161–80.

Donnison, D. and Ungerson, C. (1981) *Housing Policy*, Harmondsworth: Penguin.

Doyal, L. (1979) *The Political Economy of Health*, London: Pluto.

Drewry, G. (ed.) (1985) *The New Select Committees: A Study of the 1979 Reforms*, Oxford: Clarendon Press.

Duncan, S. and Goodwin, M. (1988) *The Local State and Uneven Development: Behind the Local Government Crisis*, Cambridge: Polity Press.

Duncan, S., Goodwin, M. and Halford, S. (1988) 'Policy variation in local states: uneven development and local social relations', *International Journal of Urban and Regional Research*, 12, pp. 107–28.

Dunleavy, P. (1979) 'The urban basis of political alignment: social class, domestic property ownership and state intervention in consumption processes', *British Journal of Political Science*, 9, pp. 409–43.

Dunleavy, P. (1980a) 'The political implications of sectoral cleavages and the growth of state employment, 1: the analysis of production cleavages', *Political Studies*, 28, pp. 364–83.

Dunleavy, P. (1980b) 'The political implications of sectoral cleavages and the growth of state employment, 2: cleavage structures and political alignment', *Political Studies*, 28, pp. 527–49.

Dunleavy, P. (1981) *The Politics of Mass Housing in Britain, 1945–75*, Oxford: University Press.

Dunleavy, P. (1987) 'Class dealignment in Britain revisited', *West European Politics*, 10, pp. 400–19.

Dunleavy, P. and Husbands, C. (1985) *British Democracy at the Crossroads*, Hemel Hempstead: Allen and Unwin.

Dunn, R., Forrest, R. and Murie, A. (1987) 'The geography of council house sales in England, 1979–1985', *Urban Studies*, 24, pp. 47–59.

ECMT (European Conference of Ministers of Transport) (1987) *Statistical Trends in Transport 1965–1984*, Paris: OECD.

Economist, The (1978) 'Appomattox or Civil War?' 27 May.

Elliot, B. and McCrone, D. (1987) 'Class, culture and morality: a sociological analysis of Neo-Conservatism', *Sociological Review*, 35, pp. 485–515.

Elson, M. (1986) *Green Belts: Conflict Mediation in the Urban Fringe*, London: Heinemann.

European Commission (1983, 1986) *The Europeans and their Environment*, Brussels: Commission of the European Communities.

Farmer, M. and Barrell, R. (1981) 'Entrepreneurship and government policy: the case of the housing market', *Journal of Public Policy*, 1, pp. 307–32.

Farrington, J. and Mackay, T. (1987) 'Bus deregulation in Scotland: a review of the first six months', *Fraser of Allander Institute Quarterly Economic Commentary*, 1, 13, pp. 64–70.

Financial Times (1987) 'Larger unions continue to lose members', 25 June.

Financial Times (1988a) 'TUC unions' membership declines 1.3%', 26 April.

Financial Times (1988b) 'Single union car plant has AEU membership of 7%', 26 April.

Finch, J. and Groves, D. (eds) (1983) *A Labour of Love: Women, Work and Caring*, London: Routledge and Kegan Paul.

Fine, B. and Harris, L. (1985) *The Peculiarities of the British Economy*, London: Lawrence and Wishart.

Fine, B. and Millar, R. (1985) *Policing the Miners' Strike*, London: Lawrence and Wishart.

Finer, S. E. (ed.) (1975) *Adversary Politics and Electoral Reform*, London: Anthony Wigram.

Fitzgerald, M. (1987) *Black People and Party Politics in Britain*, London: Runnymede Trust.

Fleming, M. (1980) 'Industrial Policy' in Maunder, P. (ed) *The British Economy in the 1970s*, London: Heinemann, pp. 141–68.

Flett, H. (1979) 'Dispersal policies in council housing: arguments and evidence', *New Community*, 7, pp. 184–94.

Forrest, R. and Murie, A. (1985) *An Unreasonable Act? Central–Local Government Conflict and the Housing Act 1980*, Bristol: School for Advanced Urban Studies.

Forrest, R. and Murie, A. (1986a) 'Marginalisation and subsidised individualism: the sale of council houses in the restructuring of the British welfare state', *International Journal of Urban and Regional Research*, 10, 46–66.

Forrest, R. and Murie, A. (1986b) 'If the price is right', *Roof*, March/April, pp. 23–5.

Forrest, R. and Murie, A. (1987a) 'Fiscal reorientation, centralisation and the privatisation of council housing', in Van Vliet, W. (ed) *Housing Markets and Policies under Fiscal Austerity*, Westport, Connecticut: Greenwood Press, pp. 15–31.

Forrest, R. and Murie, A. (1987b) 'The pauperisation of council housing', *Roof*, Jan./Feb., pp. 20–2.

Fothergill, S. and Gudgin, G. (1982) *Unequal Growth: Urban and Regional Employment Change in the UK*, London: Heinemann.

Fowle, J. (ed.) (1987) *Applications of Biotechnology: Environmental and Policy Issues*, London: Western Press.

Frankel, M. (1974) *The Alkali Inspectorate*, London: Social Audit.

Franklin, M. (1985) *The Decline of Class Voting in Britain: Changes in the Basis of Electoral Choice 1964–1983*, Oxford: Clarendon.

Franklin, M. and Page, E. (1984) 'A critique of the consumption cleavage approach in British voting studies', *Political Studies*, 32, pp. 521–36.

Fredrickson, G. (1981) *White Supremacy*, New York and Oxford: Oxford University Press.

Freeman, G. (1979) *Immigrant Labour and Racial Conflict in Industrial Societies*, Princeton, NJ: Princeton University Press.

Frenkel, S. and Western, J. (1988) 'Pretext or prophylaxis? racial segregation and malarial mosquitos in a British tropical colony: Sierra Leone', *Annals, Association of American Geographers*, 78(2), pp. 211–28.

Fry, G. K. (1975) 'Economic policy-making and planning 1945–70', *Public Administration Bulletin*, 18, pp. 3–22.

Fyfe, N. (1987) 'Contesting consultation: the local political response to Section 106 of the Police and Criminal Evidence Act 1984 in the Metropolitan Police District', Paper presented at the British Criminology Conference, Sheffield.

Gaffikin, F. and Nickson, A. (1984) *Jobs Crisis and the Multinationals: the Case of the West Midlands*, Birmingham: Birmingham Trade Union Resource Centre.

Gallie, D. (1987) 'Patterns of similarity and diversity in British urban labour markets: trade union allegiance and decline', paper presented to the Sixth Urban Change and Conflict Conference, University of Kent, Canterbury, 20–23 September.

Gamble, A. (1981) *Britain in Decline: Economic Policy, Political Strategy and the British State*, London: Macmillan.

Gamble, A. (1985) *Britain in Decline: Economic Policy, Political Strategy and the British State*, 2nd edn, London: Macmillan.

Gamble, A. (1988) *The Free Economy and the Strong State*, London: Macmillan.

Game, A. and Pringle, R. (1984) *Gender at Work*, London: Pluto.

Geary, R. (1985) *Policing Industrial Disputes: 1983 to 1985*, Cambridge: University Press.

Gellner, E. (1964) 'Nationalism' in *Thought and Change*, London: Weidenfeld and Nicolson, pp. 147–78.

Giddens, A. (1985) *The Nation – State and Violence*, Cambridge: Polity Press.

Goldthorpe, J. (1988) *Social Mobility and Class Structure in Modern Britain*, Oxford: Clarendon Press.

Goodwin, M. (forthcoming) 'The replacement of a surplus population: the employment and housing policies of the London Docklands Development Corporation' in Allen, J. and Hamnett, C. (eds) *Housing and Labour Markets*, London: Unwin Hyman, forthcoming.

Gordon, P. (1984) 'Community policing: towards the local police state', *Critical Social Policy*, 10, pp. 39–57.

Gordon, P. and Klug, F. (1986) *New Right Racism*, London: Searchlight.

Gourvish, T. (1986) *British Rail: A Business History*, Cambridge: University Press.

Grant, W. (1982) *The Political Economy of Industrial Policy*, London: Butterworth.

Greater London Council (1982) *The Policing Aspects of Lord Scarman's Report on the Brixton Disorders*, London: GLC.

Greater London Council (1983) *Policing London*, 7, p. 14.

Green, D. (1987) *The New Right*, Brighton: Wheatsheaf.

Greve Report (1986) *Homelessness in London*, Bristol: School for Advanced Urban Studies, Working Paper no. 60.

Grove, J. (1967) *Government and Industry in Britain*, London: Longmans.

Guillebaud Committee (1956) *Report of the Committee of Inquiry into the Cost of the NHS*, London: HMSO.

Guiver, J. and Turner, R. (1987) 'Buswatch: the passengers' viewpoints on deregulation' in *PTRC 15th Annual Summer Meeting, Seminar A: Transport Policy*, pp. 179–90.

Gyford, J. (1985) *The Politics of Local Socialism*, Hemel Hempstead: Allen and Unwin.

Hagerstrand, T. (1987) 'Human interaction and spatial mobility: retrospect and prospect' in Nijkamp, P. and Reichman, S. (eds) *Transportation Policy in a Changing World*, Aldershot: Gower, pp. 11–28.

Haigh, N. (1984) *EEC Environmental Policy in Britain*, London: Environmental Data Services.

Hall, P. (1986) *Governing the Economy: the Politics of State Intervention in Britain and France*, Cambridge: Polity Press.

Hall, S. and Jacques, M. (eds) (1983) *The Politics of Thatcherism*, London: Lawrence and Wishart.

Hamer, M. (1987) *Wheels within Wheels: a Study of the Road Lobby*, London: Routledge and Kegan Paul.

Hamnett, C. (1983) 'The conditions in Britain's inner cities on the eve of the 1981 riots', *Area*, 15, pp. 7–13.

Hamnett, C. (1984) 'Housing the two nations: socio-tenurial polarisation in England and Wales, 1961–1981', *Urban Studies*, 21, pp. 389–405.

Hamnett, C. (1987) 'Conservative Government housing policy in Britain, 1979–1985: economics or ideology?' in Van Vliet, W. (ed) *Housing Markets and Policies under Fiscal Austerity*, Westport, Connecticut: Greenwood Press, pp. 203–20.

Hamnett, C. (1988) 'The owner-occupied market in Britain: a north–south divide?' in Lewis, J. and Townsend, A. (eds) *North versus South? Industrial and Social Change in Britain*, London: Paul Chapman.

Hamnett, C. and Randolph, W. (1988) *Cities, Housing and Profits: Flat Break-Up and the Decline of Private Renting*, London: Hutchinson.

Hansard (1988) *Parliamentary Debates*, vol. 126, no. 79, c. 323–411, 27 January.

Harloe, M. and Paris, C. (1984) 'The decollectivisation of consumption: housing and local government finance in England and Wales, 1979–1981', in Szelenyi, I. (ed) *Cities in Recession*, London: Sage, pp. 70–98.

Harris, C. (1987) 'British capitalism, migration and relative surplus population: a synthesis', *Migration*, 1, pp. 47–96.

Harvey, D. (1982) *The Limits to Capital*, Oxford: Basil Blackwell.

Harvey, D. (1985) 'The geopolitics of capitalism' in Gregory, D. and Urry, J. (eds) *Social Relations and Spatial Structures*, London: Macmillan, pp. 128–63.

Hayek, F. von (1944) *The Road to Serfdom*, London: Routledge.

Hayek, F. von (1960) *The Constitution of Liberty*, London: Routledge.

Heald, D. (1983) *Public Expenditure: its Defence and Reform*, Oxford: Martin Robertson.

Heath, A., Jowell, R. and Curtice, J. (1985) *How Britain Votes*, Oxford: Pergamon.

Heath, A., Jowell, R. and Curtice, J. (1987a) 'Trendless fluctuation: a reply to Crewe', *Political Studies*, 35, pp. 256–77.

Heath, A., Jowell, R. and Curtice, J. (1987b) 'Attitudes, values and identities in the British electorate', paper presented to the annual meeting of the American Political Science Association, Chicago.

Henderson, J. and Karn, V. (1984) 'Race, class and the allocation of public housing in Britain', *Urban Studies*, 21, pp. 115–28.

Heseltine, M. (1988) Speech to the Brick Development Association, London, 18 May.

Hewison, R. (1987) *The Heritage Industry*, London: Methuen.

Hillyard, P. (1987) 'The normalization of special powers: from Northern Ireland to Britain' in Scraton, P. (ed) *Law, Order and the Authoritarian State*, Milton Keynes: Open University Press, pp. 279–312.

Himmelweit, H. *et al.* (1985) *How Voters Decide* (2nd edn) Milton Keynes: Open University Press.

Hindess, B. (1987) *Freedom, Equality and the Market*, London: Tavistock.

Holloway, J. (1987) 'The red rose of Nissan', *Capital and Class*, 32, pp. 142–64.

Holmes, M. (1982) *Political Pressure and Economic Policy: British Government, 1970–74*, London: Butterworth.

Holmes, M. (1985) *The First Thatcher Government*, London: Wheatsheaf.

Holzapfel, H. and Sachs, W. (1987) 'Speed and prospects for our way of life' in *PTRC 15th Annual Summer Meeting, Seminar A: Transport Policy*, pp. 223–30.

House of Commons Expenditure Committee (1977) *Planning Procedures*, London: HMSO.

House of Commons (1984) *Fourth Report from the Social Services Committee, Session 1983–4: Public Expenditure on the Social Services*, London: HMSO.

House of Commons (1985) *Second Report from the Social Services Committee, Session 1984–5: Community Care with Special Reference to Adult Mentally Ill and Mentally Handicapped People*, London: HMSO.

House of Commons (1987) *Third Report from the Transport Committee, Session 1986–1987: Financing of Rail Services*, vol. 1 HC–383–I, London: HMSO.

House of Commons (1988) *First Report from the Social Services Committee, Session 1987–8: Financing the National Health Service: Short-Term Issues*, London: HMSO.

House of Lords Select Committee on Overseas Trade (1985) *Report*, House of Lords Session 1984–5 (238–I) London: HMSO.

Howell, D. (1987) 'The future of the education service under the Conservatives', paper presented at a Political Studies Association conference, Birmingham, 31 October.

Howkins, A. (1985) *Poor Labouring Men: Rural Radicalism in Norfolk, 1870–1923*, London: Routledge and Kegan Paul.

Hudson, R. (1985) 'The paradoxes of state intervention: the impact of nationalized industry policies and regional policies in the northern region in the post war period' in Chapman, R. (ed) *Public Policy Studies: North East England*, Edinburgh: University Press, pp. 57–79.

Hudson R. (1986a) 'Nationalized industry policies and regional policies: the role of the state in capitalist societies in the deindustrialization and reindustrialization of regions', *Society and Space*. 4, pp. 7–28.

Hudson, R. (1986b) 'Producing an industrial wasteland: capital, labour and the state in north east England' in Rowthorn, B. and Martin, R. (eds) pp. 169–213.

Hudson, R. (1988) *State Policies, Party Politics and Regional Change: an Analysis of North East England*, London: Pion.

Hudson, R. and Sadler, D. (1985a) 'Coal and dole: employment policies on the coalfields', in Beynon, H. (ed) pp. 217–30.

Hudson, R. and Sadler, D. (1985b) 'The development of Middlesbrough's iron and steel industry 1841–1985', *Working Paper 2: Middlesbrough Locality Study*, Departments of Geography and Sociology, University of Durham.

Hudson, R. and Sadler, D. (1987a) 'Manufactured in the UK? Special steels, motor vehicles and the politics of industrial decline', *Capital and Class*, 32, pp. 55–82.

Hudson, R. and Sadler, D. (1987b) 'National policies and local economic initiatives: evaluating the effectiveness of UK coal and steel closure area reindustrialisation measures', *Local Economy*, 2, pp. 107–14.

Hudson, R. and Sadler, D. (1989) *The Steel Industry: Global Restructuring and Local Impacts*, London: Routledge.

Hudson, R. and Williams, A. (1989) *The Divided Realm: an Anatomy of Mrs Thatcher's Britain*, London: Radius.

Incomes Data Services (IDS) (1987) *IDS Report 505*, London: IDS.

Incomes Data Services (IDS) (1988) *Skill Shortages in the South East*, IDS Report no. 516, Labour Market Supplement, no 2, March, London: IDS.

Independent, The (1988) 'Shop staff present crucial challenge', 3 May, p. 5.

Jackson, P. (ed.) (1987) *Race and Racism*, Hemel Hempstead: Allen and Unwin.

Jefferson, T. and Grimshaw, R. (1984) *Controlling the Constable*, London: Frederick Muller, in association with the Cobden Trust.

Jenkins, P. (1987) *Mrs Thatcher's Revolution*, London: Cape.

Jennings, J. (1971) 'Geographical implications of the municipal housing programme in England and Wales, 1919–1939', *Urban Studies*, 8, pp. 121–38.

Jessop, B. (1980) 'The transformation of the state in post-war Britain' in Scase, R. (ed.) *The State In Western Europe*, Beckenham: Croom Helm, pp. 23–93.

Jessop, B., Bonnett, K., Bromley, S. and Ling, T. (1984) 'Authoritarian populism, two nations, and Thatcherism', *New Left Review*, 147, pp. 32–60.

Johnson, M. R. D. (1987) 'Ethnic minorities and racism in welfare provision' in Jackson, P. (ed.) pp. 238–53.

Johnston, R. (1981a) 'Regional variation in British voting trends: tests of an ecological model', *Regional Studies*, 15, pp. 23–32.

Johnston, R. (1981b) 'Testing the Butler–Stokes model of a polarization effect around the national swing in partisan preferences', *British Journal of Political Science*, 11, pp. 113–17.

Johnston, R. (1983) 'Spatial continuity and electoral variability', *Electoral Studies*, 2, pp. 53–68.

Johnston, R. (1985) *The Geography of English Politics: The 1983 General Election*, Beckenham: Croom Helm.

Johnston, R. (1986a) 'A space for place (or a place for space) in British psephology', *Environment and Planning A*, 19, pp. 599–618.

Johnston, R. (1986b) 'The neighbourhood effect revisited: spatial science or political regionalism', *Environment and Planning D: Society and Space*, 4, pp. 41–55.

Johnston, R. (1986c) 'Places and votes: the role of location in the creation of political attitudes', *Urban Geography*, 7, pp. 103–16.

Johnston, R. and Pattie, C. J. (1987) 'A dividing nation? An initial exploration of the changing electoral geography of Great Britain, 1979–1987', *Environment and Planning A*, 19, pp. 1001–13.

Johnston, R. and Pattie, C. J. (1988) 'Are we all Alliance now? Discriminating by discriminant analysis', *Electoral Studies*, 7, pp. 27–32.

Johnston, R., Pattie, C. and Allsopp, J. (1988) *A Nation Dividing? The Electoral Map of Britain, 1979–1987*, Harlow: Longman.

Jones, T., Maclean, B. and Young, J. (1986) *The Islington Crime Survey: Crime, Victimisation and Policing in the Inner City*, Aldershot: Gower.

Karn, V. (1983) 'Race and housing in Britain: the role of the major institutions' in Glazer, N. and Young, K. (eds) *Ethnic Pluralism and Public Policy*, London: Heinemann, pp. 162–83.

Karn, V., Kemeny, J. and Williams, P. (1986) *Home Ownership in the Inner City: Salvation or Despair?*, Aldershot: Gower.

Kavanagh, D. (1987) *Thatcherism and British Politics: the End of Consensus?*, Oxford: Clarendon Press.

Keith, M. (1987) '"Something Happened": the problems of explaining the 1980 and 1981 riots in British cities' in Jackson, P. (ed.), pp. 275–303.

Kelly, J. (1987) *Labour and the Unions*, London: Verso.

Kemp, R., O'Riordan, T. and Purdue, M. (1986) 'The public examination of radioactive waste disposal', *Policy and Politics*, 14, pp. 9–25.

Kennedy, W. (1987) *Industrial Structure, Capital Markets and the Origins of British Economic Decline*, Cambridge: University Press.

Kettle, M. (1985) 'The national reporting centre and the miners' strike' in Fine B. and Millar R. (eds), pp. 23–33.

Keynes, J. M. (1937) 'How to avoid a slump – looking ahead: the problems of the steady level', *The Times*, 12 January.

Kilroy, B. (1982) 'The financial and economic implications of council house sales' in English, J. (ed.) *The Future of Council Housing*, Beckenham: Croom Helm, pp. 52–95.

Kimber, R. *et al.* (1974) 'Parliamentary questions and the allocation of departmental responsibilities', *Parliamentary Affairs*, 27, pp. 287–93.

King, D. (1987) *The New Right: Politics, Markets and Citizenship*, Basingstoke: Macmillan.

Kinsey, R., Lea, J. and Young, J. (1986) *Losing the Fight Against Crime*, Oxford: Basil Blackwell.

Klein, R. (1983) *The Politics of the National Health Service*, Harlow: Longmans.

Klein, R. (1984) 'The politics of ideology and the reality of politics: the case of

Britain's health service in the 1980s', *Milbank Memorial Fund Quarterly: Medicine and Society*, 62, pp. 82–109.

Kleinman, M. and Whitehead, C. (1987) 'Local variations in the sale of council houses in England, 1979–1984', *Regional Studies*, 21, pp. 1–12.

Knowles, R. (1988) 'The age of the bus – or is it?', *Geographical Magazine*, LX(6), pp. 36–8.

Kolko, J. and Kolko, G. (1972) *The Limits of Power: The World and United States Foreign Policy, 1945–54*, New York: Harper and Row.

Krieger, J. (1986) *Reagan, Thatcher and the Politics of Decline*, Cambridge: Polity Press.

Labour Research Department (1987) 'Unions face fall-out from industrial decline', *Labour Research*, September, 13–15.

Lancaster City Council (LCC) (1987) *Lancaster Local Plan*, Lancaster: LCC.

Lane, T. (1982) 'The unions: caught on an ebb tide', *Marxism Today*, September, pp. 6–13.

Lash, S. and Urry, J. (1987) *The End of Organised Capitalism*, Cambridge: Polity Press.

Lea, J. and Young, J. (1982) 'The riots in Britain 1981: urban violence and political marginalisation' in Cowell, D., Jones, T. and Young, J. (eds), pp. 5–20.

Leach, B. (1987) 'Conservatism, local government and the community charge', paper presented at a Political Studies Association conference, Birmingham, 31 October.

Leitch, G. (1978) *Report of the Advisory Committee on Trunk Road Assessment*, London: HMSO.

Leonard, T. (1985) 'Policing the miners in Derbyshire', *Policing*, 1 (2), pp. 96–101.

Levitas, R. (ed.) (1986) *The Ideology of the New Right*, Cambridge: Polity Press.

Levitt, R. (1980) *Implementing Public Policy*, Beckenham: Croom Helm.

Lewis, W. (1978) *Growth and Fluctuations 1879–1913*, Hemel Hempstead: Allen and Unwin.

Leys, C. (1985) 'Thatcherism and British manufacturing', *New Left Review*, 151, pp. 5–25.

Lloyd, P. and Shutt, J. (1985) 'Recession and restructuring in the north west region 1975–1982: the implications of recent events' in Massey, D. and Meegan, R. (eds) *Politics and Method*, London: Methuen, pp. 13–60.

Loach, L. (1987) 'Can feminism survive a third term?', *Feminist Review*, 27, pp. 24–36.

London Health Emergency (LHE) (1987) *Hitting the Skids: A Catalogue of Health Service Cuts In London*, London: LHE.

Loveday, B. (1985) *The Role and Effectiveness of the Merseyside Police Committee*, Liverpool: Merseyside Police Committee.

Loveday, B. (1987) 'Progress of the joint boards', *Policing*, 3(3), pp. 196–213.

Lovering, J. and Boddy, M. (1988) 'The geography of military industry in Britain', *Area*, 20(1), pp. 41–51.

Low Pay Unit (1987) *Low Pay Review*, 31, p. 33.

Lowe, P. (1988) 'Environmental politics and rural conservation in Western Europe' in Ollerenshaw, J. and Whitby, M. (eds) *Land Use and the European Environment*, London: Francis Pinter.

Lowe, P. and Goyder, J. (1983) *Environmental Groups in Politics*, Hemel Hempstead: Allen and Unwin.

Lowe, P. *et al.* (1986) *Countryside Conflicts: The Politics of Farming, Forestry and Conservation*, Aldershot: Gower.

Lowe, P. and Morrison, D. (1984) 'Bad news or good news: environmental politics and the mass media', *Sociological Review*, 32, pp. 75–90.

Lustgarten, L. (1985) 'The long-distance policemen', *New Society*, 3, pp. 24–5.

Lustgarten, L. (1986) *The Governance of the Police*, London: Sweet and Maxwell.

McAllister, I. (1987) 'Social context, turnout and the vote: Australian and British comparisons', *Political Geography Quarterly*, 6, pp. 17–30.

MacInnes, J. (1987) *Thatcherism at Work*, Milton Keynes: Open University Press.

Macrory, R. (1986) *Environmental Policy in Britain: Reaffirmation or Reform?* IIUG DP–86–4, Berlin: International Institute for Environment and Society.

Malpass, P. (1983) 'Residualisation and the restructuring of housing provision', *Housing Review*, March/April, pp. 1–2.

Malpass, P. (ed.) (1986) *The Housing Crisis*, Beckenham: Croom Helm.

Marshall, J. (1968) 'The pattern of housebuilding in the interwar period in England and Wales', *Scottish Journal of Political Economy*, XV (2), pp. 184–205.

Martin, R. (1986) 'Thatcherism and Britain's industrial landscape' in Martin, R. and Rowthorn, R. (eds) (1986), pp. 238–90.

Martin, R. (1988a) 'Industrial capitalism in transition: the contemporary reorganisation of the British space economy' in Massey, D. and Allen, J. (eds) *Uneven Redevelopment*, London: Hodder and Stoughton, pp. 202–32.

Martin, R. (1988b) 'The new economics and politics of regional restructuring: the British case' in Albrechts, L., Moulaert, F., Roberts, P. and Swyngedouw, E. (eds) *Regional Planning at the Crossroads*, Newcastle: Roger Booth.

Martin, R. (1988c) 'The political economy of Britain's north–south divide', *Transactions, Institute of British Geographers*, 13, pp. 389–418.

Martin, R. and Hodge, J. (1983) 'The reconstruction of British regional policy, 1: the crisis of conventional practice', *Government and Policy*, 1, pp. 133–52.

Martin, R. and Rowthorn, R. (1986) (eds) *The Geography of Deindustrialisation*, London: Macmillan.

Massey, D. (1984) *Spatial Divisions of Labour*, London: Macmillan.

Massey, D. (1986) 'The legacy lingers on: the impact of Britain's international role on its internal geography' in Martin, R. and Rowthorn, R. (eds), pp. 31–52.

Massey, D. and Meegan, R. (1979) 'The geography of industrial reorganisation: the spatial effects of the restructuring of the electrical engineering sector under the Industrial Reorganisation Corporation', *Progress in Planning*, 10(3), pp. 155–237.

Massey, D. and Miles, N. (1984) 'Mapping out the unions', *Marxism Today*, May, pp. 19–22.

Merrett, S. (1979) *State Housing in Britain*, London: Routledge.

Miles, R. (1984) 'The riots of 1958: the ideological construction of "race relations" as a political issue in Britain', *Immigrants and Minorities*, 3, pp. 252–75.

Miles, R. (1987) 'Recent Marxist theories of nationalism and the issue of racism', *British Journal of Sociology*, 38, pp. 24–41.

Miliband, R. (1969) *The State in Capitalist Society*, London: Weidenfeld and Nicolson.

Miller, W. (1977) *Electoral Dynamics*, London: Macmillan.

Miller, W. (1984) 'There was no alternative', *Parliamentary Affairs*, 37, pp. 364–74.

Minford, P., Peel, M. and Ashton, P. (1987) *The Housing Morass: Regulation, Immobility and Unemployment*, Hobart Paperback 25, London: Institute of Economic Affairs.

Ministry of Health (1962) *A Hospital Plan for England and Wales*, London: Ministry of Health.

Mitchell, A. (1987) 'Beyond socialism', *The Political Quarterly*, 58, pp. 389–403.

Mohan, J. and Woods, K. (1985) 'Restructuring health care? The social geography of public and private health care under the British Conservative Government', *International Journal of Health Services*, 15, pp. 197–217.

Moore, B., Rhodes, J. and Tyler, P. (1986) *The Effects of Government Regional Policy*, London: HMSO.

Morgan, K. (1984) *Labour in Power 1945–51*, Oxford: University Press.

Morgan, K. (1986) 'Reindustrialisation in peripheral Britain: state policy, the space economy and industrial innovation' in Martin, R. and Rowthorn, R. (eds) , pp. 322–59.

Morgan, K. and Sayer, A. (1984) 'A modern industry in a mature region: the remaking of management–labour relations', *Urban and Regional Studies Working Paper 39*, University of Sussex.

Morgan, R. (1985) 'Police accountability: current developments and future prospects', paper presented to the Police Foundation Conference, Harrogate.

Morgan, R. (1987) 'The local determinants of policing policy' in Willmott, P. (ed.) *Policing and the Community*, Discussion Paper 16, London: Policy Studies Institute, pp. 29–44.

MORI (1987) *Public Attitudes to the Environment*, London: MORI.

Mottershead, P. (1978) 'Industrial policy' in Blackaby, F. (ed.) *British Economic Policy 1960–74*, Cambridge: University Press.

Moyes, A. (1988) 'Travellers' tales in rural Wales', *Geographical Magazine*, LX(6), pp. 40–1.

Murie, A. (1982) 'A new era for council housing' in English, J. (ed.) *The Future of Council Housing*, Beckenham: Croom Helm, pp. 34–51.

Murray, N. (1986) 'Anti-racists and other demons: the press and ideology in Thatcher's Britain', *Race and Class*, 27, pp. 1–19.

Nairn, T. (1977) *The Break-Up of Britain: Crisis and Neo-Nationalism*, London: New Left Books.

Nairn, T. (1981) 'The crisis of the British state', *New Left Review*, 130, pp. 37–44.

Nairn, T. (1983) 'Britain's living legacy' in Hall, S. and Jacques, M. (eds) *The Politics of Thatcherism*, London: Lawrence and Wishart, pp. 281–90.

National Association of Health Authorities (NAHA) (1986) *NHS Economic Review*, Birmingham: NAHA.

National Association of Health Authorities (NAHA) (1987) *The Financial Position of District Health Authorities: Autumn Survey 1987*, Birmingham: NAHA.

National Audit Office (1987) *The Regulation of Heavy Lorries*, London: HMSO.

Nationwide Anglia Building Society (1987) *House Prices in 1987*, London: Nationwide Anglia Building Society.

Nationwide Building Society (1987) *House Prices: the North-South Divide*, London: Nationwide Building Society.

Navarro, V. (1978) *Class Struggle, the State, and Medicine*, Oxford: Martin Robertson.

Newcastle Health Concern (1986) *Cause for Concern: the State of Newcastle's NHS*, Newcastle: North East Trades Union Studies Information Unit.

Nicholson, P. (1984) 'Politics and force' in Leftwich, A. (ed.) *What is Politics? The Activity and its Study*, Oxford: Basil Blackwell, pp. 33–45.

Norpoth, H. (1987) 'Guns and butter and Government popularity in Britain', *American Political Science Review*, 81, pp. 949–59.

Northedge, F. (1974) *Descent from Power: British Foreign Policy 1945–1973*, Hemel Hempstead: Allen and Unwin.

OECD (1984) *Environment and Economics*, Background Papers, Vol. 1, Paris: OECD.

OECD (1985a) *Compendium of Environmental Data*, Paris: OECD.

OECD (1985b) *The State of the Environment*, Paris: OECD.

Olivierin, A. *et al.* (1985) 'Ground water contamination in Silicon Valley', *Journal of Water Resources, Planning and Management*, 3, pp. 346–58.

Orridge, A. (1981) 'Uneven development and nationalism', *Political Studies*, 29(1), pp. 1–15 and 29(2), pp. 181–90.

Overbeek, H. (1988) *Global Capitalism and Britain's Decline*, unpublished PhD thesis, University of Amsterdam.

Owens, S. (1986) 'Environmental politics in Britain: new paradigm or placebo?', *Area*, 18 (3), pp. 195–201.

Paddison, R. (1983) *The Fragmented State*, Oxford: Basil Blackwell.

Pahl, J. (1983) 'The allocation of money and the structuring of inequality within marriage', *Sociological Review*, pp. 237–62.

Parekh, B. (1986) 'The "New Right" and the politics of nationhood' in G. Cohen *et al.* (eds) *The New Right: Image and Reality*, London: Runnymede Trust, pp. 33–44.

Paris, C. and Lambert, J. (1979) 'Housing problems and the state: the case of Birmingham, England', in Herbert, D. T. and Johnston, R. J. (eds) *Geography and the Urban Environment*, vol. 2, Chichester: Wiley, pp. 227–58.

Park, C. (1987) *Acid Rain: Rhetoric and Reality*, London: Methuen.

Parsons, W. (1986) *The Political Economy of British Regional Policy*, Beckenham: Croom Helm.

Paterson, T. (1984) *Conservation and the Conservatives*, London: Bow Group.

Peach, C. (1981) 'The growth and distribution of the black population in Britain, 1945–80' in Coleman, D. (ed.) *Demography of Immigrants and Minority Groups in the United Kingdom*, London: Academic Press, pp. 23–42.

Pearce, F. (1986) 'Dirty water under the bridge' in Goldsmith, E. and Hildyard, N. (eds) *Green Britain or Industrial Wasteland?*, Cambridge: Polity Press, pp. 231–46.

Pettigrew, W. (1984) *Volunteers in the Environment*, Berkhamsted: Volunteer Centre.

Phillips, A. (1987) *Divided Loyalties*, London: Virago.

Phillips, A. and Taylor, B. (1980) 'Sex and skill', *Feminist Review*, 27, pp. 24–36.

Phillips, D. (1986) *What Price Equality?*, London: GLC.

Plowden, S. (1985) *Transport Reform: Changing the Rules*, London: Policy Studies Institute.

Policy Studies Institute (PSI) (1983) *Police and People in London vol 3: A Survey of Police Officers*, London: PSI.

Pollitt, C. (1986) 'Performance measurement in public services: some political implications', *Parliamentary Affairs*, 39, pp. 315–29.

Public Accounts Committee (1988) *26th Report, Session 1987–8: Community Care Developments*, London: HMSO.

Radical Statistics Health Group (RSHG) (1987) *Facing the Figures: What is Really Happening to the NHS?*, London: RSHG.

Rankin, M. (1987) *A Fistful of Tinsel: the Effects of the Community Programme on Local Voluntary Activity*, Berkhamsted: Volunteer Centre.

Rayner, G. (1987) 'Lessons from America: commercialisation and growth of private medicine in Britain', *International Journal of Health Services*, 17, pp. 197–216.

Reeves, F. (1983) *British Racial Discourse*, Cambridge: University Press.

Reiner, R. (1985a) *The Politics of the Police*, Brighton: Wheatsheaf.

Reiner, R. (1985b) 'Policing strikes: an historical U-turn', *Policing*, 1(3), pp. 138–48.

Reiner, R. (1985c) 'Police and race relations' in Baxter, J. and Koffman, L. (eds) *Police: The Constitution and the Community*, Oxford: Professional Books, pp. 149–87.

Research Working Group (1979) 'Cyclical rhythms and secular trends in the capitalist world-economy', *Review*, 2, pp. 483–500.

Reynolds, D. (1981) *The Creation of the Anglo-American Alliance 1937–1941: A Study in Cooperative Competition*, London: Europa.

Rich, P. (1986a) *Race and Empire in British Politics*, Cambridge: University Press.

Rich, P. (1986b) 'The impact of South African segregationist and apartheid ideology on British racial thought: 1939–1960', *New Community*, 13, pp. 1–17.

Richardson, G. *et al.* (1982) *Policing Pollution*, Oxford: Clarendon Press.

Richardson, J. and Watts, N. (1985) *National Policy Styles and the Environment* IIUG DP-85-16, Berlin: International Institute for Environment and Society.

Riddell, P. (1985) *The Thatcher Government*, Oxford: Blackwell.

Roberts, J. (1987) 'Autolatry: a detumescent force?' in *PTRC 15th Annual Summer Meeting, Seminar A: Transport Policy*, pp. 243–58, London, PTRC.

Rose, R. (1982) 'From simple determinism to interactive models of voting', *Comparative Political Studies*, 15, pp. 145–69.

Rose, R. and McAllister, I. (1986) *Voters Begin to Choose: from Closed Class to Open Elections in Britain*, London: Sage Publications.

Rothwell, V. (1982) *Britain and the Cold War 1941–1947*, London: Cape.

Rowthorn, R. and Wells, J. (1987) *Deindustrialisation and Foreign Trade: Britain's Decline in a Global Perspective*, Cambridge: University Press.

Royal Commission on the Depression of Trade and Industry (1886) *Final Report*, Cmnd. 4893, Parliamentary Papers XXIII, London: HMSO.

Rüdig, W. and Lowe, P. (1989) *The Green Wave: Ecological Parties in Global Perspective*, Cambridge: Polity Press.

Sanders, D., Ward, H. and Marsh, D. (1987) 'Government popularity and the Falklands war: a reassessment', *British Journal of Political Science*, 17, pp. 281–313.

Sarlvik, B. and Crewe, I. (1983) *Decade of Dealignment*, Cambridge: University Press.

Saunders, P. (1983) '"We can't afford democracy too much": findings from a study of regional state institutions in south east England', *Urban and Regional Studies Working Paper 43*, University of Sussex.

Saunders, P. (1985) 'The forgotten dimension of central–local government relations: theorising the "regional state"' *Environment and Planning C: Government and Policy*, 3, pp. 149–62.

Sayer, A. (1986) 'New developments in manufacturing: the "just-in-time" system', *Capital and Class*, 30, pp. 43–72.

Scarman, Lord (1981) *The Brixton Disorders, 10–12 April 1981*, Cmnd. 8427, London: HMSO.

Scarman, Lord (1985) 'Police and public consultation' in Cranfield Institute of Technology, *Models of Police/Public Consultation in Europe*, Bedford: Cranfield Press, pp. 10–15.

Schott, K. (1982) 'The rise of Keynesian economics in Britain, 1940–64', *Economy and Society*, 11, pp. 292–316.

Scruton, R. (1980) *The Meaning of Conservatism*, Harmondsworth: Penguin.

Segal, L. (1987) *Is the Future Female?* London: Virago.

Simey, M. (1982) 'Police authorities and accountability: the Merseyside experience', in Cowell, D., Jones, T. and Young, J. (eds) pp. 52–7.

Simey, M. (1985) 'The true purposes of police–public consultation' in Cranfield Institute of Technology *Models of Police/Public Consultation in Europe*, Bedford: Cranfield Press, pp. 16–20.

Smith, J. (1984) 'The paradox of women's poverty: wage earning women and economic transformation', *Signs*, 10, p. 300.

Smith, N. (1984) *Uneven Development: Nature, Capital and the Production of Space*, Oxford: Basil Blackwell.

Smith, S. (1986a) 'Police accountability and local democracy', *Area*, 18 (2), pp. 99–107.

Smith, S. (1986b) *Crime, Space and Society*, Cambridge: University Press.

Smith, S. (1987) 'Racial segregation: a geography of British racism' in Jackson, P. (ed.), pp. 25–49.

Smith, S. (1988) 'Political interpretations of "racial segregation" in Britain', *Environment and Planning D: Society and Space*, 6.

Smith, S. (1989) *The Politics of 'Race' and Residence: Citizenship, Segregation and White Supremacy in Britain*, Cambridge: Polity Press.

Solomos, J. (1986) 'Riots, urban protest and social policy', *Policy Papers in Ethnic Relations*, 7, Warwick: Centre for Research in Ethnic Relations.

Spencer, S. (1985) 'The eclipse of the police authority', in Fine, B. and Millar, R. (eds), pp. 34–53.

Stapleton, R. (1981) 'Why recession benefits Britain', *Journal of Economic Affairs*, 1 (2), pp. 7–11.

Starkie, D. (1982) *The Motorway Age*, Oxford: Pergamon.

Steed, M. (1987) 'How to nobble the Thatcher vote', *New Statesman*, 27 November, p. 16.

Stevens, L. *et al.* (1982) *Race and Building Society Lending in Leeds*, Leeds: Leeds Community Relations Council.

Stewart, J. (1984) 'Storming the town halls: a rate-cap revolution', *Marxism Today*, April, pp. 8–13.

Stoker, G. (1988) 'The growth of non-elected local government', paper presented at Political Studies Association conference, Plymouth, 12–14 April.

Taylor, P. J. (1979) 'The changing geography of representation in Britain', *Area*, 11, pp. 289–94.

Taylor, P. J. (1985) *Political Geography: World Economy, Nation–State and Locality*, Harlow: Longmans.

Taylor, P. J. (1987) 'The poverty of international comparisons: some methodological lessons from world-systems analysis', *Studies in Comparative International Development*, 22, pp. 12–39.

TEST (Transport and Environmental Studies) (1984a). *BR: A European Railway*, London: TEST, 177 Arlington Road.

TEST (Transport and Environmental Studies) (1984b) *The Company Car Factor*, London: TEST, 177 Arlington Road.

Thompson, E. P. (1987) 'The rituals of enmity' in Smith, D. and Thompson, E. P. (eds) *Prospects for a Habitable Planet*, London: Penguin, pp. 11–43.

Thompson, G. (1986) *The Conservatives' Economic Policy*, Beckenham: Croom Helm.

Thornley, A. (1981) *Thatcherism and Town Planning*, London: Polytechnic of Central London, Planning Studies no. 12.

Thornley, A. (1986) 'Thatcherism and simplified regimes', *Planning Practice and Research*, 1, pp. 19–22.

Thornley, A. (1988) 'Planning in a cool climate: the effects of Thatcherism', *The Planner*, 74 (7), pp. 17–19.

Thorns, D. (1982) 'Industrial restructuring and change in the labour and property markets in Britain', *Environment and Planning A*, 14, pp. 745–63.

Townsend, P. *et al.* (1987) *Poverty and Labour in London*, London: Low Pay Unit.

Townsend, P., Phillimore, P. and Beattie, A. (1988) *Health and Deprivation: Inequality and the North*, London: Croom Helm.

Urry, J. (1981) *The Anatomy of Capitalist Societies*, London: Macmillan.

Vanke, J. (1987) *Better Roads for a Better Economy? a Literature Review*, London: Friends of the Earth.

Van Rest, J. (1985) 'Policies for Major Roads in Urban Areas in the UK', Birmingham: University of Aston Integrated Higher Degree Working Paper.

Vogel, D. (1986) *National Styles of Regulation: Environmental Policy in Great Britain and the United States*, Ithaca: Cornell University Press.

Voûte, C. (1987) 'Whose Europe? A View from the West' in Smith, D. and Thompson, E. P. (eds) *Prospects for a Habitable Planet*, London: Penguin, pp. 149–71.

Walker, B. (1987) 'Public sector costs of board and lodging accommodation for homeless households in London', *Housing Studies*, 2, pp. 261–73.

Wallerstein, I. (1983) *Historical Capitalism*, London: Verso.

Wallerstein, I. (1984) *Politics of the World Economy*, Cambridge: University Press.

Wallerstein, I. (1988) *European Unity and its Implications for the Interstate System*, in Hettne, B. (ed.) *Europe: Dimensions of Peace*, London and New Jersey: Zed, pp. 27–38.

Ward, R. (1982) 'Race, housing and wealth', *New Community*, 10, pp. 3–15.
Ward, R. (1987) 'Race and access to housing' in Smith, S. and Mercer, J. (eds) *New Perspectives on Race and Housing in Britain*, Glasgow: Centre for Housing Research, pp. 182–218.
Watt, D. (1984) *Succeeding John Bull: America in Britain's Place 1960–1975*, Cambridge: University Press.
Weatheritt, M. (1986) *Innovations in Policing*, Beckenham: Croom Helm, in association with the Police Foundation.
Weatheritt, M. (1987) 'Community policing now' in Willmott, P. (ed.) *Policing and the Community*, Discussion Paper no. 16, London: Policy Studies Institute, pp. 7–20.
Webster, C. (1988) *The Health Services Since the War, Vol 1: Problems of Health Care to 1957*, London: HMSO.
Whitehead, C. (1983) 'Housing under the Conservatives: a policy assessment', *Public Money*, June, pp. 15–21.
Whitelegg, J. (1984) 'The company car in the UK as an instrument of transport policy', *Transport Policy and Decision Making*, 2, pp. 219–30.
Whitelegg, J. (1985a) *Urban Transport*, London: Macmillan.
Whitelegg, J. (1985b) 'Road building and the urban economy' in *Cities and Roads: Proceedings of a Conference held at the City University, London, 26.11.85*, London: Transport 2000.
Whitelegg, J. (1987) 'Rural railways and disinvestment in rural areas', *Regional Studies*, 21, pp. 55–63.
Whitelegg, J. (1988a) 'High speed railways and new investment in Germany', paper presented to the Annual Conference, Institute of British Geographers, Loughborough.
Whitelegg, J. (1988b) *Transport Policy in the EEC*, London: Methuen.
Whitelegg, J. and James, A. (1987) *Bringing the Tunnel to South Yorkshire: A Case for Rail Freight and Rail Investment*, Lancaster: Straw Barnes Press.
Whiteley, P. (1983) *The Labour Party in Crisis*, London: Methuen.
Whiteley, P. (1984) 'Perceptions of economic performance and voting behaviour in the 1983 general election in Britain', *Political Behaviour*, 6, pp. 395–410.
Whiteley, P. (1986) 'Predicting the Labour vote in 1983: social backgrounds versus subjective evaluations', *Political Studies*, 34, pp. 82–98.
Wiener, M. (1981) *English Culture and the Decline of the Industrial Spirit*, Cambridge: University Press.
Williams, B., Nicholl, J., Thomas, K. and Knowelden, J. (1984) 'Contribution of the private sector to elective surgery in England', *Lancet*, 14.7.84, pp. 88–92.
Williams, C. H. (1980) 'Ethnic separatism in Western Europe', *Tijdschrift voor Economische en Sociale Geografie*, 71, pp. 142–58.
Willis, E. (1987) *Community Programme – A Volunteer Dream*, Berkhamsted: Volunteer Centre.
Wilson, E. (1987) 'Thatcherism and women: after seven years' in Miliband, R., Panitch, L. and Saville, S. (eds) *Socialist Register 1987*, London: Merlin, pp. 199–235.
Winterton, J. (1985) 'Computerized coal: new technology in the mines' in Beynon, H. (ed.) (1985), pp 231–44.
Wintour, P. (1987) 'Manufacturers shift spending to overseas jobs', *The Guardian*, 5 May.
Wolmar, C. (1984) 'Neighbourly nosing', *New Statesman*, 21 September.
Young, K. (1985) 'Concern for the environment' in Jowell, R. and Witherspoon, S. (eds) *British Social Attitudes: the 1985 Report*, Aldershot: Gower, pp. 159–76.

Notes on Contributors

James Anderson is Lecturer in Geography at the Open University.

Simon Duncan is Lecturer in Geography at the London School of Economics.

Andrew Flynn is a Research Associate at the University of Kent.

Nicholas R. Fyfe is a Research Fellow at Sidney Sussex College, Cambridge.

Andrew Gamble is Professor of Politics at the University of Sheffield.

Mark Goodwin is Lecturer in Geography at Goldsmiths' College, London.

Chris Hamnett is Senior Lecturer in Geography at the Open University.

R. J. Johnston is Professor of Geography at the University of Sheffield.

Ray Hudson is Reader in Geography at the University of Durham.

Philip Lowe is Lecturer in Countryside Planning in the Bartlett School of Architecture and Planning, University College, London.

Linda McDowell is Senior Lecturer in Geography at the Open University.

Ron Martin is Lecturer in Geography at the University of Cambridge and a Fellow of St Catharine's College.

Doreen Massey is Professor of Geography at the Open University.

John Mohan is Lecturer in Geography at Queen Mary College, London.

Joe Painter is a Research Student at the Open University.

C. J. Pattie is Research Fellow in Geography at the University of Sheffield.

Susan J. Smith is a Research Fellow in the Centre for Housing Research and the Department of Social and Economic Research at the University of Glasgow.

Peter J. Taylor is Reader in Geography at the University of Newcastle upon Tyne.

John Whitelegg is Lecturer in Geography at the University of Lancaster.

Index

298